# FIRST-GENERATION PAKISTANI MIGRANTS IN THE UK

# FIRST-GENERATION PAKISTANI MIGRANTS IN THE UK

Zeibeda Sattar

TRANSNATIONAL PRESS LONDON

2021

MIGRATION SERIES: 36

First-Generation Pakistani Migrants in the UK

Zeibeda Sattar

Copyright © 2021 Transnational Press London

First Published in 2021 by TRANSNATIONAL PRESS LONDON in the United Kingdom, 13 Stamford Place, Sale, M33 3BT, UK. www.tplondon.com

Transnational Press London® and the logo and its affiliated brands are registered trademarks.

Requests for permission to reproduce material from this work should be sent to: sales@tplondon.com

Paperback
ISBN: 978-1-80135-083-9
Digital
ISBN: 978-1-80135-084-6

Cover Design: Nihal Yazgan
Cover image is from the authors' family archive

Transnational Press London Ltd. is a company registered in England and Wales No. 8771684.

# CONTENTS

# ABOUT THE AUTHOR

Dr Zeibeda Sattar (Zeb) is Lecturer in Health Policy and Programme Lead in Master for Public Health. She is a second-generation migrant and was born in Newcastle upon Tyne, a Northern part of United Kingdom. She has experiences of working in public, private and third sectors. She was an Electronics Engineer/Quality Assurance Manager for over 10 years before pursuing a career in Health and Social Care. Her interdisciplinary research experiences have included managing national and culturally diverse cross sector projects. Her health inequalities research includes 'Holiday Hunger' food provision across England and has extensive experience of working with minority ethnic communities to design and implement culturally appropriate services, e.g. sustainable physical activity interventions to reduce obesity and addressing older South Asian women's health and social care needs. Prior to beginning her PhD in South Asian communities and mobilities in Newcastle upon Tyne, she owned and managed a care home for 3 years, looking after older people and people with learning disabilities. It was the premature death of her father (aged 48) that led her to pursue a career in service design and delivery to improve and prevent health inequalities. This book contributes towards the growing field of migration studies.

# FOREWORD

It gives me great pleasure to write the foreword for this book. Zeb's work on the migration and settlement experiences of Pakistani migrants in the north east of England sheds light on both the historical and contemporary lives of the Pakistani diaspora. In her exploration of personal biographies, she develops insight into how the push and pull of economic, political and cultural factors influenced the decision of people to migrate to the UK. Zeb charts their experiences of life in the UK, focusing on how their identities were shaped by connections both within the UK-based Pakistani community and outside it. Maintaining links with the homeland through travel was important for many, but influenced by socio-economic status. Zeb's work is relevant to not only the Pakistani community, but also helps better understanding of how migrant communities generally maintain connections and develop new ones and adapt to new environments. Her work has implications for how we view migrant communities, and in particular, how we shape health and social services to support them.

Professor Jonathon Ling

University of Sunderland

# PREFACE AND ACKNOWLEDGEMENTS

As a second generation migrant, I observed the challenges and issues my parents faced living in a new country in which they could not speak, read or write English. I have vivid memories of sitting in solicitor's offices, after walking for miles, trying to interpret for my dad at the tender ages of nine, ten, eleven and onward. This book presents my research work which I undertook in the area of migration and settlement experiences that was inspired during my work in my care home as an owner and Registered Manager. Looking after older people and people with disabilities, I was approached by members of the South Asian community who were struggling with their health asking if I could help them. I was amazed with their stories of settling in the UK and how they displayed pure resilience in all areas of their lives. Some stories were uplifting while others were tragic. The book, 'Myth of Return' by Anwar in 1979 was highly influential and relevant as a key theme in most of the conversations that took place with the first-generation migrants.

My father was a first-generation migrant and entered the UK in 1963. He relied on friends to support him in his early days. I recall him saying that there were several people to a room and when the night shift people came back from work, they would sleep in the same beds as the people who left them to work dayshifts. A big pan of curry was made by one person in the room/house and they all shared the food. This is as far as I could remember my late father's stories. He sadly passed away in 1990 while I was in my final year of my first degree.

I tried to find out more information about my father's life here in the UK but could not find anything -apart from stories of people living in the community. After ten years or so I took this initiative and decided to record the experiences of the first-generation of migrants.

Locally, research was being promoted in the migration agenda and it was during this period I realised that I needed to document the experiences of the first-generation Pakistani migrants before it is lost. My first supervisor, Professor Tony Hepburn, a Historian was very supportive of my work and I never looked back. Sadly, he passed away after I carried out the empirical work. Professor Kevin Hannam took over the challenge of supervising this work from a, 'Travel and Tourism', standpoint, hence the implementation of the 'Mobilities Theory' in the book.

This book reports how modern life is constantly being affected by increasing forms of mobility. These mobilities allow for people to carry out activities that form and maintain relationships and networks on a social and obligatory basis. Complex mobility systems have enabled greater movement for many at local, national and international levels. Migration theories have been influenced by the mobilities paradigm and have led to the creation of new terminology such as 'transnational migrants'. Both the needs of post-Second World War labour shortages and the political and economic climate of Pakistan (after partition in 1947) led to significant post-colonial Pakistani migration. This directed attention to life in the UK and resulted in and created new mobility dynamics. In terms of the research on which this book is based, face to face interviews took place, with a total of twenty eight interviewees that were carried out in two parts with the Pakistani diaspora living in the city of Newcastle upon Tyne who migrated up until the 1970's. Evidence from the interviews supports the notion of the Pakistani diaspora holding on to its values and solidarity. Nevertheless a fluidity of identities has become the norm for this diasporic group and the concept of transnational citizenship has become a reality. Examples of social integration and identity formation are documented as are the political and health issues of main concern. Finally, the leisure and tourism activities have been analysed. A theme that is central to the group was health and as the natural ageing process sets in there are motility issues that affect their lifestyle significantly and health care needs. Network capital, mainly the telephone has therefore become more prominent in interviewees lives whereas social capital has reduced as a result of immobility. It is concluded that diverse mobilities have enabled the Pakistani diaspora links to be maintained locally, nationally and internationally as well as the religious requirements to be met. I literally sold my care home to write up my research as my passion to document the experiences of first-generation migrants took over my life. Little did I know that I would be working in Public Health, many years later, currently as the Programme Lead for MPH in Public Health at Northumbria University to reduce health inequalities of disadvantaged communities across the globe. The aim of this book is to enhance the understanding of the conditions and lifestyles this community group has lived from the 1960s. Within the wider context this community group are now older people, yet are facing contemporary challenges such as the disproportionate impact of COVID-19 during the pandemic on Black and Minority Ethnic communities and the Black Lives Matter movement. Working with people in a minority ethnic community has been a privilege, whilst many researchers state that it is hard to engage with such groups, my experiences have been the opposite. Perhaps belonging to the group and being able to take on an emic and etic position has its advantages. I hope this book provides the reader with an insight into the experiences of first-generation migrants in a Northern area of United Kingdom.

# INTRODUCTION

This book critically analyses post-migration mobilities of the Pakistani diaspora living in Newcastle upon Tyne. There are three conceptual lenses that are incorporated into the analysis from an explanatory standpoint. These are the mobilities paradigm, the transnational approach and diaspora studies. The first two chapters describe the background to these theories and the fluid aspects of identity conceptualising migration as a continuing dynamic between the homeland and the host country (UK) thus affecting how we think about migration.

'Without mobility we could not live. Without mobility we could not get to work or the nearest food source, neither could we stay healthy and fit. We could not make and sustain social relationships and we could not travel so far off or nearby destinations' (Adey, 2010, p.1). One kind of mobility leads to another mobility. Migration is one type of human mobility that is understood to be facilitated by the use of communication technologies. With the term 'trans' denoting moving through space or across lines and the changing nature of something the word 'transnationalism' and 'flexible citizens' is used to denote international migration (Ong, 1999). Urry, (2007) states mobilities may create structures and fixities that may influence further movement but in terms of identity one cannot easily step in and out of one's own positioning (Adey, 2010, p. 26). At the same time there is an understanding that there are problems with the 'grand narrative' narrative of mobility and fluidity (King and Christou, 2011, p. 454). Politically contested mobilities have enabled and shaped mobilities through policy and regulation. In the aftermath of 9/11 new policies were developed and immigration was 'securitized' (Papastergiadis, 2010, p. 343), thus, policy itself travels and is shared and copied (Adey, 2010, p. 5). The issues of unequal access to mobility at an international level have also been recognised and immobility or moorings (Hannam et al., 2006) have also become significant factors in the arena. An 'immigrant' is someone who moves on a permanent level as opposed to a 'migrant' moves backwards and forwards to and from the home country and host country (Suarez-Orozco, 2003) although are used in literature interchangeably (Horevitz, 2009, p.748). For the purposes of this study 'migrant' will be used.

It is suggested that there are three types of transnationalism: economic, political and cultural (Ellis and Khan, 2002, p. 169). Hence, the 'push' of lack of economic opportunities in Pakistan and the 'pull' of economic expansion in the West as well as the political decision to build Mangla Dam in Mirpur Azad Kashmir, Pakistan precipitated migration (chain migration) to the UK. Once families joined the men the 'Myth of Return' (Anwar 1979) was dismissed and the diaspora began to develop (Ellis and Khan, 2002, p. 174). The UK has the 'largest settlement of Kashmiris and for diasporic activities is the most important centre' (Ellis and Khan, 2002, p. 174). However, it has been argued that the reception a migrant receives from its country helps give 'direction to their adoptive strategies' including those of a transnational character'. Thus, questions over identity and racism confrontations have led to alliances being forged with those of similar positions. These include 'South Asians'; 'Black', 'Muslims in Europe' (as Islamaphobia is widespread); 'British' and 'English' identities (Ellis and Khan, 2002, p. 174). It has been argued that the social field of these migrants is relatively simple and consists of a bipolar pairing of the natal village and the urban neighbourhood compared to other kinds of transnational migrants embedded 'in more geographically diffuse migration systems- the relationships and scales will probably be more complex' (King and Christou, 2011, p. 456). The migrant diasporic groups create places in between and away from their places of departure and enact a process of deterritorialisation. This process leads the migrants to live in continual reference to their diaspora and to their place of origin Adey, (2010, p. 79) and these are described as pathways (Werbner, 1999). Thus migrants visit their homeland frequently while ostensibly on holiday (Coles and Timothy, 2004) with 'translocal' places that extend the sociality of home into somewhere else (Adey, 2010, p. 79). It is the forgrounding acts of 'homing' that direct the complexities 'between travel and dwelling, home and not-home' and necessitating the (re)positioning of tourism from the mobilities theoretical perspective (Hannam and Knox, 2010, p. 162). There has been an emergence of ethnic tourism through studies of diaspora including their experiences of tourism, the spaces they occupy and the production of tourism for and by the diasporic tourists; these are themes Coles and Timothy (2004, p. 163) have highlighted with discussions on diaspora identities being creolised or hybridised (Friedman, 1999).

The mobilities turn and its studies have enabled a new form of sociological enquiry that remedies the neglect academically of movements such as people, objects, information and ideas, but also there is important social and material phenomena relating to the global society emerging (Urry, 2010). There is attention to'fluid' and new ways of understanding the relationship between theory, observation and engagement (Buscher and Urry, 2009, p.99).

Social life takes place across borders and the theoretical developments and debates are on the one hand new assimilation theories and the new research relating to living transnationally and the discovery that poverty and powerlessness is overcome by accumulating capital i.e. finance, and terms such as translocalism (Barkan, 2006) and bi-localism are proposed. Many scholars of migration accept the transnational practices and attachments for the first-generation (Alba and Nee, 2003) and such links are seen to be multiple to states rather than disappearing. Organic and mechanistic metaphors have been employed to underpin the classical paradigm but the persisting anxiety towards the social impact of migration and the status of people on the move has been a 'lucanae' in the social sciences and a more general understanding of mobility missing in public debates (Papastergiadis, 2010). It is argued that the 'global patterns of migration and the contemporary forms of hybrid subjectivity do not fit well with this paradigm' and these limits and kinetophobic associations are examined through an alternative conceptual framework based on the complexity theory, although it also has its setbacks.

It has, however, been noted that this conceptualisation has already being used as through a set of metaphors and concepts as a new toolkit in the social sciences (Urry 2007) and therefore stresses that before it becomes a 'map to explain the totality of social relations' (Papastergiadis, 2010, p. 355) there is still a sense that the vocabulary and techniques for representing social change are lagging behind the dynamism that has exploded from the major events of our time. Most importantly, 'it produces a more optimistic view towards mobility and difference', (Rosenau, 2003, cited Papastergiadis, 2010, p. 355). Thus it is argued that the complexity theory is a relational process that exists between and within the 'closed' spaces of structure and the 'open' spaces of chance (Papastergiadis, 2010, p. 355).

The aim of this book is to critically analyse the post-migration mobilities of the Pakistani diaspora living in Newcastle upon Tyne

This book is the first of its kind that captures the mobilities of Pakistani migrants settling in a Northern part of United Kingdom. Its main objectives are listed below:

1.  To collate the in-depth biographies of key members of the Pakistani diaspora in Newcastle upon Tyne.

2.  To develop a critical analysis of the diverse mobilities of the Pakistani diaspora in Newcastle upon Tyne.

3.  To critically analyse the extent to which 'access' plays in the public and social practices of the Pakistani diaspora in Newcastle upon Tyne.

4.  To critically analyse the leisure and tourism mobilities of the Pakistani diaspora in Newcastle upon Tyne.

The earlier studies of migration reflected a simplistic model that 'held sway at the time' (King and Christou, 2011, p. 453). From the dismissal of the 'Myth of Return' (Anwar, 1979) the exploration of the ontology and the return of migrants has recently embraced a variety of mobilities beyond the original migrants and fundamentally reframed the study of migration (King and Christou, 2011, p. 453). The social sciences and the humanities regarded the nation from a residential viewpoint and as a reference for geo-political affiliation, cultural attachment and socio-economic organisation. However, Cresswell (2006) has summarised this desire to have roots as a fundamental human need to under-estimate the social value of mobility and entrenching a kinetophobic view towards migrants. The new mobility paradigm 'unpicks these negative assumptions and the viability of attachments and seeks to affirm both the agency of the person in movement and the viability of attachments that are formed across boundaries. This fluid form of agency and social belonging has re-ignited the social and political debates on cosmopolitanisms (Papastergiadis, 2010, p. 356). Hence, an attempt is made in this work to analyse the behaviour of the Pakistani diaspora and identify the activities and lifestyles in order to establish their fluidity and identities on display. This process has considered insights from three paradigm shifts, namely, the mobilities paradigm, the transnational approach and diaspora studies.

The methodology is therefore qualitative and interpretive for this analysis especially where the analysis of multiple and intersecting mobility systems is an adapting and evolving relationship with each other. Thus, it is a process for 'post-human analysis' (Hayles, 1999) and it is argued that humans are co-constituted by various material agencies and we have never simply been human (Buscher and Urry, 2009, p.100) but 'life and matter come to matter and are made meaningful as people, objects, information and ideas move and are (im)mobilised' (Barad, 2007 cited Buscher and Urry, 2009, p.100).

## Methodological Considerations

This section will review the qualitative approaches to research that are available and the methods that were undertaken to pursue this study. The research methods from a qualitative standpoint are discussed with a section on the latest developments on mobile research methods. The validity and reliability of these methods is also reviewed followed by a discussion of the demographics of the research participants. Data collection and data analysis methods are discussed and the role of the researcher with the limitations of the research.

As stated, the purpose of this research was to critically evaluate the experiences of the Pakistani Diaspora currently living in Newcastle upon Tyne. It aims to investigate the historical and contemporary experiences of the Pakistani diaspora to evaluate the nature of 'fluid identities' practiced relating to the 'ways of being' and the 'ways of belonging' that enact identity and demonstrate consciously a connection to a particular group (Morwaska 2007, cited Levitt and Jaworsky, 2007, p.133). This has been carried out by aiming to establish an understanding of the way of life of migrants from Pakistan from 1945 onwards.

## Qualitative Research Methods

The main research method was interviewing for this qualitative study. Semi-structured interviews were used for qualitative data collection. They are non-standardised and although there is generally a set of questions and issues to be covered they may not be formally structured and the order may change depending on the direction the interview takes. Additional questions may be asked depending on the response and documented by note taking and recording the interview. These type of interviews allow for probing of views and opinions which is an important angle in exploring subjectivity (Gray, 2010, p.373). Although interviewer bias can creep in many subtle ways, consistency is required in the measurement of outcomes. Oppenheim (1992 cited Gray, 2010, p.377) have listed a number of ways bias can occur, from a poor maintenance of rapport with the respondent to a rephrasing of attitude questions, biased probes and departures from the interviewing instructions.

The criteria for a successful interview includes being clear at the outset about the research, showing interest and knowledge. The structure of the interview needs to be clear and the researcher needs to have the ability to steer conversations, be critical and listen carefully and remember what has been said as well as have the ability to interpret statements (Kvale, 1996, cited Creswell, 2007). Transcribing the interviews also involves time and skill to record the words of an interview and thus there is an advantage to transcribing your interviews by becoming closer to the data (Creswell, 2007).

### Qualitative Data Analysis

Analysis for Woolcott (1994b, p.26; cited in Creswell, 2009, p.162) 'is a sorting procedure – the quantitative side of the qualitative research. There are of course systematic procedures that when adhered to enable the findings to be presented in a user friendly manner e.g. tables, charts, diagrams, figures and patterned regularity. To establish patterned regularity comparisons and evaluations are derived through drawing thematic connections and theoretical frameworks. There is also the 'critiquing of the research process and research redesign proposal' that is another step in analysis (Creswell, 2009 p.162). It is the thematic connection that is the main process in data analysis in this study this involves coding and, although it can be exhaustive, is also mandatory.

Collect, code, and collect is another principle from which themes may be noticed at an early stage helping with theoretical sampling. Other helpful principles are familiarisation, focussed reading, review and amending codes, and generating theories by looking for threads and connections between categories and concepts. However, narrative analysis consequently has gained greater popularity because no matter how well these principles are applied the coding tends to fragment the data and the connection between text and context is sometimes lost (Gray, 2010, p.496). Most importantly analysis needs to move beyond using isolated quotations from a number of interviewees.

Finally relating the analysis to the field and theory requires some care especially when applying the 'etic' and 'emic' rules. Although it can be argued these rules exist in many people's thoughts and actions of 'practical consciousness' (Pierre Bourdieu (1984) and Anthony Giddens (1984) cited Crook and Crang, 1995, p91). The purpose of data analysis is to find a means of understanding the versions of reality and the inter-relations as opposed to developing a distinct account (Crook and Crang, 1995).

### Mobile Research Methods

The development of the mobilities paradigm has lead to offshoots in other disciplines and areas to advance the neglect of various movements of ideas, information, people and objects. In research methods this detail has evolved into mobile research methods. Mobile research methods consider new empirical sensitivities and analytical methods and motivations to examine important social and material phenomena (Buscher and Urry, 2009, p.99). 'Existing methods deal, for instance, poorly with the fleeting – that which is here today and gone tomorrow, only to re-appear again the day after tomorrow. They deal poorly with the distributed - that is to be found here there but not in between - or that which slips and slides between one place and another. They deal poorly with the multiple-that which takes different shapes in different places. They deal poorly with the non-causal, the chaotic, and complex. And such methods have difficulty dealing with the sensory-that which is subject to vision, sound, taste, smell; with the emotional – time-space compressed outbursts of anger, pain, rage, pleasure, desire, or the spiritual; and the kinaesthetic – the pleasures and the pains which follow the movement and displacement of people, objects, information and ideas' (Law and Urry, 2004 cited in Buscher and Urry, 2009, p.103).

The suggestions by Buscher and Urry (2009) on developing research methods with the above in mind need to involve 'being on the move' and is achievable by:

1.  Tracking subjects - including physically travelling with their research subjects. Sheller and Urry, 2006 have referred this to the many and interdependent forms of intermittent movement of

people, images, information and objects.

2.  Allowing themselves as researcher to be moved. Interpreting this simply means to follow or move with the subjects. This will give an interesting and challenging edge of the method as to why, how and when people move (Law and Mol, 2002, cited in Buscher and Urry, 2009).

Another view by several researchers mentioned by Buscher and Urry (2009) is that the methods employed need to 'follow the thing'. To elaborate on this issue what is termed as an object and its purpose have been described earlier. The main feature is that objects move as part of international trade and travel. An example given by Marcus (1995) is that of computer components that travel the equivalent of a journey to the moon. Whereas some objects lose their value i.e. cheap souvenirs, others gain. For this reason Lash and Lury (2006; cited Buschman and Urry 2009) call for a 'cultural biography of objects' as part of the appropriate methodology.

**Research Design**

It was anticipated from the outset that this study would be a qualitative programme with in-depth interviewing. In order to ensure there were sufficient questions to ascertain the interviewees' perceptions, feelings and tactics on stories, themes issues and topics the interview protocol resulted in the development of a structured questionnaire with open-ended and closed-ended questions. Ethical consideration was given to the study and a consent form was developed alongside each questionnaire. The plan of the research method was to target no less than 20 interviewees (and no more than 50 interviewees) to conduct structured interviews of first-generation Pakistani migrants through the snowballing technique. The primary goal was to identify the first-generation Pakistani migrants through researcher reflexivity. Hence, knowledge of the community and local areas as well as conducting interviews in their homes. The aim was also to conduct interviews with an equal number of male and female interviewees. It was felt necessary to carry out in-depth interviews as opposed to focus groups. It was felt that behaviour or the experiences would be more openly discussed on a one to one interview basis hence a deeper insight of issues and needs being addressed. Arguably, the male and female Pakistani interviewees may not feel comfortable talking in a group and also gendered only interviews may have limitations .

The interviews were to take place in 2005 and there was no plan to re-interview these individuals. Thus, I was the only investigator and it was anticipated that material would be translated at interview from Urdu/Mirpuri dialect to English rather than translate material or use interpreters (also for transcriptions). It was felt this would allow for consistency in the results as well as reduce costs and time. The requirement was therefore for the interviewer to be literate in both English and Urdu, which was the case.

### Conducted Fieldwork Experiences

The aim of this section is to describe exactly what the process of data collection was. Hence interviewing has its own challenges depending on the form it takes. In-depth interviewing involves conducting interviews with individuals intensively. These interviews provide detailed information on the issues being researched as well as exploring the thoughts and behavioural patterns of the individual. These interviews are usually carried out with a small number of interviewees to explore the situation. This was the case in this study.

Interviews took place in two stages. All the fieldwork was of the semi-structured nature. The first set of interviews took place in 2004/ 2005 (28 interviews) and the second set in 2011. The second set of interviews were innovative in that the same group were approached with an additional remit. The questionnaires for the first set of interviews were modified and the same structured approach was followed. It was felt this was an important requirement in order to establish rapport and to gain the trust of the interviewee, although prompts were frequently required to discuss specific issues. A few interviews were carried out in other places i.e. workplaces, this was at the request of the interviewees. More females were interviewed than males. A demographic profile of these interviewees is included in the appendix together with a sample of three part transcripts.

There was also the issue of individuals not speaking English that was resolved by the interviewer interpreting the questions for the interviewee in Urdu or Mirpuri to answer. This was felt to be expensive and a time consuming exercise. For each interview a set of rules was adhered to in order to ensure consistency between each interview and the reliability of the findings. Consent and confidentiality issues were explained and asked prior to the interview. A brief outline of the guide adhered to included thanking the interviewee for taking part, giving the name of the interviewer and describing the purpose of the interview. The interviewees were then assured of the confidentiality aspect of the study. This meant that their names would not be used in any format and all responses would be anonymous on analysis. They were then informed that the interview 'should not take more than an hour' and that a tape recording would be made of the interview. It was explained that this was to ensure all the information would be recorded as by writing alone all the notes may not be recorded. The interviewee was made aware of the fact that if they did not feel comfortable answering a question they did not need to answer and finally asked if they had any questions before they were asked to complete a consent form. The interviewees' age range was between 48 and 74 years (where dates of birth were available). In some cases interviewees did not know their date of birth and gave approximate ages.

It was anticipated that I would be in a position to take an 'etic' approach by sharing the same ethnicity but also constructive by taking an 'emic' position. This position is clarified by Harris (1990, p.49, cited in Ali et al, 2006, p.228) specifying 'emics of the observer must be categorically distinct from the 'emics' of the participants'; especially as the researcher 'emics' are bias towards the research itself.

As stated earlier there were two parts of the interview process. The first part involved 28 interviewees of whom 16 were male and 12 were female. These interviewees were identified through the snowballing technique but also significantly with the researcher's background knowledge of living and being an active member within the community from childhood played a major role in obtaining this number. Interviewees were contacted by telephone or visiting homes on spec, in some cases interviews were carried out at the time of visiting or telephoning and for a small number of interviewees an appointment was made. There were several interviewees who did not want to take part. The majority of the interviews took place in the interviewee's homes, although there was a need for the researcher to be flexible and one person wanted the interview to take place at his workplace, another in his daughter's house and there were a couple of interviews in coffee shops. Although there were many leads given as to who could be interviewed by the initial interviewees, the time frame of interviews being conducted and the number of interviewees obtained became a valid reason to end the interviewing process. The first set of interviews therefore took place in the winter of 2004 and 2005.

The structured questionnaire required a degree of flexibility to allow for the sensitivities and emotional aspects of the 'thick descriptions' being recorded and adopted. The reflexivity of the researcher was also important as was the researcher skills in making the interviewee feel comfortable and interested in the topic of conversation. Hence, a part-structured questionnaire followed, to allow for the continuity of data collection. Thus, I probed on questions that were related to the questions when deemed necessary, in particular where there were open ended questions. The interviews were mainly conducted in English, however, there were interviewees who did not understand English and therefore the researcher translated each question and conducted the interview in Urdu, or Mirpuri (a dialect of Urdu). Interestingly, some of the interviewees talked in Urdu or Mirpuri despite speaking English for which the same language was spoken by the researcher. It was felt that this was a means of displaying trust and comfort in answering the questions. The interviewees were thanked for their time at the end of the interviews.

The second part of the interviews involved re-visiting the same interviewees from the first set for which a semi structured interview was designed. This process did not take as long as the first set of interviews, especially since they had already given consent and were familiar with the research set up. A dictaphone was used (for the first set there were tape recordings) and therefore more reliable. There were 19 interviewees for the second part of the research. There were ten males and nine females. Thus, nine interviewees did not take part for several reasons apart from one person who refused to be interviewed again the other reasons given were either ill-health, hospitalisation, no longer living in the same place and death.

The interview questions were both open-ended and close-ended but not as long as the first questionnaire where a lot of the demographic information was collected. All interviews were transcribed in English, for the majority there were tape or dictaphone recordings from which data was coded and analysis carried out.

## Researcher Reflexivity

Within the realms of qualitative tourism research Ali (2012) has discussed a framework to include 'emotionalisation of reflexivity' (|Ali, 2012, p. 23). An attempt has been made in this section to focus and explore this subject. It requires the awareness of the researcher from the personal and epistemological presence. Hence, personal reflexivity reflects the self-conscious emotions.

The first stage of the research process is known as pre-research. The research setting was moulded by conducting the 'Who am I' test. This examines my position as an insider and /or outsider in the research and the following statements are applicable:

I am a:

1) Pakistani, 2) Muslim, 3) British citizen, 4) member of an ethnic minority, 5) Mirpuri and Urdu literate, 6) second-generation Pakistani born to first-generation migrants to England, 7) student, 8) mother, 9) married women, 10) Geordie, 11) researcher, 12) participant in return visits to Pakistan, 13) practising Muslim, 14) wearer of hijab, 15) Pakistani living amongst the community, 16) Pakistani community in Newcastle upon Tyne, 17) researcher in my 'own' field.

I am not:

1) A migrant, 2) born in Pakistan, 3) regularly wearing the traditional dress outside my home, 4) a grandparent.

This test enabled me to identify my strengths and weaknesses in conducting the research with the Pakistani migrants and gave me the confidence in pursuing the interviews. The second process was the surfacing of emotions during the research. Hence, I was in a position to empathise and understand most of the practices emerging at interview.

The third process was the post – research emotionalisation of reflexivity. Hence, an overview of my 'emic' and 'etic' positioning during the research was visible. On analysis of greater significance was the positive and negative aspect of the results. These affected my 'inward' personality as well as enriching my 'outward' personality to date. Arguably due to the nature of the research, I have been left with a feeling of 'helplessness' or perhaps better defined as 'emptiness' by my lack of influence and ability on some of the dilemmas identified. Infact, the depth of emotional entanglements have surfaced in this area despite critically interpreting the positioning of my emotions and myself in the research setting. This is an argument that Ali, (2012, p. 22) supports.

## Limitations of Research Methods and the Role of the Researcher

The interview process was a lengthy and time consuming process. Unfortunately, timing was such that the first set of interviews took place in the winter of 2004 and 2005 when the weather was cold and wet and, for some time, snowing too. This hindered the study in that it took longer to get from one place to another in sometimes dangerous conditions. However, this also set the scene for the interview to take place where there was a big welcome for arriving to the interviewee's house and especially with those who lived alone and were looking forward to the conversation.

The second set of interviews were innovative in that the same interviewees were approached for a separate theme of research and the results were surprisingly thick and descriptive and the interviewees were extremely co-operative and perhaps even delighted to be of further help.

It was advantageous for me to have local knowledge and also knowing the interviewees from the community and the role of the researcher was re-defined as a daughter, sister, social worker, interpreter, helper. Nevertheless, there were drawbacks to this familiarity and several times during interviewing it was necessary to bring back conversations that drifted to talk unrelated to the study. This of course also complicated the issue of 'emic and etic' for the researcher where these moments were difficult to distinguish otherwise emotional reflexivity. This also resulted in other members of the family taking part in answering for or with the interviewee; it was difficult to prevent this especially when they only had one room to sit in and also wanted to help with the research. This resulted in the interviews in some cases taking twice as long as anticipated to complete, but it was felt that the interview was easy for the interviewee as it was opinions, experiences and expressions that were being sought. This had consequences for the analysis of the data which took a lot longer to decifer. Attempts were made to take notes at the interview by laptop but several technical issues at the first interview (battery running out etc.)

were abandoned and questionnaires completed by hand together with the recordings enabled sufficient for coding the data.

It was felt that it was advantageous to belong to the same ethnic group studied but it was also felt advantageous to live amongst the community. Hence, in relation to the 'who am I test?' there have been benefits to a longer list. This enabled greater access to specific issues and deeper probing on sensitive issues. The group was small, but rich and in-depth responses were obtained. Another factor that helped was the fact that it was a woman interviewing. This meant the many religious and ethnic sensitivities were overcome i.e. male was not interviewing females. A disadvantage was that as a member of the community it has been expected that my role involved social work and was asked to carry out additional work from the interviewees i.e. read letters, phone utility companies, help to sort out finances, give lifts, buy groceries…and there were some requests I was unable to help with, although as a second-generation Pakistani women those interviewed viewed the researcher as a daughter and the researcher called most of them 'Aunties and Uncles' out of respect of the culture.

## Summary

In this section, a description of the research methods are outlined and the strategies of enquiry explained. The research method involved interviewing using questionnaires. The research has spanned over six - seven years and a further dimension of travel and tourism was added to the study. This resulted in a richer data and analysis. Researcher reflexivity positioning was considered and emic and etic positions have been acknowledgement. The first set of interviews were carried out in 2004/2005 and the second set in 2011 (see appendix for exact dates). Although mobile research methods are discussed the application has been limited. The next chapters describe the frameworks of the mobilities paradigm, the transnational approach and diaspora studies with reference to the reconceptualization of the study of migration. The implications, policies and regulations post-September 11th have been summarised by addressing border controls and security issues in the forefront. The themes identified are: Experiences of Pakistani Settlement in Newcastle; Experiences of Public Services in Newcastle and Experiences of Leisure and Tourism of Pakistanis in Newcastle.

# CHAPTER 1

# MOBILITIES THEORY

## Introduction

On its own mobility simply means movement. But when mobilities are contextually referenced to, or relative to a concept, it is not simply movement. Cresswell (2006) expanded on this and states there is much more to mobility than this superficial meaning especially when it is described through the production that is linked to mobilities. The movement carries the burden of meaning and rarely just movement (Cresswell, 2006). Mobilities with meaning opens a spectrum of fields and concepts for all walks of life and technology; hence taking a central role or recognition in all social sciences. From a pictorial angle the scenario of an abstract mobility from 'a' to 'b' is demonstrated below.

**Figure1.1.** Abstracted mobility

a--------------------------------------------------------b

Cresswell (2006, p.2)

Mobilties are, however dependent upon other factors, they are rarely about the bare facts. It is the context in which a mobility occurs and the significance of it. A whole new picture can be built up with many complex rhythms, trajectories and synchronicities, this is illustrated below:

**Figure 1.2.** Mobility in context

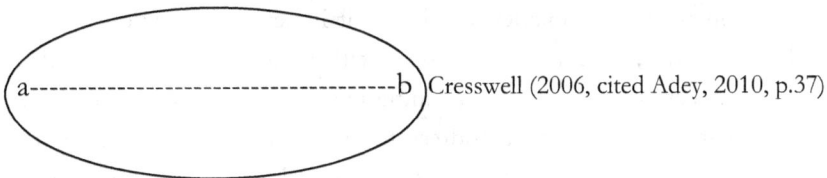

a-----------------------------------b Cresswell (2006, cited Adey, 2010, p.37)

A simple walk in this instance could be a simple walk but to a landowner it could be viewed as trespass and an intrusion to their private property. Someone walking may interpret another walker walking towards them as a threat. This is a more-than-representational mobilities of 'doing' and can be defined as the enactment of the act and all that goes with it. Another example is how Thrift (1997) has noted of Isadora Duncan 'if I could say it, I would not have to dance it' (cited Adey, 2010, p.134). In other words, the attributes of mobility gain as well as attribute meaning by those who interpret and make sense of it. It is the more -than-visual and emotional registers which are equally significant and the multi-sensorial and felt characteristics. This section and the next describe the impact of mobilities and the 'mobilities paradigm' (Urry, 2007).

### The Mobilities Paradigm

The mobilities paradigm refers to 'mobility systems'. These mobility systems are functional and the systems developed through this process or usage as Urry (2007) defines. The usage is referred to as mobilities and it is this role that identifies the different kinds of movement and who and what the movement is. The mobility system has been associated with pavement and paths; public trains; cars and roads; and aeromobility. Urry (2007) has developed five main interdependent 'mobilities', namely corporeal, physical, imaginative, virtual and communicative mobilities. The movement of people, images, ideas and objects are explained through this paradigm.

The fact that people go on holiday, walk, drive, phone and fly is a means of confirming that movement exists but these activities have mostly been ignored by the social sciences (Urry, 2007). These activities also confirm degrees of personal and cultural behaviour, however, the underlying physical and material infrastructures have rarely been considered (Cresswell, 2006). The analysis of 'mobilities' and 'immobilities' provides new forms of sociological inquiry and a deeper insight into human processes. Mobility always involves other mobilities and hence it is never singular but always plural (Adey, 2010). Therefore, mobilities is either about being mobile with a relation between the mobility and immobility; or, on the other hand, mobilities can involve how we address the world and make sense of the relations made. Societies should then be understood as mobility systems that are shaped through relations with other such systems (Jamal and Robinson, 2009). These are 'sedimented practices requiring extensive networks and flows of mobilities on order to stabilize' such as institionalised narratives, information, networks mediating transporting, social relations etc' (Baerenholdt et al, 2004, cited Jamal and Robinson, 2009, p.649).

Major changes due to the advancements in networks and communication over the last decade have resulted in different styles of socialising and working. Adey (2010) has taken on board these concepts and has considered three dominant approaches stating mobilities are more-than-visual and emotional registers from a performance and practicing point of view of nomadism and sedentarism. Scholars have been attempting 'to move beyond the primacy of representation and meaning towards body-centred experiences and forms of knowledge that are rooted in philosophical traditions such as phenomenology' (Adey, 2010, p.137). The three main approaches taken are all relational but can be identified separately. They are practices, performance and more-than-representational mobilities. Thus, by examining performances, habits and practices of nomadism and sedentarism mobility the sensorial characteristics and emotional registers all play a role depending on the context of the mobility. For example, the most simple is that of a 'flaneur' who visually absorbs the sights from the position of wanderings. Of course, others have proved that mobility and visuality is never purely an optical endeavour or a simple and practical exercise. Hence, other practice such as site-seeing (tourism), walking and cycling are all made up of various forms of mobile multi-sensorial activities. Urry (2007) refers to the tourist activities as 'the tourist gaze' and the elements that build the tourism symbol. That is a series of movements and pauses taking place while on holiday such as staying and going, leaving and arriving, hence, a status symbol of many societies along with many other mobile practices (Urry, 2007). Hannam and Knox (2010) have developed the daily or mundane tasks to be called banal to state that these activities are also part of the tourist's journeys too.

Mobility can thus be felt but it can also be moved and moved by. This means mobility can be felt in both an emotional and affective sense. Bachelard (1988) has described our hopes and fears have a vertical differential in how they might make us lighter or heavier. Thus moods and emotions have been taken as movements in and of themselves (Adey 2010, p162). Adey (2010) has named several main movement patterns for the mediation of mobility systems and has distinguished between three separate mediation mobilities. They are:

1) Mobilities are often diffused,

2)  Mobilities mediate between,

3)  Mobilities augment relations and other mobilities.

(Adey, 2010, p.177)

Transport and activities can be distinguished and the mobilities paradigm posits that activities occur while on the move. According to Cresswell (2006) it is being on the move that sets of 'occasioned' activities. The 'activities' may be specific forms of talking, information gathering and work. On the other hand, they could involve simple connections, maintaining a moving presence with others that hold the potential for many different convergences or divergences of physical presence. In summary, 'people perform mobilities when they are on the move. Travelling from one location to another should not be regarded as a 'dead time that people always try to minimize' but rather as 'dwelling in motion' (Sheller and Urry, 2006). Sheller and Urry (2006) also state that there is a growing interest in ways in which material 'stuff' helps to constitute tourism. This 'stuff' is always in motion, changing configuration by being assembled and reassembled. 'Stuff' can be cars being sold at an auction, the mobility of people buying cars from car magazines at a distance; 'stuff' can be geared to the cosmo-pharmaceutical industry, when individuals travel internationally and nationally for treatment, hence sold as packages.

Within this context Urry (2007) argues the need of a mobilities framework to be implemented in sociology. Urry's (2007) 'mobilities paradigm' removes the need for looking at parts as separate and trying to fit subjects into boxes; but welcomes the overlapping or intersecting of the social subjects, especially in travel and communication. It is also clear that social relations at distances need to be investigated from the social sciences perspective (Urry, 2007). Social life can, with this in mind, be examined by 'analysing' the role of 'movement of people, ideas, objects and information'. The term mobilities therefore refers to the broader aspect of establishing movement. It is not just being mobile individually and independently or with other people but as the world must be mobile too (Adey, 2010). But it is important to note that 'our life-worlds are mobile for us, with us, and sometimes they are against us' (Adey, 2010, p.4).

The emphasis on the mobilities paradigm with those objects which are ready-to-hand and highly varied, provide different affordances, especially many variables enabling or presupposing movement. These are referred to as 'moorings' which are relationally placed (Urry (2007). Objects can be distinguished and categorised as being fixed and temporary immobile: hence augmenting mobilities. For example, satellites are fixed in geo-synchronous orbit for the functioning of GPS navigational systems; but a passenger en route staying in a motel is the temporary immobility. Below is a list with further examples of such immobile and stationary or temporary time-space immobilities:-

'-held in place (prisoner, clamped car, poster, rhetoric figure);

-fixed in place (railway track, agrophobic building, library book,);

-temporarily stationary (visitor, car in garage, graffiti, a presentation);

-portable (baby, laptop, souvenir);

-part of a mobile body (foetus, iPod, ID card, designer label);

-prosthetic (disability assistant, contact lenses, name badge, gender)

-constitutive of a mobility system (driver, road, timetable, speed);

-consisting of code (cyborg, BlackBerry, digital document, computer virus).'

(Buscher and Urry, 2009)

It is this process of circulation that has impacted the social world. In other words the creative power of the worldly life can clash or suppress the forces of life. Buscher and Urry (2009) theorise that it is the systems around which serve the human subject. Humans are nothing without objects and meanings are organised into various systems. The systems around serve the individual human subjects their ideas and information (Urry, 2007).

There are the negative aspects of mobility too (Urry, 2007). In certain places, cultures and societies a downward mobility is often attributed with negative significance (Adey, 2010, p.37). Game (2000, cited Adey, 2010, p.37) has shown 'how falling is associated with a kind of passivity and the loss of self-determination over one's fate'; whereas moving away for a job is seen as vertical social mobility. Research by Zelinski (1973) refers to the American citizen as' never arriving, always on his way'. In fact mobility is seen as a social good and immobility confers defeat, failure and being left behind. Social connections are made or maintained through this network of different forms of communication and distances, whether the moments of immobility involved are voluntary or enforced, temporary or long-term, enjoyable or troublesome moments.

The 'mobilities paradigm' also refers to 'tools' to unlock and interpret the paradigm including rhythm and direction; connections, meetings, positioning and synchronising of mobilities. Said (1993, cited Adey,2010, p.26) argued that 'travellers must suspend the claim of customary routine in order to live in new rhythms and rituals...the traveller crosses over, traverse territory, and abandons fixed positions all the time'. In terms of identity in this scenario it is as if one can step in and out of one's own positioning (but fluid positioning of individuals has its limitations). Probyn (1996) emphasises identity as a process of continuous departure. Urry (2007) describes how synchronicity and other tools are necessary components and how they justify some extensive mobilities that people make.

According to Urry (2007, p.47) there are five interdependent 'mobilities' that produce social life organised across distance. These are:

1) 'Corporeal' travel. This travel of people for work, leisure, family life, pleasure, migration and escape, organised in terms of contrasting time-space modalities (from daily commuting to once-in-a-lifetime exile).

2) The 'physical' movement of 'objects' to producers, consumers and retailers; as well as the sending and receiving of presents and souvenirs.

3) The 'imaginative' travel effected through the images of places and peoples appearing on and moving across multiple print and visual media.

4) 'Virtual' travel often in real time thus transcending geographical and social distance.

5) The 'communicative' travel through person- to-person messages via messages, texts, letters, telegraph, telephone, fax and mobile.

(Urry, 2007, p.47)

The argument here is that social networks weak or strong, involving close family friends, colleagues or others can be maintained through the complex assemblage of the above mobilities. For example, weak corporeal travel intermittently can be maintained globally. Thus bodies are not fixed and as they move they 'sense' technology in its surroundings. Travelling usually involves 'corporeal' movement and as bodies move it is the 'mechanics of space' of touching; the feet on the grass; the hand on the rock -face. Thus, in summary, this kinaesthetic sense is facilitated by objects and everyday mundane technologies. However, the need to be face-to-face remains strong. There are five processes that describe this face-to-faceness. They are legal, economic, familial, social obligations to be co-present. Durkheim (1915, cited Urry, 2007, p.49) has explained this face-to-faceness is likely to incur a 'powerful force' or 'a rush of energy' that is felt when there is togetherness. It is significant that Urry (2007) believes it to be the core of social life connections whether close or at a distance. Adey (2010, p.211) has called this the concept of mobility substitution and the formulations vary in their assessment of the severity of substitution.

Here it is emphasised how systems are significant and the metabolic relationship of human societies with nature is in and through time-space by distributing people, activities and objects; namely, the rail system, aeromobility, automobility and the pedestrian system. Nevertheless, there is the fact that richer societies have a wider range of mobility systems. The two new mobility systems that have developed over the last decade or so are 'networked computers' and 'mobile telephony'. Just as route-ways have a spatial - fixity there is the perception that these new systems will change mobility and motility patterns this century. Moreover, as technical expertise has become available so has dependency on this increased expertisation. There is, of course, a distinction between the various socio-spatial patterns of mobility. These include migration, leisure, travel, and nomadism and for each category the social form is distinct 'in the case of a wandering group in contrast to a spatially fixed one' (Urry 2007, p.21).

The proposal of a 'mobilities paradigm' takes into account the imagined presence which occurs through objects, people, information and images travelling, and carrying connections across, and into, multiple and other social spaces (Urry, 2007). The emphasis is on the presence being intermittent and always interdependent with other processes and encompasses all the above senses of mobility. It is these changes that are creating notable political effects on nation states, citizenship, culture and ethnicity. The next section considers the human aspect of mobilities.

## Human Mobilities

People make their lives significant through experiences. Tuan's (1977) theory on place states that movement takes time and occurs in space. Thus, a break or a pause in movement allows it to become a centre of meaning with space organised around it. This is shown below:

A schematic of Tuan's theory of place

Figure 2.3

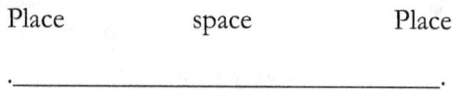

Place space Place

(Adey, 2010, p.54)

The 'focus here is on the points, not abstract dots but points as foci of meaning and significance with space lying in between them' (Adey, 2010, p.54). Tuan's theory has given context and significance to these points in space as opposed to spatial theorists who refer to these nodes or points as physical and economic attractors. These points are places with 'centres of meaning' which is where we organise our social and inherently meaningful lives. Places become meaningful but that does not mean they are on the move. It is the migration element that is critically analysed in this research. Previously, studies of migration, diasporas and transnational citizenship viewed individuals within a static category of nation, ethnicity, community, place and state. It is theorised that 'the actors are still classed, raced, and gendered bodies in motion in specific historical contexts, within certain political formations and spaces' (Smith, 2005, cited Adey, 2010, p.78). It is the 'emplacement' of these individuals in society 'when moving through and acting that is contextually significant' (Mol and Law, 1994, cited Urry, 2010, p.353).

The portrayal and impression of equality within mobilities is noted from the outset as a mis-conception. Ahmed (2000) argues that bodies are characterised as different and access to mobility is highly uneven. It is therefore necessary to examine such zones that are central, empower and connect but also on the other hand disconnect, exclude socially and may be often inaudible (Sheller and Urry, 2006). The processes of globalisation create 'criss-crossing' of individuals in the world and on comparison a single pair of countries contains highly uneven and skewed rights to travel (Gogia, 2006, Timothy, 2001). It has thus been argued that it is these differential mobility empowerments that exacerbate structures and hierarchies of power and position by race, gender, age and class, ranging from the local to the global (Tesfahuney, 1998). Critically different types of human mobilities have different types of mobility empowerments. Turner (2010, p.241) argues that although goods travel relatively freely in a global market the same cannot be said for people.

The recent credit crunch and financial crisis have 'forced social scientists to reconsider existing assumptions about globalisation' and perhaps need to consider the prospect of de-globalisation, in particular the notion of spatial mobility (Turner, 2010, p.241). As 'society' means the nation state the notion 'liquid modernity' and citizenship has interested many, including the diaspora. There is also interest on the issue of entitlements of human rights addressing the rights of migrants moving across national borders (Blau and Moncada, 2005).

At a local level the increase in the concept of the enclave is evident and societies have been described as communities that are gated or ghettoed, as well as quarantine zones (Turner, 2007). The inference is that people have become akin to commodities and can be bought or sold. Ideas of flows, networks, and mobility can be implemented in the enclave society where in an enclosed society, the state regulate spaces. Enclavement thus refers to 'segregation and containment of social groups', exemplified by bureaucratic barriers, legal exclusions and registrations. Entrapment can be viewed as the management and isolation of individuals; hence the 'state' has opted for security over liberal democratic principles (Turner, 2010).

Meanwhile, coerced movement can generate deprivation amongst migrants and refugees around the world. This is also the same for 'forced re-settlement schemes for tribal populations in the face of tourism mobilities'

(Hannam, 2005). It is these mobilities that create and require deeper examination and explanation. With reference to citizenship and the contested multiple identities, identities have become fluid and are negotiated by 'tourists' or 'migrants' particularly at the interstices of different countries in so-called 'contact zones' (Pratt, 2008, cited Hannam and Knox, 2010, p. 165). Places, technologies and 'gates' enhance the tourism mobilities of some while reinforcing the immobilities (or demobilisation) of others' (Hannam et al., 2006).

An important question to ascertain is when does a tourist become a migrant? A definition of a tourist can be defined as 'practices involving the notion of 'departure' of a limited breaking with established routines of everyday life and allowing one's senses to engage with a set of stimuli that contrast with the everyday and the mundane' (Urry, 2007, p.2). It can be argued that tourism is in the broader context part of global human mobilities. With migration, it is 'characteristically' different but 'local' concerns regarding daily transport, material cultures and spatial relations similar. Tourism mobilities involves the use of distinct social spaces such as stations, hotels, motorways, resorts, airports, leisure complexes, cosmopolitan cities, beaches, galleries, roadside parks etc. Social life is full of the multiple and extended connections, and often across long distances and are organised through such nodes or platforms.

It has been recognised with migrants that the subject is either one of 'fixing' and 'placing', whereby one becomes 'part of' the places in which they are located. Migrants and those living at a distance are placed in continual reference to their diaspora and to their place of origin. Appadurai (1995) termed this as 'trans-locality'. Common among South Asian diasporic communities is the traffic of clothing and fashion goods as a significant bridge (Werbner, 1999). Thus, this acts to 'foreground acts of 'homing and 're-grounding which points towards the complex inter-relation between travel and dwelling, home and not-home' (Hannam and Knox, 2010, p.162).

Urry, (2007) explains that although there are numerous new means of communicating, i.e. through the internet and the mobile phone, the need for face-to-face contact is maintained. This could be that one is living as part of a family from a distance, to establish and or maintain business networks, or for friendship purposes. On the other hand, there is the 'forced migration' which as a result of economic and or political reasons results mainly from developing countries. Such migration becomes complex in particular when the receiving countries (mainly developed) have their own legal and social systems (Marfleet 2006). In general, 'economic processes, climate-related disasters and political conflicts continue to create increasingly mobile populations and hybrid resident tourists. Cross-border migrations, refugees and diasporas, globally situated second-home owners and amenity migrants, regular short stay commuters and longer stay economic migrants, all contribute to a global landscape characterised by hybridities, postcolonial identities and roots-seeking homelessness' (Hollinshead, 1998 cited Jamal and Robinson, p.649).

Castles (2009, p.442) has examined the ongoing debates of migration and its development relationship. Migration can be positive (Newland, 2007) or pessimistic (Newland, 2007; Ellerman, 2003). An academic and political debate exists despite it being a 'process of social transformation' that is a central concept for analysing the links between human mobility and global change. However, rural livelihoods are affected in third world countries and factors such as intensification of agriculture are some setbacks when people exercise their agency to improve their livelihoods (Castles, 2009). Castles (2009) also notes the following in relation to migration and development:

-'Migrant remittances can have a major positive impact on the economic development of countries of origin.

-Migrants also transfer home skills and attitudes-known as 'social remittances'-which support development.

-'Brain drain' is being replaced by 'brain circulation', which benefits both sending and receiving countries.

-Temporary (or circular) labour migration can stimulate development.

-Migrant diasporas can be a powerful force for development, through transfer of resources and ideas.

-Economic development will reduce out-migration'.

(Castles, 2009, p.458)

## The Concept of Diaspora

The concept of home has been defined as static as opposed to dynamic, with processes, involving the acts of imaging, creating, unmaking, changing, losing and moving 'homes' (Armbruster and Nadje, 2002). The traditional meanings of home known as the physical place of dwelling and shelter, 'home' commonly been linked to 'family', community or 'homeland / nation' have been subject to social, cultural, economic and political changes and has also been radically re-defined.

Homelands, lands of settlement and spaces for travel can all be re-worked through the concept and object of the diaspora. Diaspora, by definition, is dispersion which effectively compresses time and space such that it enables the experiences of many places at what would appear to be one moment. Today such multiplicity and simultaneity has become particularly pronounced. Barber's (2001) definition of diaspora is 'communities that define themselves by reference to a distant homeland from which they once originated' (cited Hannam and Knox, 2010, p.163). Within this topic of diaspora there is also tension between the specific and the general that may be variously dictated as the local and the global, the particular and the universal, or the national and the regional. Shukla (2001) uses the phrase 'changing same' illuminates the apparent paradox of the persistence of South Asian traditions and forms of expression around the world and the increased visibility of innovative renderings. On the one hand, diasporic tourism may be seen as 'in search for their roots' of self-discovery and identity affirmation (Adey, 2010, p.163) but also these communities also engage in everyday tourism in their host country. For example, the Pakistani community in the UK will visit the beach (Adey, 2010, p.163).

Diaspora has therefore created ideal sites to explore the effects of globalisation. Hannam and Knox (2010, p.165) have distinguished that a resident diasporic population is certainly helpful for outbound tourism and their activities when visiting the co-members of the diaspora 'become an object of a wider tourist gaze'. Coles and Timothy (2004, cited Hannam and Knox, 2010, p.165) have noted that 'when residents of the original homeland' make a trip to diaspora spaces they may visit sites of heritage or attend festival and events targeted specifically at them such as 'Bollywood Britain'.

Moving from country to country is a dislocating experience (Werbner,

2005). Following the riots by young South Asians in northern British towns the historical migration and settlement in Britain was identified to generate two paradoxes. The first was that 'encapsulated 'communities' are formed by being set apart culturally and socially; to sink roots in a new country. Secondly, within these communities culture is conceived as an 'embodied ritual' 'in social exchange and in performance, conferring agency and empowering different social actors: religious and secular, men, women and youth' (Werbner, 2005). Thus, it is conflictual, open, hydridising and fluid while trying to conform to sentimental and morally compelling forces. Werbner (2005) has identified the diasporic Pakistani community in South Manchester to have always been a non-localised network, marked by class divisions and social relations cutting across class and neighbourhood boundaries and linking the whole of Britain to their homeland. The notion of culture is displayed through ritual gift giving, embodiment (such as displayed in wedding ceremonies), and the following of a religious figures in Islam. In summary these intersecting transnational cultural spaces do not coincide with the UK nation state (Islamic, South-Asian and Inter-national). Werbner (2002, cited in Werbner, 2005) has argued that identity can thus be a series of projected imageries for a diaspora. Thus migration entails more than cultural transplantation or translocation. Acts of cultural and material creativity are entailed which all need to be created from scratch which can be inescapably hybrid and permeable. With this theory in mind the vulnerability of all diaspora Muslims after September 11th is a predicament of 'being forced to make impossible choices between deeply felt loyalties' (Werbner, 2005).

The diasporic migration patterns and return visits involve complex relations. The contemporary term by Benson and O' Reilly (2009, p.608) is 'lifestyle migration'. As it has been stated 'the political, technological, financial and transportational changes have been critical in significantly lowering the barriers to mobility. Hence, the frequent visits of migrants returning home visiting friends and family while ostensibly 'on holiday' in their country of origin. In fact, this diaspora tourism may be seen in turn as genealogical (Nash, (2002). There is on the other hand visits made to the diasporic homelands that are 'troubling, disconcerting and ambiguous experiences as well as new found ambivalences' (Duval, 2003; Hannam, 2004; Stephenson, 2002, cited in Hannam and Knox, 2010, p.163).

Historically, the concept of a 'myth of return' has been explored in terms of post-colonial economic migrants experiences (Anwar, 1979). This has been an ongoing predicament for the first-generation who have memories and stories of an identity have been that blurred through assimilation and integration from settling in the UK. As Tolia-Kelly (2004) argues the notion of 'land' and 'nation' seem imperative to the survival of these myths and memories. Brah (1996, p16) also claims that these 'diasporas sustain an ideology of return' but according to Hall (1996, p.10) these diasporas will hardly ever return to their roots or origins.

After the 11 September 2001, an over-emphasis on 'culture' and cultural differences that leads to 'othering' of minority groups has contributed to shifts in ethnicity and diaspora, leading contemporary theorists in diaspora, such as Paul Gilroy and Stuart Hall to re-conceptualise culture in different ways. While 'diaspora culture' may produce ethnic absolutisms as part of its political project, they are not objective givens. In the case of Afro-Caribbean experiences identity is not fixed or dependent on a given culture but the outcome of shifting positions. Studies by Homi Bhabha during the 1990s transpose previous ideas of hybridity and argued the loss of the colonial authority to be a factor of hybridity. Migrants fall into the notion of the 'third space' within the diaspora, creating cultural hybridity, that is, 'the jarrings of a differentiated culture which challenges the centred, dominant cultural meanings' (Young 1995, cited Gardner, 2002 p.10). However, 'research conducted with educated young Bangladeshis in Tower Hamlett in the early 1990's showed how the second generation put together new 'hybrid' identities that build upon Bangladeshi, Muslim, Bengali, British and solidarities' (Eade, 1994, cited Gardner, 2002, p.12). Increasing exposure to the cultures of the new homeland becomes hybridity, however, it is the younger generations that are affected not the parents who remain orientated to their place of origin. Thus, older models of assimilation with time and cultural change need to be treated with caution.

**Transnationalism, Mobility and Belonging**

Transnational migration is but one aspect of a series of accelerated changes in post-modernity that has unsettled previously bounded, singular and stable conceptualisations of home (Rapport and Dawson, 1998). It has been suggested that some international migrants have always displayed transnational characteristics (King and Christou, 2011). It has been argued that technologies involving transport and communications and the creation of 'corridors' of migration, remittances and transnational economic and social activities (Guarnizo, 2003) have enabled a different order of connections to the previous eras. Progressively, there has been a subversion of the rhetoric, policy and scholarly concentration on integration and assimilation (Vertovec, 2001) to that of 'transmigrants' or 'floaters' who live simultaneously in two or more worlds (King and Christou, 2011, p. 456). Thus, transnational social spaces (Faist, 2000; Ali and Koser (2002) and translocal social fields have been the definitions pursued with the social fields that the migrants inhabit.

Existing literature has challenged the fact that the people they studied found their home in movement and people engaged in transnational practices, this led them to express an uneasiness, a sense of fragmentation, tension and even pain. There are many facets of transnationalism including the emotional, social and cultural effects. Belonging to a place has therefore created studies at a transnational level. Therefore certain studies are briefly reviewed in the light of the concept of the mobilities turn considering the theoretical developments on migrants and the social and cultural implications of places while on the move. An emphasis has been placed on mobility and belonging from this perspective. As an example, the most vulnerable, the poor, women, illegal immigrants and refugees; although the existence of the more positive experiences of the migrants living across physical and cultural boundaries are not denied and enjoying a multiplicity of fixed and / or moving homes (Rapport and Dawson, 1998). One of the defining characteristics of transnational migrants is that they have multiple allegiances to places they consider home or a place of residence. Thus, the concept of 'home' is complex and multi-dimensional. Armbruster and Nadje (2002, p.6) have thus defined home as:

'Home is also 'a universe of moral strength'. It is a memory of a place and an imagination of a space where 'proper values and functioning social relationships can be found'. Home is multi-located – it could be in the country of origin (Turkey) or the country of residence (Germany), but maybe more significantly, 'it could be a tension between the two'.

The micro-level analysis of 'home' and 'community' also consists of the individual's sense of identity and belonging. On the one hand the analysis of 'home' is the making of 'tradition' and 'culture', (Fabos, 2002) and, on the other, a dual belonging allowed by transnational practices can also be accompanied by a sense of rupture and discontinuity whereby a contradictory feeling of home is used as a tool to negotiate identities and establish continuities (Salih, 2002).

Studies have shown that in relation to tourism and diaspora important connections are made with their places of origin. Their 'identities are creolised or hybridised' (Featherstone, 1995, Friedmann, 1999, Lowe, 1991, Nurse, 1999, cited Hannam and Knox, 2010, p.163) and can be related back to forms of so called 'ethnic tourism'. King (1994, cited Hannam and Knox, 2010, p.163) explains this term as: 'a desire to delve into family histories through travel to the relevant country. It might or alternatively might not involve actually staying with family... and this type of ethnic tourism has tended to be regarded as virtually synonymous with the visiting friends and relatives or VFR traffic.'

Transnationalism or broadly speaking distance and sense of mobility also affects the 'relationship of belonging'. It is assumed that if one is mobile they do not possess the strong sense of belonging as that of a person who remains immobile. Gustafon (2009, p.249) has demonstrated that there are two important parameters that need to be taken into account when referring to mobility and belonging. These are the different kinds of mobility such as daily commuting, long-distance travel, residential mobility, and international migration. The second is the examining of local, regional, national and European belonging. Human mobility may take different forms such as frequency, distance, and duration (Bell and Wood, (cited in Gustafson, 2009, p.491). Feldman, Pollini, Savage, Bagnell and Longhurst, (cited in Gustafson, 2009, p.491) have found that mobile people have a strong sense of belonging.

A basic assumption in migration research holds the view point that over a period of time the feeling of belonging to the host country increases and assimilation and integration occurs. Castles and Miller (1998) have suggested that there is actually a more complex picture on transnationalism and international migrants where a sense of belonging is developed in both sending and receiving countries. Fog-Olwig (1999) shows in her ethnography of West – Indians on Nevis, that their propensity to migrate is balanced by an equally strong attachment to what she terms cultural sites, such as family houses or land.

On the other hand, Gustafson's (2009) research showed that residential mobility has a strong negative relationship with local belonging. Strong regional belonging was more common with women than men; on a national level white collar workers were more likely to have a strong national belonging than blue collar workers although over seventy percent did have a strong sense of belonging to national belonging. People who travelled to other parts of the country expressed a strong sense of belonging nationally; but for residential mobility and immigration, the relationship with national belonging was negative. Both immigration and temporary residence abroad were associated with a stronger sense of belonging to Europe. Migrants usually maintain bonds (locally, regionally, and nationally) with their former home countries, such that bonding into a new home country is often a lengthy process (Castles and Miller, (1998).

Although, there have been suggestions that certain elements are required for 'national attachment'. Renshon (2005, cited Renshon, 2008, p.82) has 'listed a warmth and affection for; an appreciation of; a pride in; a commitment and responsibility toward, and; support for the USA (its institutions, its way of life and aspirations, and its fellow citizens'. In summary, the research shows 'love' may cover these terms but it is the importance of each on its own that has significance in culture and identity. In particular, these elements are essential for understanding the national attachment related to the integration of immigrants.

Holding dual identity has shown to provide the most satisfaction with one's situation than the other forms of cultural adaptation (Gonzaz and Brown, 2003; Sam and Berry 2006, cited Klanderman et al., 2008). In addition, it has been shown that those with dual identity are more likely to participate in social and political situations as well as collective action. This highlights the importance of the degree of identification of the nation to stimulate such activities (Klandermans et al, 2004). Research by Klanderman et al, 2008) also considered emotions as antecedents of movement participation. Emotions can either be avoidance when one does not participate out of fear or approach orientated. The latter can be described as anger which is antecedent of protest participation (Van Zomeren et al, 2004, cited Klandermans et al, 2008). The relationship between emotions and efficacy is apparent and also shows that anger is an important stimulant of protest participation. Van Stekelenburg (2006, cited Klandermans, 2008) demonstrates that rather than functioning as a separate pathway to collective action, emotions amplify already existing motivations. Thus in addition to grievances, efficacy, identity and emotions the involvement in civil society organisations or social embeddedness has been determined as meaningful on collective action.

Given the 'increased distrust Muslim immigrants have endured from the host population since 9/11' results from this study may not be wholly representative in engaging in collective action. Conclusions showed two clusters, a social embeddedness cluster and a grievances cluster. The first cluster consists of feelings of efficacy and embeddedness in social networks. Hence the more efficacious migrants feel and the more involved they are in civil society organisations, the more they participate in collective action. They also are more involved in social networks and especially those involved in ethnic networks. The latter consists of political cynicism, perceived unfairness, and identity. Political cynicism is associated with the perception of unfair treatment which in turn reinforces action participation. Interestingly those participants with dual identity have a stronger identification with the host nation and expect fair treatment and if not react in a stronger fashion; although are not disloyal to the nation. But feelings of efficacy determine whether grievances generate fear or anger which in turn are results of social networks and the characteristics of these networks. Forcing assimilation has proven to be the least beneficial as there is a tendency to produce the opposite effects. 'The view of social capital as a resource which is mobilised in purposive action is akin to the central tenet of resource mobilisation theory' and social embeddedness and dual identity are closely related although it is stipulated more work needs to be done. Strengthening people's feelings of political efficacy and reinforcing people's dignity is the result of integration and migrants can turn discontent into action. (Klandermans et al., 2008).

### Mobility Systems

A key main concept focussed on in the mobility paradigm is 'systems'. Systems make possible movement and most significantly it is in these moments of 'spaces of anticipation' are made, that the message will get through, that the parcel will arrive. Examples from the twentieth century have been the car-system, the national telephone system, air power, high speed trains, modern urban systems, budget air travel, mobile phones and networked computers. The twenty first century has moved further into expert systems, is more involved and more complicated as well as much more interdependent of each other. Personalisation has resulted in greater dependency on these systems to facilitate human life. And as we move forward into the twenty first century these 'mobility systems' are even more complicated (Urry, 2007).

'Human beings are nothing without objects organised into various systems' (Urry 2010, p. 272). Hence, these systems serve humans to carry out their requirements, but also develop significant powers themselves. McLuhan (1964) first noted this division in telecommunications and transport; there is the informational mobility and the physical mobility which are inter-connected. On separation of messages from these mediums the fluidity of the physical transport, infrastructures, roads and wagons is untied and creates informational mobility. This is concerned with words, ideas and imagery from the physical objects on the other hand, for example, such as stones, coins and papyrus. Thrift (1990) for example, has pointed out how the evolution of newspapers are tightly coupled with the Post Office history, as is the railway and telegraph scenario and transport and communications rely on each other. This is the same for all mediating mobilities that are part of people's lives that are wrapped in and wrapped around their lives (Thrift, 1990). The processes through which mobilities mediate require vast fixed infrastructures and other systems of mediation to control and regulate them. Adey (2010, p.223) has called the carrying and the 'facilitation function parasitic'. Adey (2010) has noted the transport systems of the car and the aeroplane as the two main forms of mediation today. Although in other countries it may be a different form of mediation such as trains in India.

When 'doing mobility' (Adey, 2010), seeing, sensing and moving are all practised and experienced. This could be purely visual (as initially described by Urry (2007); site-seeing; walking and cycling all part of the activity. Urry (2007) has described walking as a movement which underpins the other modes of mobility and focuses on pavements and paths. However, with time the thinking behind walking has transformed to several connections. There is now what can be termed the 'mundane walk' to the shops or the leisurely walking, perhaps walking to the countryside. The hybridised character of the paths can be connected with other technologies of movement e.g. clothing, footwear, rules and regulations. Recently Sony Walkmans, the ipod and mobile phones create the image of a cool walker and re-organises the sound-scapes of city-life (du- Gay et al., 1997). Walking has three nodes according to Urry (2007), namely: walking for an adventure; walking without adventure e.g. parks, promenades, camps (Diken and Lautsten, 2005); and walking and personal fitness. Adams (2001,cited Adey, 2010 p.157) 'writes how walking through a place demands an 'involvement' with senses such as 'sight', 'hearing', 'touch', 'smell' , 'the kinetic sense called proprioception' and even 'taste'. Sounds could 'range from the call of birds to the sounds of traffic horns' whereas the sensation of touch 'might include the brush of tall grass, the spray of passing cars on wet roads, and the jostling of strangers in crowded places'. Wylie (2002) has explained this process to continuously fold and unfold through which subjectivity and meaning may emerge. This has been agreed to be the most egalitarian of the mobility systems, regardless of how unequal services and access may be. To summarise, there are these paths for walking for the able-bodied, but it may not be an option to walk to family and friends because of the 'supermarket of friends available globally'.

A new connectedness was initially developed though with the era of the public railway. Sheller and Urry (2003, cited in Urry, 2007 p.91), described this as 'public spaces becoming mobile and connecting, a set of circulating process that undercuts the spatial divide of the 'public' and the 'private' A 'nexus' defined by Laing (cited in Urry,2007, p.94) as 'a group, whose unification is achieved through the reciprocal interiorisation by each of each other...The nexus is everywhere'; in other words, the 'whole only functions with all its parts', without the 'nexus' the separate elements are non-existent. The train was an invention exploited by the Victorians who themselves had a global outreach and with the advent of the train came 'clock time' disciplining passengers. The noticeable effects were the shrinkage of space by bringing places close together and in parallel connecting spaces that would not be accessible. Travelling through such a confined vision disembodied the traveller from the land and panoramic views were able to be sighted, (Schivelbusch, 1986). Other activities relating to the railway was the rise of micro-spaces, the train journey thus planned, with the intention to read, to work taking the laptop or make use of the time with the mobile phone. The most important deduction is that it is not seen as dead time and the stations are another hub reflecting its sociability.

Described as 'diffused mediation' (Adey, 2010) or 'diffused mobility' (Urry 2007) the automobile and aeromobility have provided a means for the individual to move away from timetables and gain degrees of freedom and flexibility. Hence, the car has fast become recognised as monopolistic, as an individualised desire for privatised flexibility. There is the notion of the car being associated with comfort, pleasure, of security, emotion and dwelling. When considering listening to music in the car it is another diffusion of music, as has already been mentioned by Adey (2010) who has termed this system to a 'diffused mediation'. Although it has less flexibility than the car, with the introduction of cheaper airlines is still more flexible than rail systems.

However, after September 11th there is the perceived pressure of terrorism, but at the same time globalisation and global competition are central to aeromobilities. 'Aero and automobility enable people to perform social activities as well as the obligations required to form and sustain relationships and networks' (Adey, 2010, p.180) aeromobility has been described as corridors of travel (Lassen, 2006). Airports are a place of 'cybermobilities' (Adey and Bevan, 2006, cited Hannam, Sheller and Urry, 2006). This has created new forms of socio-economic spaces and connections.

Augmentation between the mobilities has also increased enormously with the advent of ICT (Information Communication Technology) systems. ICT includes the movement of information such as telephone signals and Internet data packets, or the sunken formations of cables, wires and infrastructures which all take significant consequences and social inflections for mobilities. Thus, virtual reality; the emergence of powerful, independent knowledge-based systems through continuous developments of software are 'increasingly organising production, consumption, travel, and communications around the world' (Urry, 2007, p.159). Corporeal movement is continuously and perhaps obsessively utilised by texting etc. with less of a need for an obligatory visit. Thus, the notion of 'making space for time' can be applied again with 'complementarity implementation'. This is when ICT and other forms of virtual mobility have augmented and created new physical journeys. Transport and communication technologies have now been described as partners and these components are known as network capital (Urry, 2007). It is seen as 'a new form of social networking and physical travel which is enhanced by new communications'. There is the 'shift of relationships further to a person-to-person connectivity and engendering new kinds of sociability's on the move'. They develop 'interspaces' and shift time systems from 'punctuality' to a more informal fluid' system of coordination. These mobile means of communications are increasingly combined with humans, forming new material worlds inhabiting machines. These mechanic hybrids involve 'a contradiction between nearness and remoteness, or mobility and fixation... at the push of a button, territories dissolve, oppositions of distant and close, motion and stasis, inside and out, collapse; identities are marginalised and simulated, and collectivises lose their borders' (Bogard, 2000 cited Urry 2007, p.181).

As a result of technology people from near and far, can have strong and weak ties. Meetings although costly in terms of time, money and effort have a twofold benefit. They reinforce strong links and maintain weak ties through intermittent co-presence. The maintenance of weak ties is an interesting analogy in that research has shown that 83 per cent of jobs were acquired through people who they did not 'know' very well. Thus, the extensive weak ties of aquaintanceship and informational - flow central to job success (Granovetter, cited in Urry, 2007, p.214). These network hubs can take several forms but in summary it is the increase of very weak ties; whether friend, family or work and arguably 'knowing'. Larsen, Urry, Axhausen (cited in Urry, 2007, p.220) theorise for maintaining social networks 'people have to spend much time planning and sustaining meetings with a fairly small proportion of those who are 'known communicating and then travelling from a distance so as to keep in touch'. Meetings are central to people's lives, but even to maintain even the weakest ties it can be done by minimal effort. When meetings occur it can be seen as an opportunity of expanding networks in both work and play situations.

Sustenance of relationships can only be partially through various communication and technologies. As Urry (2007) argues in order 'to 'cement' the weak ties and people have to occasionally 'meet' face-to-face or even body-to-body (Urry, 2004). Urry (2007, p.233) has identified five processes within social networks that engender travelling, meeting and normally much talk. These are legal, economic and familial obligations that are relatively formal meetings. Social obligations and obligations to be co-present with others. The first three obligations can be a 'mobility burden' as it involves travelling at specific times for specific reasons because of expectations of presence and of attention (Urry, 2004). However, as these meetings all involve some kind of movement, the better the technology, it increasing motility and therefore greater are the obligations to meet (Urry, 2007). Social capital practices are processes that also enable resources to be secured by individuals or groups through the social networks (Heisler, 2000). These are divided into four categories, namely:

1) 'Value introjection is a source of social capital and is considered to be the driving force behind the collective good, encouraging members to behave in a socially acceptable ways.

2) Reciprocity transactions refer to norms of reciprocity, when an established pattern exists of individuals asking for and reciprocating favours or assistance from one another. In this way good deeds, information and approval are constantly given and reciprocated within a group.

3) Bounded solidarity refers to the unified collective, formed when a group is faced by a common adversarial situation.

Enforceable trust refers to the ability of the group, being to its cohesiveness and collective group norms, to govern and hold accountable individual group members.' (Portes and Sensenbrenner, 1993, cited in Lee, 2009, p.740-742)

Listing the reasons to travel to be at another place intermittently is extensive, but the general reasons are: travelling to family events for a wedding, funeral, birthday party, christening, Thanksgiving, Christmas; visiting a lawyer or court, to attend hospital, or school, university or public office; to travel to work or a job interview. The social obligation refers to the quality of time being spent with the other (family, friend or colleague). This can be another mobility burden as its requirement is being face- to- face; present and attentive (ranges from the formal handshake to sexual intimacy). Being present intermittently enables the weak network to gain strength and trust by members being able to 'read' what the other is thinking and observe the body language. It is also an opportunity to hear 'first hand' what they have to say, to sense a response and to observe emotions. 'Co-presence renders persons uniquely accessible, available, and subject to one another' (Goffman, cited Urry, 2007, p.233). Such a requirement for the trust and commitment to one another over periods of distance and solitude 'create a temporal feel for the moment, separate from and at odds with 'normal' life (take time out)' (Urry, 2007, p.234).

Meetings are for conversation and important for facework between people in interaction order. The conversation can be diverse but as already mentioned through this embodiment follows trust and interaction order. Meetings can be held from the work point of view and also family and friendship point of view. In the latter it has reported that half of Sweden's travel stems from meeting up with friends and family (O'Dell, cited in Urry, 2007, p.245). Another study in the UK reported by Gordon, (cited by Urry, 2007, p.246) states that, 'There are social customs, obligations and activities that substantial majorities of population... identify as among these necessary events are: celebrations on special occasions such as Christmas' (83%) and 'attending weddings, funerals' (80%) 'visits to friends or family' (84%), especially those in hospital (92%). In other words, to maintain and reproduce familial relationships travel and communication is the core. If one is unable to attend to a dinner meal, apologies are necessary. The same applies to shopping for the family and geographical distance and obligatory meetings (even more so for the 'family fragments' as a result of residential migration and diasporic communities).

Travel for the migrants and diasporic cultures meeting in places they grew up in or in old schools is an experience of value and remembered until the next time. This is particularly so for those in stretched-out social networks. Mason (cited in Urry, 2007, p.249) found in her research that the Pakistani migrants in the North West of England fondly remembered their visit to Pakistan. This lasted between two weeks to several months and almost all the respondents were enthusiastic about their visit whatever their age. Larsen, Urry, Axhausen (cited in Urry, 2007, p.249) highlighted how a death of a family member resulted in the individual wanting to be present at the funeral in an embodied and social way more than is possible by phone or email.

## Conclusion

The current era of globalisation has impacted on mobilities and has resulted in the recognition from all the social sciences. Mobilities have become central (Adey, 2010) within the theoretical climate and empirically proven. This chapter has reviewed mobilities from an abstract position and contextually (Cresswell, 2006). It outlines the mobilities paradigm that has five main interdependent variables including the five processes that describe face-to-faceness (Urry, 2007). These are described in relation to human mobilities and how people make their lives significant through experience (Adey, 2010) hence altering travel, tourism and migration patterns (Hannam and Knox, 2010). A major change has culminated in the approaches to nation, state, ethnicity, community, place and space which were previously defined from static entities to a contemporary fluid approach. Literature on dual-identity; border security re-assessment and control; tourism and migration were reviewed taking into account the changes since September 11 and the July Bombings of 2005. The post-colonial Pakistani community falls into the category of a diaspora and a section on the definitions, perceptions and processes that have been challenged in the contemporary world discussed this above. Diasporas have been regarded to be ideal sites to explore the effects of globalisation (Hannam and Knox, 2010) and the theoretical concepts on integration and assimilation has been reviewed. Cultural aspects were discussed and the transnational, translocality patterns and hybridisation of the community were compared with the 'myth of return' analogy and mobility and belonging. This was followed by an evaluation of cultural adaptation and the behaviour of individuals within the context of this adaptation (Klanderman et al., 2008).

It has been defined that 'human beings are nothing without objects organised into various systems' (Urry, 2007, p.272). The processes and behavioural patterns of the diaspora have thus been visualised through these lenses with the different types of mobility systems. Adey (2010) has defined this to be 'mediated', for which the two core mediators are the car and aeroplane or as Urry (2007) terms automobilty and aeromobility. These have been enhanced with the increase of Information Communication and Technology (ICT) to the level where there is complimentarity implementation (Plaut, 1997). This has led to a more fluid system of coordination and its effects on social mobility are reviewed. To illustrate this point the accessibility of the capital rich and capital poor was discussed. The impact of mobility systems, the benefits and disadvantages were also discussed. For example evaluations of the mediations of aeromobility can be a good indicator of individual members of the diaspora returning to their home country Pakistan but also there are stringent controls on entry and departure at the terminals or hubs i.e. airports, particularly since September 11th. However, the next chapter critically analyses migration policies and in particular empirical studies of South Asian migration and findings of the Pakistani community living in other UK cities.

# CHAPTER 2

# PAKISTANI MIGRATION TO THE UK

## Introduction

After the Single European Act (1986) and of greater urgency since the 11 September 2001 events and 7 July and 21 July 2005 bombings; migration, freedom and security have been under microscopic screening leading to greater legislation and controls (Geddes, 2008, p.68). Over the last two decades there has been a 'sea change in migration' (Levitt and Jaworsky, 2007, p.129). Large numbers of people are on the move within and out of their home countries who maintain ties with the homelands as well as incorporating these ties into the receiving country (Levitt and Jaworsky, 2007). When referring to these groups living outside their homeland they are referred to as 'diaspora', although a new concept of cosmopolitanism to capture the 'diaspora in motion' has been developed. Migration and diaspora are seen as social historical processes overlapping with transnationalism. This also falls into the mobility range where people occupy 'in-between spaces of identity, culture and communication' (Rajan and Sharma, 2006, cited Brettel and Hollifield, 2008, p.121). Transnational migration 'signal(s) an abatement of national boundaries and the development of ideas or political institutions that spanned national boundaries. Transnational processes are increasingly seen as part of a broader phenomenon of globalisation, marked by the demise of the nation-state and the growth of world cities that serve as key nodes of flexible, capital accumulation, communication and control' (Schiller et al, 1995, cited Kim, 2009, p.681) as discussed in the previous chapter.

A speech given by Margaret Thatcher referenced immigration in January 1978 talked about the British way of life and concluded that 'this country might be swamped by people with different culture'. Although immigration was reduced greatly in 1971 (Immigration Act) this was a popular speech and the party was voted into parliament. New Immigration rules came into effect in the 1980s targeting the South Asians and the 'arranged marriage system'. The 1970s was also a period of economic recession together these issues fuelled conflict and fascist organisation movement (Brah, 2006, pp.50-51).

Renshon (2008) has taken the issue of racism out of the 'box' and used terms such as giving 'access and support' to the immigrants to aid the stages of integration, the third one to be attachment. It has also been recognised that dynamics such as race and ethnicity are involved in the assimilation process (Portes and Zhou, 1993) as well as the 'rates of immigration' and the time that has elapsed for the society to adapt before further migration (Massey, 1995)

The male post-colonial Pakistani's that came for work in the UK from the 1950's to the 1970's are known as 'pioneers' and it can be demonstrated that there were essentially two types of post-colonial Pakistani men, namely those who were educated and initiated programmes for the community at large and those who were the recipients of these pioneering developments e.g. the purchase of a building for conversion to a mosque that was used by all the Muslim's to pray in, hold wedding ceremonies etc.

A shift in the study of migration has resulted due to the failure of the assimilation model to explain the 'resurgence' of ethnicity and the persistence of racial inequality and conflict. This was due to the naïve images of the melting point and being out of touch with the contemporary realities (Alba and Nee, 1997). Levitt and Jaworsky have stated that the 'process of assimilation into a melting pot or a multicultural salad bowl' has never been one-way but migrants are 'simultaneously embedded in the multiple sites and layers of the transnational social fields in which they live' (2007, p.129). This has resulted in separate strands of migration literature (Hein de Haas, 2010). Migration is multi-faceted and multiform, with social change (individuals changing over time and the successive replacements of generations) it is important for theories to account for these changes (Alwin and McCammon, 2003). However, it is also important to understand how these theories have developed and evolved from different disciplines to further advance knowledge in the area.

The motives for immigration vary into the UK; some groups come to make money and then return home and there are the groups that come to stay; it is their integration which needs to be addressed. Integration or 'fitting in' takes three stages, namely, acculturation in terms of symbolic ethnicity (Alba, 1990); assimilation in terms of fitting in and then attachment which has been the ultimate goal of many immigration policies. Recognition is given to the fact that this may occur in the second or third-generations rather than the first (Renshon, 2008). From a contemporary perspective, fluid identities are evident (Urry, 2007).

These stages in detail of integration are:

1. Acculturation (symbolic ethnicity) where one alters behaviour to another culture.

2. Assimilation (fitting in) Modood (2007) defines this as a one way process where newcomers do little to disturb the host society thus identifying primarily with the culture of the country.

3. Attachment (a key aim of many immigration policies). Renshon (2008) however, defined the process of 'complete integration' when love and loyalty to the host society is developed. Previous empirical studies have also shown the transnational relationship and the diasporic link has kept this 'myth alive' and in some cases 'revived' it (Ali and Holden, 2006). Arguably, the embodiment of being in 'reviving the myth' can take on the form of being a tourist and taking part in leisure activities

Waters and Jimenez (2005, p.107) have pointed out that in contrast to previous migration, an ongoing replenishment of new immigrants requires the need to rethink the concept of generation. 'At any point in time each generation has a mix of cohorts and each cohort has a mix of generations' (Water and Jimenez, 2005, p.121). Thus we cannot study migration solely from a host-country perspective anymore and a general agreement that a set of more focussed themes and questions are more relevant than mere descriptions. Directions point towards space, place and the nature of embeddedness, the variable consequences of transnationalism and international and internal migration comparative studies (Levitt and Jarwosky, 2007).

Migrants within cities have been understood to employ a mechanistic model with levels of adaptation in residential or occupational clustering from a statistical basis to a new and unfamiliar environment. The concept of 'adaptation' takes into account the inherent qualities of the migrant group responding to an independent set of circumstances. This can be visualised by relating to the collection of characteristics of a migrant group, for example, the Irish groups, Jewish groups and the South Asians. At the extreme ends, the demography and geography of the Jews tends to be ahead of the dominant population and the Gypsies living in the worst conditions and known to be poorer and among a non-industrialised population. Using these two examples as a barometer, minorities and emigrants fall in between these two categories (Panayi, 2000, p.21).

De Haas (2010) has outlined the main developments in research on migration from 1945 in relation to the policy field. Optimism was felt up to 1973 in the migration field with the link to return strong in the development area. It was expected that the capital and knowledge obtained would help the developing countries in 'development take-off' (De Haas, 2010, p.230). During the period 1973 and 1990 scepticism grew with brain drain concerns and the emphasis on integration in receiving countries and the tightening of immigration policies. From 1990 to 2001 there was a readjustment towards subtle change in approaches as a result of empirical work. But continuous scepticism and a further tightening of immigration policies were implemented by policy development. However, it is only since the millennium that research has shown there may be a positive approach de-linking development with return and a change of view on remittances. There was renewed hope on the 'development contribution of migration often framed within renewed hopes put on circular and return migration', diaspora involvement has been seen as a vital tool development tool, remittance boom, a turn around on views of remittances and brain gain (De Haas, 2010, p.230). In addition to the pessimistic frameworks migration is noted to affect the traditional care systems and disruption of kinship, breaking down traditional institutions regulating village life and culture (King and Vullnetari, 2006).

### Policy Implications of Migration to the UK

The effects of policies and legal requirements in the UK in an attempt to control the movement of migration have been significant. An informed analysis of such changes can only be made considering all of the complex and changing patterns of migration to the UK itself. Commonwealth immigrants who came before 1971 were given all the rights as British citizens on admission. This has now changed to the need for the legal residence in the UK for five years by the 1971 Immigration Act and the 1981 British Nationality Act. The Commission for Racial Equality was set-up through a series of Race Relations Acts in 1965. In the 1980's there was a shift away from 'interventionist anti-racist policies' and an attempt to approaches that were more market-orientated (Home Office, 1981, 1989, Banton, 1984, Beyon, 1986, Layton-Henry, 1986, OECD, 1992;1997, Solomos, 1993, cited Castles and Miller, 1998, p.223).

Joining the European Union has also had its own effects on the values and judgements towards the global migration changes. A Member of State of the European Union is a State that has agreed to the conditions known as the 'Copenhagen criteria' or referred to as the 'Treaties of the European Union (EU). The country maintains its own national military and foreign policy but is bound by its laws. In return the EU's legislative and judicial institutions then represent the country. Disparities between the member countries are noticeable and therefore it is obvious that variations of regulation and requirements are needed for some whereas others are well advanced, shaping and leading policy. The UK was one of the initial seven countries to form part of the now EU.

In terms of migration the monitoring of movement across borders and pooling of information has led to significant developments of tools such as Schengen Information Systems (SIS), the Visa Information System (VIS) and the Eurodac system which involves the sharing of data on asylum seekers and illegal immigration (Geddes, 2008). When referring to migration and asylum policies there are three types of borders that are defined. That is, territorial borders, organisational borders (work and welfare) and conceptual borders. The first two are self-explanatory and it is the last type of border which is more unclear referring to identity, belonging and entitlement (Geddes, 2008, p.25). A resident citizen and a member of the EU is normally entitled to the country's benefits. In terms of entitlement a long term resident is also entitled to equal treatment with nationals. This includes social security benefits, tax benefits, access to housing, employment, education and vocational training and freedom of association (trade union membership etc). Hence, since the end of the 1990's softer approaches have been employed for 'immigration integration' although the 'national' has played a key role in defining the European (Geddes, 2008, p167). The EU has acted as an international body as a result of the external dimensions of non-EU states. A recent common scenario is the highly skilled worker, 'door opening' for one state but a 'brain drain' for another (Geddes, 2008, p.171).

The phases of migration governance from phase 1 (intra EU migration) to phase 2 (developing the concept of 'neighbourhood' partnership) has not been without its issues. In the latter although dialogue has been made with countries such as African and Caribbean states (Bicchi, 2007, p.177, cited Geddes, 2008) there has been an absence of EU competencies for legal migration channels which are required for a relationship between migration and development. Difficulties with phase 1 has taken the EU longer to achieve its objectives. However, as it can be illustrated theoretically and empirically international migration is integral to the European state system and needs to define its relation to the rest of the world (Geddes, 2008, p.184-191).

State legitimacy is assessed by fairness; accumulation; security; and institutional legitimacy. These four areas come into play within migration policy as restrictionism policies are limited for migration control. This is so that public confidence is maintained by the state with formal conditions (rule of law, preservation of democracy etc.). Security issues are however of greater significance in today's global climate. Together, to control migration and provide conditions for wealth accumulation; state control and competencies to manage the economy create increased pressure for the state. It is the immigration aspect that is a contributor to accumulation but where contested the liberal policies have been developed discretely in certain industries. There is the protectionist aspect of fairness but in general the policy promotes exclusion of people who are from outside the country; the term 'intentionally fudging policies' has been used in cases where there is conflict. Boswell, (2007) has noted that emphasizing the urgency of security takes over clear liberal policies. A five configuration scenario has been developed by Boswell (2007) to understand the four functional imperatives of the state. These are shown in Figure 3.1.

Rarely will these be adapted in their pure form but a prominent feature of one type will be displayed of one type. Type 1 was characteristic of labour migration and asylum policies (early 1950's and 1970's) which was not perceived to conflict with the fairness and security issues of today. The UK displays more of type 2 and/or type three characteristics on areas of immigration policy. Type two is an elitist category and refers back to the UK policy prior to 1970's. Type 3 is characteristic of less liberal states implying a high degree restriction e.g. Gulf States. The fourth is of many European countries where there is a struggle to balance the requirements with public opinion. Type 5 is a highly restrictionist policy where irregular migration is tolerated and encouraged periodically. It has been concluded with the notion that through the functional imperative the state adopts its choice of policy. But where conflicts arise two strategies are adopted, that is- types four and five (intentional coherence) and type three (protectionist) (Boswell, 2007).

**Figure 3.1** Types of Policy Responses (Boswell, 2007, p.94)

| | Type 1: Non-political | Type 2: Elitist | Type 3: Populist | Type 4: Nontransparent | Type 5: Uncontrolled |
|---|---|---|---|---|---|
| Security | / | / | / | / | Unstable |
| Accumulation | / | / | x | / | / |
| Fairness | / | X | / | Unstable | / |
| Institutional Legitimacy | / | / | x | / | Unstable |

The concept of 'citizenship' has thus many implications when trying to allocate people to a state. This concept has further complicated matters when referring to dual citizenship notably when considering equality of individuals and people who are fit for society are the two main principles citizenship rests upon. Thus as Wolf (2001) states migration is not a new phenomena, it is the increasing migrants who maintain ties which is creating the patterns of belonging in different places called global migration. The integration of political, cultural, economic and social systems over geographical boundaries creates pressure externally and internally. Globalisation trends are seen as 'external reasons'. Soysal (1994) has carried out work on concepts of citizenship and looks at both external and internal factors. She also looks at how initially immigrants are granted civil rights then social and finally political. The linking of states and citizenships has created many discussions on de-territorialization although debates revolve around the active role of citizenship its duties and the passive role enables rights and entitlements too (Ignatieff, 1991). Increasing external pressure on nation-states, have resulted in questions on future nation-states and lead a process of a continuum to emerge. Dual citizenship is at one end of the continuum and 'statelessness' (Weil, 2001, cited in Sejerson, 2008) without legal resident status and limited rights at the other end. Peter Nyers (2003) has referred to refugees, asylum seekers, undocumented workers, illegals and overstayers as 'the abject class' of global migrants.

Many European countries who allow dual citizenship encourage diasporic ties with their country of origin (Howard, 2005). Some countries only allow dual citizenship in certain circumstances (e.g. Denmark and Germany); although many have introduced legislation in the last decade or two. From this angle Gustafson (2002, 2002a, 2009) argues that individuals should be able to vote in their country of residence. Incidences of cross-national marriages have increased and children leading to multiple citizenships from these marriages. Hence, the changes from 'immigrant' to 'emigrant' follows legislation for dual citizenship. The creation of a 'European citizen' is another innovation of the Maastricht Treaty. Thus, the law reflects the eventual integration and experience of the migration process (Brettel and Hollifield, 2008, p.254). However, this also poses questions of identity and entitlement issues in addition to many other complex anomalies.

More significantly for this study, directly and indirectly British rule has had migration effects in Asia, Africa and Middle East over the past two centuries. In 1947 Pakistan and India separated and it is at this time period when mass migration to the UK was first clearly recorded. London, Yorkshire, West Midlands and Lancashire became home to many settlers and foundations were laid 'for the formation of BrAsian 'nation' (Ali N., 2006, p.160). The next sections discuss the research in this area in detail.

### South Asian Migration to the UK

The term South Asian refers to people who at some point in the past come from the Indian subcontinent (Boyarin, 1992; Gilroy, 1993, cited in Shukla, 2001). Although the presence of South Asians in Britain can be traced back to the seventeenth century (Ansari, 2006) it was in the post-Second World War period that there was mass immigration to fulfil labour shortages in the UK and hence 'subsequent natural growth' (Peach, 2006, p.169). In the early 1940's the Ministry of Labour sent from amongst the arrivals merchant seaman to Birmingham to 'work in factories producing military material (Ansari, 2006, p.155). It is at this point 'colonial contact and appropriation into particular relationships can be seen as the beginning of the process by which South Asians began to be incorporated into the international system of labour divisions based on their mobility' (Ali N., 2006, p.164). This mass migration, however, tailed off at the intervention of immigration policies from the 1970s onwards (Ali N., 2006).

There are five key areas from which migration from South Asia has taken place. These areas are the Punjab, Azad Kashmir, Sylheti, Gujarat and East Africa. The constant threat of war between India and Pakistan also has, to date leads to the displacement from Mirpur. There was also the large displacement of people when the Mangla Dam was constructed where 100,000 people were displaced (Ballard, 1990). Peach (2006, p.160) has however stated that although at first glance there appears to be large numbers of South Asians in comparison to other regional populations, the difference is small on a comparative basis. In terms of immigrants in the UK - the Chinese is 3%, which is just 1% less than South Asians. The figure by comparison is 20% for Europeans and 54% for Africans.

Figures from the 2001 census and the Office of Population Census (OPCS) are evaluated for South Asian migration. Recent estimated figures have also been considered. There were 750, 000, Pakistanis, 280 000 Bangladeshis and a total of one million Indians (Ali et al, 2006, p.168). Birmingham and Bradford have been two major cities in the UK with a larger population of resident Pakistanis, Newcastle is much lower.

The total population figure for England has been recorded to be 53 million at 2011 compared with 51 million in 2001 (Census, 2001). It is helpful to note when comparing cities, that Newcastle upon Tyne has the lowest population of Pakistani migrants. Bradford's population of Pakistanis is14.5 percent when compared nationally and in Birmingham there is over10 per cent of Pakistanis recorded (2001 census). Luton has 10 per cent residents of Pakistani origin; for Newcastle upon Tyne it has been recorded as two per cent. (Census, 2001). Unfortunately, the 2011 figures have not been published at the time of submitting this research. However, there are increases inevitable (figures are due to be released in November 2012) and arguably mainly through natural growth (Peach, 2006). It is not anticipated that these will effect the ranking relative to other cities in the UK.

As a brief overview the North - East has a population of 2,564,500.0 recorded in 2001 (Census, 2001). There are over two million people of South

Asian ethnic origin living in Britain. For the number of Muslims (Pakistanis and Bangladeshis are mainly Muslims) a figure of 1.6 million (70% together with Indian Muslims) living in Britain. Although in terms of the country of origin matters become complicated as Bangladesh was classed as East Pakistan until 1971 when establishing the country of origin.

The post Second-World War was the beginning of mass migration from the South Asian subcontinent to fulfil the labour shortages of Britain. South Asian is the social construct referring to people from the South Asian subcontinent including India, Pakistan and Bangladesh. Pakistani's arriving in Britain can hence be defined as an 'immigrants' or a 'migrants'. Hence, the policy adopted for the welfare of these immigrants when arriving into the country (mainly between 1940s and 1950s) was to meet the needs of the mainly unskilled but also that of 'return' (Mason, 2000). It was this which led to assumptions that 'assimilation' would take place should this not be the case. This theory has been written into the dialogue of the 'Myth of Return' for which Anwar (1979) has been notably famed for 'ringing' the dilemmas Pakistanis have been challenged with throughout their time living amongst the 'white' host society. Khan (1977) stated that the 'myth' was also partially supported by 'institutions of migration' through tourism participation. This encompasses travel agents and airlines such as Pakistan International Airlines (PIA), (Ali and Holden, 2006, p.218).

The Parekh report in 2000 was focussed on the 'rethinking of multiculturalism' because of the tensions that were felt when establishing culturally sensitive approaches which 'tended to strip culture of its broader socio-economic context' (Ahmad, 2000, cited in Atkin, 2006, p.247). Although the term 'institutional racism' which is defined as 'the uncritical application of policies and procedures that ignore the needs of an ethnically diverse society' (Atkin, 2006, p.247) has been written into law for agencies to identify and tackle as 'institutional racism'. One example is that of health; Atkin (2006) has reported on the lack of understanding and development on issues of health and the National Health Service inability. The diversity required has thus led to the term of misrepresentation of healthcare needs of the South Asian population (Atkin, 2006, p.249).

During the first stages of migration the majority of South Asians were mainly men living in all - male households. They were mainly from rural backgrounds and their new jobs demanded many adjustments and adaptations in an industrialised environment. At this point culture and identity was not a major issue (Brah, 2006). It was from the early 1960s that this became a political topic. Once financial investments were made and families reunited the Asians began to accept 'their stay would not be temporary' and attention was directed towards life in Britain in the 1970s. Asians became aware of the need for them to organise against forces that would undermine their identity. The 'anti- immigration' and 'alien culture' thus resulted in the immigration acts and institutional racism became widespread. (Brah, 2006, cited Ali et al., 2006, pp.50-51). Cultural issues became greater as the second-generation emerged and were living in-between two cultures'. Difference and conflict resulted from this inter-generational development and at times violence and riots were continuously in the news in the 1980s (Brah, 2006).

Tolia Kelly (2006, pp.149-170) has worked on a study of postcolonial connections of South Asian women in North London. Her insight into the diasporic community as a member helped the development of the relationship as a researcher and hence a greater depth of information accomplished. Her findings 'related artefactual records of domestic cultures connecting the remembered landscapes, lived environments and natures'. Thus material cultures are embedded in South-Asian homes signifying the history, heritage and identity creating the illusion of security and stability. These patterns have been noted in other post-colonial studies and the presence of material cultures has shown to disturb and shift notions of Britishness. In this study Tolia-Kelly (2006) identified four modes of environmental memory:

-the suitcase-pieces of jewellery, toys etc (thus constituting pathways of connections of the diasporic community,

-ecological fragments-double migrant reflections,

-landscapes of films- cinema was and is a cultural magnet for the Asian community, and

-ecological icons- narratives describe the context of natural textures such as planting back home'. (Tolia-Kelly, 2006, p.149-170).

Many of the earlier studies reflected the pioneer experiences of Pakistani labour migration. In Bradford it was established that the Pakistani population was extremely homogenous (Khan, 1977, p.57). It was thought that a family life with the fair treatment of society would maintain a 'distinctive identity and life-style' (Khan, 1977, p.87) i.e. have arranged marriages, not conforming to existing patterns of English behaviour. At the time of study there were 30,000 Pakistanis from a population of 300,000 and 60 to 70 percent from the Mirpur District of the Azad Kashmir province of Pakistan. Alison Shaw's study of Pakistanis in Oxford in 1994 (p.37) showed that its 2000 members were from either the Mirpur Districts, Jhelam Districts and Attock Districts too. This was also the case in the Luton study (Ali and Holden, 2006). Hence, movement of individuals and groups is powerfully shaped by kinship loyalties (or 'biradari' loyalties). These loyalties had a powerful impact on the migration process and settlement of the migrants (Shaw, 2001).

Ballard and Ballard (1977, p.21) identified four phases of South Asian development from rural backgrounds; it is the chronological ordering that is of interest. Individual pioneers and later pedlars were the first phase (initially almost all ex-seaman). A small group of South Asians worked in nearly all the major cities as pedlars. Mass migration of unskilled labour at the end of the Second World War was the development of the second phase. Workers lived in 'densely packed all-male households in inner city areas' (Khan, 1977, p.22). The third phase was marked by the large-scale entry of wives and children and moving into less crowded conditions. It has been suggested that religion was the reason why there were these distinctive features of settlement (Khan, 1977). The fourth phase was that of the moving away from the tight-knit community and ghettos into the British middle-class suburbs.

It was the third phase of Ballard's (1994) stages that the research on Bradford was carried out. The women with their children were now entering the UK and virtually no men - following the policy change. Bradford is known to be the largest South Asian diasporic city in the world. It is referred to as the story of 'Brad-istan' and has the largest proportion of Pakistanis (67,994). The ethnic category is reinforced by religion hence there are 75,188 Muslims living in Bradford compared to 4,748 Sikhs and 4,457 Hindus (Mcloughlin, 2006, p.110). Studies have captured some of the struggles experienced by the communities and their means of coping.

Watson's (1977) account at the time established that women did not work as it was considered 'un-Islamic' but they also did not have anyone to leave the children with. Men were the sole breadwinners. Although women had more control over the non-monetary economy at their country of origin, there was less emphasis on the 'purdah' (seclusion). The social aspect for women revolved around the friends and 'biradari' (kin) in Bradford or in other towns. The buffering of the initial settling issues, especially facilitating savings reduced further their participation in British society. As numbers grew the 'biradari' members trusted each other more than the unrelated kin. Neighbours were included into the social network by the ties of 'region of origin'. In the very early times these migrants would keep in touch with each other and visit friends at long distances; but, as these gaps were filled by the increase in numbers so they had the security, support and confidence. Although money was still being pooled together to start a business or by a house and 'biradari' looked after each other's children as a women went back home. An aspiration for the migrants who came to the UK was the education of their children. There were schemes to teach English for children aged from four and a half to five for a year or so until they moved to mainstream school by local bus pick-ups. There was the worry of the girls who were thought to be better off with grandparents back home because of the western influences. Thus Ballard (1994) has referred to the isolated experiences of South Asians and their challenges as having created resilience amongst its host society and success in their own self-created worlds. These accounts were criticised, however, for not challenging the way in which colonialism continues to shape contemporary Britain (McLoughlin, 2006, p.114) as she studied the experiences of Pakistanis in Bradford and the villages of Mirpur. Many of the families to be re-united were the first-generation men who returned to Mirpur to marry. The arranged marriage dilemmas were not of an issue but were predicted to be more of a second-generation problem.

Another study at the time of settlement of South Asians was carried out by John Rex (1991) and Robert Moore (1971) of Sparkbrook, the south-east side of Birmingham which looked at the tensions amongst the mixed population of Irish, Pakistanis and West Indians. The shortage of houses after the war left the lodging houses in Sparkbrook as multi-letting single rooms for the new immigrants. The Public Health Department used compulsory orders in an attempt to reduce crowding and carry out repairs.

This caused problems for those landlords buying from each other informally and not checking via solicitors for any outstanding orders. Thus, the Public Health Department became an enemy of the Pakistani and Indian lodging house landlords. Amongst other migrant groups Rex and Moore found that at that time they were known to be the most noticeable because of their language and 'apparent tightness exert a special influence' in comparison to other migrants such as the Irish, (Rex and Moore, 1971, p.115). As their role in the community progressed into landlords they became more disliked.

Religion played a part in some Pakistani migrants in Birmingham more than others. Approximately six or seven thousand Pakistanis attended Eid prayers from all over Birmingham and although the majority of respondents wanted to prayer daily they could not because of work commitments. But others did not wish to saying they had escaped since leaving Pakistan. Few respondents stated they prayed five times a day. Among community leaders approximately fifty thousand pounds was raised to build the first mosque in Balsall Heath. Members of the 'Preachers for Islam' who visited Birmingham in 1963 received only a 'lukewarm welcome' when they tried to hold immigrants to their true faith. It was noted that although the Pakistani community held separate cultural and social values to the host society, there were signs of moving away from Islam and the Pakistani culture (Rex and Moore, 1971). At the time there was great optimism that assimilation would begin as the children attended host schools (Rex and Moore, 1971, p.170). Indeed, educational values were the most prominent for the Asians although the second-generation immigrants faced culture-shock, language issues and a strange school system and about 70 per cent left school without any qualifications (Rex and Tomlinson, 1979).

A more recent study by Ali and Holden (2006) in Luton challenging the embodiment of the 'myth of return' and shows the 'myth' is still flourishing and the burden of familial obligation is passed on to the second generation (Anthias 1998, cited Ali and Holden, 2006, p.238). Bury Park in Luton has two distinct ethnic groups, that is the Pakistani and Bangladeshi. Whereas the studies of Bradford and Birmingham were carried out within the first decade of migration this research highlights how over time perceptions, economics and adaptations have a stronger sense and effect of staying in the UK. Hence, reminiscence of the past is relived by return visits and re-unions to fill the gaps. In interviews, Ali and Holden (2006, pp.230-239) documented that the first-generation Pakistanis remember and recall their homeland and childhood experiences. From their diasporic or post-colonial standpoint the 'myth' is 'hope' for the return to 'home in Pakistan' but the reality is they stay in the UK indefinitely. A temporary return was obligatory and interviewees stated that these obligations are three fold where the return is for themselves, for the relatives in Pakistan and thirdly for the community members in Luton. One respondent said if they go anywhere else their kin would not be happy. But it is the events such as funerals, burials, festivals and weddings that are the main determinants for Pakistani diaspora mobilities. Significantly 'home' ranked highly when talking to the first-generation migrants. This was where their family and friends were and where their childhood memories belonged, this is where they were born. In summary this 'myth of return' is kept alive and institutions such as specialist travel agents cater for this. Ali and Holden (2006) feel this may be a barrier to visiting other tourism destinations although assimilation and integration by the second and third-generation is attempted at the cost of the first-generation agonising over their loss of Pakistani-ness.

### Gender and South Asian Studies

Gender roles are a set of social and behavioural norms that are considered socially acceptable for a specific sex in the context of a specific culture. Hence the Pakistani migrants departed the traditional Muslim and patriarchal society where gender roles were organised in terms of sex and age of its members and arrived into an environment with greater gender equality practices on the domestic front (Khalid, 2011). Thus, from the traditional gender roles to contemporary gender observations (whether social and or cultural changes) complex historical migratory experiences have demonstrated change when conducting research with the return migrants (Khalid, 2011). There have been significant gender studies in the South Asian community that have identified the emergence of fluid identities in social and cultural settings (Ali et al., 2006; Ahmad and Modood, 2003)

In the UK 'women appear only as the victims of culturally rooted masculine control and oppression' (Macey, 1999, cited in Alexander, 2006, p. 268). This patriarchy was short lived as Bhopal (1997) described women's roles within the domestic sphere shifting and finding the South Asian women to exercise a considerable level of control over all aspects of their lives including work and choice of partner for marriage. These attitudes have been assigned to the increasing education and qualifications and /or professional employment of South Asian women although these natural manifestations to authority and growing independence of adolescence was primarily viewed as 'cultural rebellion' against the 'traditional' values. This was 'especially the case of Asian girls and the question of marriage' (Ahmad, 2006, p. 277). The rebirth of 'ethnicity' in the 1990's placed assertion on culture and increasingly the religious differences. The tracing of generational change through cultural markers including clothes, mother tongue, marriage and religious practices has resulted in theory that is inherently patriarchal and misogynist (Alexander, 2006).New research suggests younger British born and educated South Asian women are taking advantage of educational opportunities in 'their search for upward mobility' (Ahmad, 2003, p. 279).

This gendered discourse of the South Asian community has been updated from the discrete 'ethnic bubbles' defined as having different core values and traditions to the wider British society to the formation of cultural identities explained in terms of power and complexity as the 'new ethnicities' debate'. 'New ethnicities' has been defined as a process of fragmentation, change and contestation. It places ethnicity on only one axis of identity that intersects with other factors. These factors include gender as well as class, age, religion etc. The approach continues with culture remaining central in analysis but there is a state of 'becoming' rather than a 'mode of being' and power and inequality structures intersect and constrain the subordinated identities. Hence, 'identities become open ended, unpredictable and often ambiguous in the ways they appear and are lived through' with new forms of cultural production challenging dominant paradigms of ethnic minority identities (Alexander, 2006, pp.268-269). Engagement with the British cultural mainstream has been demonstrated in cinema such as 'Baji on the Beach' and 'Bend It Like Beckham' as well as literature, music and photography. The concept of the community 'being constantly imagined and re-imagined, from moment to moment, person to group, and from one second-generation to the next (second) generation' (Alexander, 2006, p. 271). Alexander (2006) argues that the second generation has the power to generating new cultural practices and new identities.

Research has demonstrated the extent of gender roles. For example, 'male members of the households mainly make the visits to the travel agents, due to the travel agents in the local area being run by males – an observation of Islamic religious practices of 'purdah' or segregation of sexes from men or women beyond immediate kinship bond' (Ali and Holden, 2006, p. 234). South Asian women have been portrayed as passive, suffering from violence, victims of honour killings and forced arranged marriages (Brah, 1996). The heavy media coverage of British Muslim males in the 2001 summer riots portrayed 'dissaffected youth' as well as tension on a racial basis (Ahmad, 2003, p.45). However, Ahmad (2003) also emphasises that differences in socio-economic status, histories, religion and family dynamics all play a part in gendered lifestyles and argues that by locating areas of high South Asian residency for fieldwork can essentially limit the scope on British Muslim families and these sites are reduced to objects for social research.

### Pakistan Community to Newcastle upon Tyne

The total population recorded in the 2001 census for (OPCS) for Newcastle upon Tyne was 259,536 with 1.87 % of this figure of Pakistani ethnic ethnicity (4,847). The City Council of Newcastle-Upon-Tyne produced a report called 'The Coloured Immigrant in Newcastle-Upon-Tyne in 1967 following a meeting in Leicester in 1965 with the National Committee for Commonwealth Immigrants. A joint committee was set up with members from health, housing and education in preparation for developing policies at trying to involve the immigrants in welfare activities. The study was carried out by Sudha Telang and she looked at the history of Newcastle and when migrants first started to come in numbers. She looked particularly at the Pakistani community and the West - Indian community. The main categories reviewed were housing; education and literacy; employment and occupation; social and medical health; and social and cultural attitudes and activities. At this time, Newcastle had not experienced the same social strains as that of the other major cities, but it was thought sensible to 'investigate without pressure' and develop welfare policies to prevent future difficulties. It was also thought that beginning this process would promote the integration process. The majority of respondents in this study were women.

From a historical point of view, it was recorded that the first coloured settlements were seamen who came off the dock areas including North and

South Shields, and students from India. By 1961 there were 4650 Indian and Pakistani students who had left their countries of origin to use or gain their technical qualifications. There was also a significant amount of migration after the partition of India and Pakistan. As word spread, relatives and friends joined them in the UK. The report noted that in 'Newcastle many of the immigrants (excluding students) are from the Punjab and this is a result of partition and subsequent economic difficulties in the area' (Telang, 1967, p.4). This was compared with the migrants from Hong Kong who had come mainly for economic reasons and did not have any intentions to stay permanently. The study established that the migrants did want to maintain contact with their home country but not whether they wanted to stay in the UK permanently. Some respondents said they would return home depending on their circumstances and others wanted to return home to visit relatives. There were some who wanted to gain British nationality and then return home.

Pakistani men who had come to Newcastle were either single and went back to get married or were already married and their wives and children came over later when they had settled with work and a place to live. A distinction was made in the study between those Pakistani students who came over and worked in higher ranking jobs (such as medicine) and those mainly from the rural areas of Pakistan who took on labouring jobs. A figure of 20% was recorded for illiterate women from rural areas of Pakistan. Notably there was a breakdown of 'purdah' (covering of head/body) for women when they realised the economic requirements required their wives to work (Telang, 1967).

The West-end of Newcastle was the most popular area for the Pakistani migrants to live in during the 1960s and 1970s. Several reasons for this were noted. The first was that the houses in the Elswick-Armstrong-Stephenson area were large and could cater for the economic conscious migrant, living in multi-occupation rented accommodation. The streets in the West end were Rye Hill, Elswick Road, Crown Street, Grove Street, Malvern Street, Ashfield Terrace, Normanton Terrace, Sceptre Street and Armstrong Road. The preference to move was also indicated by the majority of respondents to Jesmond or Heaton. It was known that status was raised by moving into these locations, but only the 'educated' lived there. Employment was relatively easy to find for the migrants as they would work long hours and jobs which the host society found tedious or involved unsociable hours. The Pakistani migrants in Newcastle also enjoyed a level of healthcare that they did not have in their home country. However, in general, the main problem that they stated was of concern for them in Newcastle was the weather. Trying to keep the houses warm and wear suitable clothing was an issue. Indian films would be screened on a weekly basis in the West End and in particular the younger ones attended and used this opportunity to show material possessions. Women stated they rarely attended the mosques and those who did would do so only on a Tuesday (Telang, 1967).

## Chapter Summary

In this chapter, South Asian migration to the UK has been reviewed to establish the events and processes that took place for settlement and establishing communities. Pakistan was part of the colonial empire and after de-colonisation and the separation of India and Pakistan in 1947, migration from the country took place in large numbers. These migrants can be referred to as economic, political or post-colonial migrants. It has been hypothesised that cities with a larger number of South Asians integration is less in comparison to cities where there is smaller number of South Asians. Empirical studies in Bradford, Birmingham, Newcastle and Luton have therefore been reviewed. 'Since settlement, the socio-economic trajectories of the three national ethnic groups have diverged significantly' (Indian, Pakistani and Bangladeshi) (Peach, 2006, p. 170) although a breakdown of socio-economic status by gender i.e. gender are not yet available.

In the next three chapters the themes that are relate to mobilities and migration of the Pakistani diaspora in Newcastle upon Tyne. They are: Settlement of the Pakistani Diaspora; Public and Health Services Accessed by Pakistani's in Newcastle upon Tyne and Travel and Tourism habits of the Pakistani Migrants

# CHAPTER 3

# PAKISTANI MIGRANT SETTLEMENT IN NEWCASTLE UPON TYNE

## Introduction

The aim of this chapter is to critically analyse and understand the historical experiences and mobility of the place and settlement process of Pakistani migration to Newcastle in the immediate post-war period up until 1960. This chapter has been divided into two sub sections, namely: experiences of arrival and experiences of work and based upon the key themes that emerged from the interviews undertaken. Although all groups are gendered, gender is mediated by ethnicity and in this scenario through Pakistani cultural norms (Maynard et al. 2008). These distinct gendered roles and gender expectations are on the same level as class and generational change. Modood (2007) has given the example of Pakistani mothers having greater freedom over choosing a partner for her children but not as much freedom over familial activities especially in public participation and work. Such differences and similarities will be noted throughout the examination of the themes. Thus, increased international migration is a common experience 'for developed, economically strong nations and the moves are shaped by patterns of supply and demand of jobs and labour' (Finney and Simpson, 2009, p.178). The post-colonial links to Pakistan has resulted in the migration of this diasporic group (Ali et al., 2006). Hence, the aim of this research was primarily to analyse first-generation experiences which has been fulfilled. Gender differences have been evident and these experiences have been categorised under male and female interviewees.

This stage is characterised by the pioneering 'Myth of Return' legacy conceptualised by Mohammed Anwar (1979). The 'Myth of Return' refers to the return of the Pakistani's to their homeland eventually. Ali and Holden (2006, p.239) show this myth is preserved for those who permanent settlement to Pakistan has not been possible and 'there is a lifelong ambition to fill this void between pasts and presents in order to return forever to the homelands'. Thus temporary migration has resulted in permanent residency of the migrants in the UK. Throughout my research the transparency of this myth is also apparent. I argue that re-visitisation (Ali and Holden, 2006, p. 231) for some migrants, namely those in the fast lane (Hannam and Knox, 2010) can be referred to as a banality (Hannam and Knox, 2010, p.90) of post migration for the diasporic group. My empirical findings have also demonstrated how 'short term plans' have developed into 'longer term experiences'; and strengthen the theory by Alba (1990) of conformance to the stages of integration. It has also been noted that integration is developed through a combination of employment, education and standards of living opportunities. Thus, in accordance to factors relating to socio-economic status as defined by Ali and Holden, 2006.

The empirical analysis has highlighted the complex 'mobile understanding' (Urry 2007) to the process of forging 'places between and away from their places of departure' (Adey, 2010, p.77) otherwise known as trans-locality (Appadurai, 1995). An attempt has therefore been made to logically explain the settlement of the post migratory group of fluid identity within the remit of mobilities; that is, 'the actors are still classed, raced and gendered bodies in motion in specific historical context, within certain political formations and spaces' (Smith, 2005 cited Adey, 2010, p.79).

The approach in analysing the themes throughout each chapter is interdisciplinary. As Urry (2010, p.347) suggests 'a global civil society' is imminent and complex interdependencies have been evident through the emplacement of the post migration of Pakistanis. I have taken this interdisciplinary approach and hence have placed an emphasis on the effects of mobility and 'our ways of knowing it' (Cresswell, 2006, p. 45). In accordance with Cresswell's (2006) theory explained in the mobilities chapter the findings support the fact that movement gains meaning and significance opposed to an abstract mobility from 'a' to 'b'. The context of the mobility therefore becomes dependent upon other factors (see fig. 1.1). Hence, migration studies are important to the study of mobilities. This is demonstrated by the extensive variables that have affected the settling process of the Pakistani migrants from the 'moment of arrival' (Adey, 2010, p. 172). Hence, the emplacement strategies adopted by the interviewees have been critically analysed and theorised. The analysis has also taken into consideration new encounters (such as lively interactions) and configurations (of energy and feelings) of the interviewee experiences and events taking place.

It has been historically recorded that through economic or chain of migration (Telang, 1967; Watson, 1977; Rex and Moore, 1971; Anwar, 1979; Ballard, 1994) that the experiences of settlement of the ethnic group have been a distinct mobility process (Adey, 2010). This has involved 'locating homes' as well as establishing the 'home' (Ali and Holden, 2006, p. 231). In addition, there are attempts towards consistency and conformance to the mundane tasks in the trans-local environment that are emplaced. My interviewees have also explained how psychological factors have played a role amongst gendered experiences. For example, the women having feelings of isolation in the initial stages of settling; but reasons for these feelings have been identified as two fold when relating to theory. Of significance, have been the ethnicity and identity formation activities (Ali and Holden, 2006, p. 233) and the fluid identities that have resulted at a global level. These have been overcome as their social capital increased. The argument I put forward is that this was enabled by diasporas through the mobility system dominant at the time; this was walking (Urry, 2007). The second analytical chapter considers some of the 'mobile complexities' (Urry, 2010) of this emplacement through the context of 'access of services' whilst the third analytical chapter critically analyses the participation in tourism of this diasporic group.

The 'home-making' process has been identified as a theme throughout the analysis chapters and it is argued that 'home-making' has been a characteristic and goal of the transnational Pakistani migrants on arrival. Those interviewees who arrived as adults into the UK (for some this is five decades ago) are now at the pensionable age and many are unable to travel (e.g. motility issues) and 're-visitation' (Ali and Holden, 2006, p.231) is not an option. Therefore, I support the fact that the 'myth of return' has been out-lived and these migrants have pursued with environmental memory (Tolia-Kelly, 2006). For some interviewees, especially those who arrived as children into the UK, they have continued (Ali and Holden, 2006, p. 237) to travel to Pakistan arguably revisiting 'myth of return'. However, my empirical findings have demonstrated that these migrants have also taken holidays to other places apart from their homeland. This finding captures the 'cosmopolitanism' of the diaspora in motion and provides evidence of the process of eliminating barriers to other tourism destinations (Ali and Holden, 2006, p.239) to have begun in an ever permeable and mobile world (Urry, 2010).

### Experiences of Arrival

The perception of 'home' was a significant factor in the settling process for both genders. However, analysis has shown that the perception of male 'home-making' has been distinctly different to that of female practices. These differences will be discussed within each section and theme. A clarification of a few terms in the area are however, explained to demonstrate the evolving nature of 'belonging from the onset'. The desire 'for a homeland' and a 'homing desire' are distinguished. 'Homing desire' does not necessarily need to sustain the 'ideology of return' of the diaspora despite the fact that diaspora is conceptualised with the home as rooted, located and bounded with memories and close ties of the imagined homeland. Mobilities research emphasises the nature of 'routes' and the transnational connections and networks of the diaspora accentuating deterritorialization yet not precluding 'homing desire' (Brah, 1996 cited in Blunt and Dowling, 2006, p. 199). Arguably, 'the home-making' process is a mobility (Adey, 2010) thus is relational within the context of migration and beyond not from point to point (see chapter on mobilities), Cresswell, (2006). A gendered critical analysis is carried out below in terms of Pakistani migrant's experiences of arrival.

### Male Interview Narratives

It was the male members of Pakistani families who came to the UK politically defined as economic migrants with the intentions of both parties that they would return home after earning 'enough money'. This intention was within the remit of the famous 'myth of return' (Anwar, 1979) as has been discussed in the earlier chapters. Households mainly comprised of men (Brah, 2006) that were living in the inner city areas (Peach, 2006). My findins has supported these theories. The initial settlement within Newcastle upon Tyne of the Pakistani diaspora was that of 'clustering' and noteable with levels of adaptation identifiable (Panayi, 2000). One of my interviewees Mr Rehmath originally from Azad Kashmir (a retired shopkeeper) said he came to England when he was a young man and recalls a conversation by his father:

...the British Government had written to the then Pakistani

President Ayub asking for men to go over to England to work as labourers, my big brother was studying and they asked for one child... so I came over in 1962. (Interview date: 18.11.05)

This narrative demonstrates that, at the time Mr Rehmath arrived in the UK, the political agenda was to recruit 'labour' and this resulted in his brother's immobility and the push – pull worldview factors came in to play. Mr Rehmath experienced 'the travel of policy or policy in motion' as theorised by McCann, 2008, cited in Adey, 2010, p.5. That is, it can be related to the degrees of mobility and / or equilibrium states of matter. I further support this notion that mobilities are enabled and shaped through policy and regulation and with lived experiences. Contemporary immigration policies have changed several times and other issues such as the recent 'brain drain' effect have been experienced by the third world countries and more recently brain circulation (see chapter 2). Bauman (1998) has defined this process as a filtering 'difference machine' where there is an uneven distribution of population at a global level (cited Adey, 2010, p.95) and the 'degrees of mobility' are variable connected with many factors including social-class and citizenship. Morley (2000, cited Adey 2010, p. 95) asks 'who has control-both over connectivity, and over their connectivity, and over their capacity to withdraw and disconnect'. Adey (2010) has concluded that control lies in a hierarchy and the higher up the hierarchy the more mobile one is.. In the case of Mr Rehmath the interplay of the push-pull worldview factors (Herbert, 2008, p. 17) was an 'opportunity turning into mobility' unlike his brother who remained 'fixed' in his home country. Upon emplacement the priorities for these Pakistani migrants varied especially with age: the priorities for males arriving into the country were an economic goal. For those who arrived as children, it was adapting and assimilating into the host society through the education process. Although the assimilation and generational cohort differences have been discussed from a mobilities and migratory and transnational perspective in the literature review, it is the 'home' and 'home-making' process and mobility systems (Urry, 2007) involving domestic work, family and social relationships that are explored historically to establish a wider sense of feeling and the change over time. Gendered behavior and patterns (Blunt and Dowling, 2006, p. 35) are themes of extraction. Mr Rehmath reminisced about the past and made the following comments:

...the English people used to be really nice...they used to 'respect' a lot...People used to get up from their seats and we learned that you stood up for the older men. When I used to go looking for work I used to look for the vacancy sign or enquiries and it was a pleasant experience and found there was a lot of love and respect for each other...we used to go knocking on doors and if you needed something like a room or a job you used to asked each other and they used to go here or there...

...Life is what you make it, I have lived there and now I have settled here...you have to adapt into the place you live...(Interview date: 18.11.05)

This narrative demonstrates that Mr Rehmath had similar experiences in comparison to other empirical studies in the field, several of these studies are summarised in the literature review. The description of living and making a home was significant for these migrants in terms of the experiences outside of home. 'Helping each other' has been a philosophy most of the first-generation of both genders recall frequently. They state this used to be the case and help was available through the pioneers many areas including settling, look for jobs, a place to stay, family issues, borrowing money and health care issues. I argue that this has been a process transformed from the dominant mobility system of walking. As the mobility system of the car became more dominant, ultimately, reducing the frequency of face-to-face meetings this reduced conversations and reducing possibilities of 'helping each other'. I assign this arrival stage for the migrants to be the beginning of the era to communicate by telephone and to arrange meetings transnationally. In Mr Rehmath's scenario, he talks of the search for work and living in rooms with several other men. He travelled 'by foot' and recalls 'knocking on doors'. Mr Rehmath and several other interviewees talked about the nature of their cultural and social values in terms of commitment and the desire to meet with each other. It was a 'close knit community' and 'people had time for each other' were some of the comments made of this time period about the community involvement.

It is felt, however, that there is difficulty in measuring and ranking the 'process of mobilities'. The experiences are personal and gendered, locality and class cut across ethnicity; other than from stating similarities and differences with theory. Research by Cohen (2004) highlights the need for such measures and a need for a theory-based tool for empirical comparisons of ethnic sub-populations. The parameters that were accessed gave an indication of the symbols that were nurtured to identify the 'ethnicity'. Creating and re-creating the home was therefore established by intersecting with the attributes of his identity from the ethnic, cultural and national traits (Ali and Holden, 2006, p. 233).

Cohen (2004) specifies three categories were used as markers for symbols of ethnic identity. These were emotional, affective and behavioural aspects. The first two were harder aspects of identity to measure as they had cognitive elements. The process used symbols that were expressions of identity such as birth place, religion, culture and education. It was argued that there was 'commitment' based on these links. Werbner (2005) has defined two paradoxes that relate to the Pakistani transnationals. She has defined these within the settlement context arguing that 'the dislocations and relocations of transnational migration generate these paradoxes' (Werbner, 2005, p.745). The first is that the migrants set themselves apart socially and culturally by forming 'encapsulated communities' and the second is that culture is seen to be 'conceived as conflictual, open, hybridising and fluid' (Werbner, 2005, p. 745). While these theories are valid I argue Urry's (2007) paradigm on the need to meet face to face and means of communicating dependent on motility is equally valid in these scenarios too. The narratives below further capture the start of the 'encapsulated community' yet fluidity notable.

The situation of the Pakistani migrants led to 'matching up people' and passing on 'ideas, emotions and fellow sentiments' through the removal of barriers by being mobile with these acts (Adey, 2010, p. 174). I theorise that a significant factor in aiding the hybridity structure and encapsulation of the community spoken of by Werbner (2005) and Ali N. (2006) was created by the 'pathways and pavements' of mobility (Urry, 2007) i.e. they lived in close proximity and were in daily contact with one another. Hence, social capital was evident within 'walking distance' and there was no need to reach out past this point. As part of daily life a 'powerful force' or 'a rush of energy' was felt when there was a togetherness: a process the interviewees described as 'chatting on streets'.

Overtime, the concept of 'cementing weak ties' was created through access of cars for social and obligatory practices. This has been in addition to gaining social and cultural capital in the process (Urry, 2007), a factor that has been notably affected through the use of a car. At the time the diaspora came to the UK the automobile and its structure was available but this application was not utilised by the community, I propose this was until capital was gained. Hence, weak-ties were also cemented through the changing availability of employment (Telang, 1967) and social and kin networks which determined the settling pattern (Herbert, 2008, p. 17). To summarise, I argue that the sustenance of all corporeal relationships was aided through the mode of walking.

For Mr Rehmath Newcastle was not the first destination of arrival, this was also significant for several other male interviewees. Previous empirical studies of Newcastle, (Telang, 1967); Birmingham, (Rex and Moore, 1971); and Bradford, (Watson, 1977) demonstrate similar settling experiences that correlate with this study. They mainly went to Bradford or Birmingham in the first instance (Anwar, 1979). Hence, I have deduced from thses findings that initial settlement patterns differed and were influenced by the existing social and kin networks as well as corporeal mobility (as was the case for Mr Rehmath). Once settlement took place I argue that weak ties were intensified during this period through regular face to face meetings by the functions of social and cultural capital enabled by the mobility system of walking. These narratives also suggest an emphasis was placed on social capital by the migrants on arrival and 'ethnic' activities were strongly supported. For example, Indian films showing at two local cinemas, converting houses into mosques and the purchase of a church on Elswick Road and being converted into a mosque.

Politically, it can be argued that the virtues of thinking geographically with the decline of British industry marked the phrase of 'mobility meaning power and power meant the promise of geopolitical dominance (Luke and O' Tuathail, 2000, cited Adey, 2010, p. 58). Hence leading into the citizenship issue; it is the passport being the object and a symbol for mobility here. As Mr Rehmath's quote 'describes the process of and after mobility, across borders, importantly there is a follow-up of a 'continuum of mobilities' with which different complexities of mobilities arise (finding a place to live, work etc). The passport is a mere means of allowing the state to monitor and manage as well as establish rights to travel (Adey, 2010, p. 105). Crossing borders and being emplaced into a society has both positive and negative effects on the host society as well as the individual (Herbert, 2008) and for some people mobility can actively weaken them (Massey, 1991, cited Adey, 2010, p104). Mr Ahmad who is a barber and is 74 years old went to Birmingham first; (as did Mr Rehmath). Mr Ahmad recalled:

> ... I was fourteen when I came on the plane I was very excited to come when I got my passport arrived in London from Pakistan and then I went to Birmingham for three or four months but I couldn't find a job. One of my friends lived here in Newcastle I trained as a barber by an English person I lived with in Grove Street I lived here with a few people...there was Malvern Street, then Crown Street then Grove Street....I used to get income support which was £ 2.50 a week everything was cheap then I had to cook on my own separately. I remember I could not afford a watch then. I used to go to the pictures every Sunday at 6 o clock. That was a young age it was carefree and I enjoyed it. (Interview date: 20.11.05)

Mr Ahmad went to Pakistan twelve years later to get married. He also opened his own Barber shop in Stanhope Street soon after arrival in Newcastle. Although not capital rich, he felt the array of people from his ethnic background was the basis of him settling in Newcastle; at the time he claimed he knew everyone in the local area, most people lived locally and used to walk. Mr Ahmad has experienced his social capital being reduced over the years. Most of his customers who were his friends have now moved into more affluent areas. Mr Ahmad explained how there was a lot of overlap of social networks and walking in the area and there were quick casual meetings with each other and his shop was a meeting place or a fixed node as described by Axhausen (2002). These narratives also demonstrate a structure of hybridity in developmental stages as suggested by Werbner, 2005. Walking played a major role in this development; the main mode of travel for this period (Axhausen, 2002, cited Urry, 2007, p. 220). Cresswell (2006) has described mobility systems including walking to provide chances of meeting friends and family en-route in the neighbourhood; defining this as 'occasioned' activities such as forms of talking, work and information gathering. Notably, an overlap of these activities existed with their personal lives and work performances with simple connections also maintaining a moveable presence with others through this travelling mode and potential of many convergences or divergences. From a geographical point of view many of the streets mentioned by the interviewees do not exist any longer. However, the place the Pakistani migrants lived within the West end of Newcastle was within a radius of a mile, hence of walking distance (see map in appendices). Sheller and Urry (2007) called this time of moveable presence as dwelling in motion. Putman (2000), stated that telephone and other home-based technologies were not widely available at the time but when they became widespread it also resulted in the loss of the 'casual co-presence'. Thus, I highlight this to be the experience of Mr Ahmad. Mr Ahmad also stressed that 'people had moved on… and there are a lot of new people from the European countries' and now he 'hardly knows the locals'. More importantly as the mobility system has advanced to the car it had affected his business and stated that it 'isn't as good as it used to be'. This is a significant statement that effects community relations and an area to investigate in terms of 'place' It can be argued that Mr Ahmad has been an indirect victim of the mobility system and / or where the 'system-ness' of mobility has led him as an individual to become 'a mere-cog' in the larger system of things and power (Urry, 2007, p.23). Hence, Urry (2007, p. 23) theorises that 'the metropolitan life, its rush and fragmentation, generates both powerful objective systems partly concerned with maintaining rules of distance and formality, and very varied personal subjectivities'. The trans-local nature of the diaspora, within the context of technology of transport and communication is connecting in a 'different order than the previous era' (King and Christou, 2011, p. 455). This can be applied to most of the interviewees experiences. In particular emphasis is placed especially on the families entering the country of the new culture of 'meeting and activities have to be punctual, timetabled, rational, a system or a 'structure of the highest impersonality'.

Another interviewee, Mr Maqsood, meanwhile, was a semi-retired businessman from the Punjab district. He came to England when he was nine years old. He described how it was very hard living in Cambridge Street in Newcastle. He said he was the only Asian when he arrived in 1957. The emphasis on meeting people of the same ethnicity was very important for Mr Maqsood. Only when a few more families arrived did he begin to 'feel more at home'. I therefore support the notion that the arrival of other families from

Pakistan 'aided' the 'bonding' into a new home for Mr Maqsood, and hybrid traits therefore became more evident (Werbner, 2005). Although, Castles and Miller (1998) have noted that bonding into a new country is often a lengthy process.

Mr Maqsood came to the UK as a child and has a personal story 'sharing a sense of a shared history' from childhood, in addition to race, gender, generational differences, class, religion and language similarities that are a basis of identity construction. This is continuously being 'constructed and reconstructed, making the diaspora spaces dynamic and shifting'. Mr Maqsood had recently taken up early retirement and his wife added that since his retirement she still intends to carry on attending her groups and social activities and will not stop because of her husband's early retirement. Although there will be discussion later this dialogue between the couple demonstrates the equality of a 'Pakistani women' from Mr Maqsood's 'viewpoint'.

Mr Ahmad and Mr Maqsood can also be used as examples of the Pakistani community setting up small businesses amongst the community in Newcastle. Both have been running businesses. Mr Maqsood himself however has moved away from the Asian area or 'enclave' but has served Asian businesses by running smaller shops and off licences in the less desirable areas as well as larger businesses such as cash n' carry's all his life. I relate this to the classification of 'the middleman minority class' that Bonacich (1987) has theorised about.

Mr Shan also went to Birmingham first before settling in Newcastle upon Tyne, he came to the UK because his father was in the British Navy and was here during the war from 1939 to 1945. He was proud to say:

> ...my father also had a Victoria Cross! (saying loudly and with a big smile on his face) and the full navy uniform and badges... (Interview date: 28.11.05)

Mr Shan's father was highly respected and used to go to the solicitors for 'others' and translate as well as write letters for them and filled in forms for them. By 'others' he was referring to the Pakistani's who were unable to do this. This type of person has been referred to as a pioneer by Ballard (1977). His father went back to Pakistan when he became ill and passed away in his home country 'as he wished'. This was a duty that was expected of children whose parents or elder relatives died they would fly the body back to Pakistan. However, death and dying has not been fully researched I can take an emic viewpoint and state that due to religious reasons and the families settling in the UK this is now less common. Mr Shan's father also wanted his only son to be educated and so Mr Shan went to 'private English classes' at the Haymarket, in Newcastle city centre and remembers:

> …We bought our chapatti flour from an English woman from a little fruit shop and she also had live chickens and most of our people bought the live chickens and they killed them at home…my father knew how to cook as he learnt from the navy and I learnt from him and became a good cook (laughing). (Interview date: 28.11.05)

Hence, an illustration of the initial 'home-making'; challenges of settling in a new place, he has had to experience leaving a customary practice at home (Pakistan) and live-in new rhythms and rituals (Said, 1993); living as a diasporic migrant in the inner city of Newcastle upon Tyne and develop specific characteristics. However, this also aided the original pioneers to collectively develop the ethnic and cultural practices. The striking support that Mr Shan exposed was his father. His father who had travelled extensively through his 'navy post' has been classed as a' middleman who developed valuable transferable skills, including business acumen (the example noted by Mr Shan was the door to door salesmanship he did with his father); language capabilities (as an educated person Mr Shan and his father became the 'official office' as the first point of call for all problems encountered for those illiterate or unable to pursue matters on their own); and also experts in the English lifestyle by living in the presence of the British imperialist (Bhachu, 1985, cited Herbert, 2008, p.18). What Mr Shan was horrified with was the amount of snow that fell in the winters. He stated:

> …The snow used to be above our knees, those were the real winters, now there is hardly any snow…we used to go to work in the freezing cold weather… (Interview date: 28.11.05)

An important consideration that favours the 'mobility system' of 'walking' is that the interviewees, including Mr Shan who walked to work did get to work. Hence, it has been argued to be the most egalitarian of the mobility systems, regardless of how unequal services and access maybe (Wylie, 2002). Unlike scenarios these days where mobility systems of the car and aeroplanes are halted as a result of adverse weather conditions, although agree-ably the systems are improving strategy to overcome bad weather. It would be interesting to establish what practicalities were implemented on the paths and the type of connections with other technologies e.g. clothing, footwear, rules and regulations and as well as the dominant senses such as sight, hearing, touch, smell, the kinetic sense called proprioception and even taste that played a apart in the mode of walking relative to contemporary lifestyle and leisure developments of today. In other words, to develop theory on the three nodes of walking identified, walking for an adventure (Diken and Lausten, 2005); walking without an adventure and walking and personal fitness (Urry, 2007, p.157). Mr Shan, a Muslim eating only halal meat spoke of how this issue was overcome (by keeping live chickens in people's backyards). Prior to this they would not eat meat i.e. vegetarian diets. Needless to say the consumption of food is another practice of diasporic home-making (Blunt and Dowling, 2006, p. 216). Mr Shan's father, through the mobilities lens thus mobilised his cooking skills and taught his son (Herbert, 2008). Halal meat, a religious requirement for Muslims now is supplied through nationally recognised schemes and wholesale halal butchers. Thus, as Giddens (1997) argues, I can reveal this as evidence in emotional culture that food 'was a principal metaphor for conceptualising emotional experience. A final comment to make is that transnational home-making was not entirely 'gendered', especially when it was only the men who migrated first, thus these findings support Blunt and Dowling (2006, p. 213). Cooking is only one of many other examples. I can conclude through the critical analysis that there has been an intensification of the ethnic culture relative to cultural assimilation to the host society. Thus a fact strongly addressed by Werbner (2005, p. 751) or at least, a home as a distinctive site reflecting 'double belonging' and a 'plural identity' both in terms of the visual and material cultures of home. Arguably, this can also be known as the 'preparation and consumption of food' (Blunt and Dowling, 2006, p. 217) - in other words a cultural practice translocation (Werbner, 2005, p. 750). Class distinctions can be identified by using Mr Shan's father and Mr Shan's initial settling experiences as partly working class and, although not rich, the socio - economic status was raised through their educated backgrounds. This was a crucial factor for the diaspora living in a host country of which they had no or little understanding or language (Werbner, 2005). This has been defined to have been a local class, gendered but also of intergenerational power struggles. In line with theory Mr Shan's father was educated and that led to a high social capital and hence the family were in a position to reproduce rituals. This is also a viewpoint taken by Werbner (2005, p.751). Significantly, I argue this may not be the case today, through mobilities in a triadic system. That is, between production, consumption and reproduction, although it will be evident later how the triadic systems of 'consumption and competitive lifestyle strategies are centred around reproductive rituals' (Werbner, 2005, p. 751). These skills i.e. attending meetings who people who did not speak the language was a specific 'embodiment'; this embodiment was also influential in terms of his religious practice and movements were made towards siting the first mosque in Newcastle by this pioneer. This may or may not have been an incidental mobility, or could be classed as a philanthropical activity. Another interviewee to arrive when he was a little boy was Yasir, he was 56 years old and was self employed:

> ...I was born in Pakistan and was six years old when I came over ...lived with my Aunty...I remember I lived in one room with my grandad, dad and uncle and one other person. This was in Hawthorn Street the next Street to Park Road...my Uncle Mushtaq came here in 1939 and Uncle Noore in the 1940s. There were only one or two other families living in Hawthorn Street and Warrington Road" (Interview date: 21.12.05)

The living arrangements again follow patterns of study with those who came into the country elsewhere in the UK post-war (Anwar, 1977). McLoughlin (2006) notes that the majority were unskilled and uneducated from the Azad (free) Kashmir in the 1940's and 1950's which may have been the case for the diaspora who arrived in the UK as adults but Mr Yasir is an example of entering the country at a younger age and achieving graduate status from the educational establishment in the UK.

This is illustrated below by Mr Yasir noting this was not a completely gendered process but connotations in the types of work women pursued. Mr Yasir described his early years in England:

...I went to Cambridge Street school and was there until I was eleven years old. I picked up stuff at school and mixed with other white children...I stayed dinners at school and played sports like hockey, football and athletics... I nearly got picked by the Northumberland Hockey Team and the England Boy's Team. My mam came over in 1968 (eight years later). I stayed on at school and did my 'A' levels. I did Chemistry in Newcastle Polytechnic in 1974... (Interview date: 21.12.05)

Mr Yasir said he considered himself to be a Geordie and doubted he would go back to

Pakistan. He reflected on his days at Cambridge School:

At first there we used to store hot water in a big pan on an open fire...back boilers and emersion heaters followed later and gas central heating in the 80's....My Uncle Mushtaq however was a carpet trader and had carpets in the 1960's and also had a telephone too! (Interview date: 21.12.05)

In order to describe the process of 'home-making' it is important to understand the three frame-works in which 'home' is understood. This is explained from a geographical discipline. These are known as housing studies, Marxist and Humanism. Housing studies have four main strands and hence a multi-disciplinary and multi theoretical framework. The strands include housing policy, economics of housing provision, housing design and the last is the experience and meaning of home. The last strand is increasingly a strong strand of study for housing studies (Blunt and Dowling, 2006, p. 8) and it is anticipated is the underpinning concept amongst the diasporic group under study and the spatialised feelings within and beyond the house as well as the concept of home can be drawn in the course of analysis. The Marxist framework was an important area of work in the 1970's and 1980's and concentrated on production, workplaces and labour ignoring the home (Blunt and Dowling, 2006, p.10). Thus explaining why the Marxist framework to have been adopted by previous empirical South Asian studies and perhaps also argued to be an element of the framework in this research. The epic investigations have, however, enabled 'thick' descriptions of living conditions. The narratives in this section highlight the conceptualised home being a social reproduction. Homes were used for food, resting, clothing and shelter and the main purpose of the home translated limited to a physical and emotional dwelling ensuring fitness for work (Blunt and Dowling, 2006, p. 1). Thus human geographers place home at the centre of their analysis…home is much more than a house, and much more than feelings of attachment to particular places and people. Home is hearth, an anchoring point through which human beings are centred. Evidently, I reinforce that the connotations are vast from this perspective for the transnational migrants and clarification on this theme sets the scene in pursuing the mobilities paradigm (Urry, 2007) in conjunction with ethnicity, socio-economic status, gender and culture.

Mr Maqsood has shown to be a prime example of this framework. He initially was amongst the hybrid Pakistani community in the west end of Newcastle. His family needed to identify with people of the same ethnicity and trans-local activities. Over time he gained capital and social status and moved strikingly upwards 'twice' with homes being bought in the more affluent areas of Newcastle (Fenham and Gosforth). He moved to a large house in Fenham for his family to live in and arguably I have demonstrated that there was a requirement to 'belong as part of rather than separate from society' (Blunt and Dowling, 2006, p. 14) and as his children grew up and left home he moved into a smaller home in Gosforth. Mr Shan and Mr Yasir have also moved from their first 'house' they lived in. Mr Yasir was an educated young man and very successful in his work (has been listed as the first and only male interviewee who went to University in this study) but these interviewees have demonstrated how they have marked their identities in two paradoxes of culture, namely, by initially setting themselves apart socially and culturally forming encapsulated environments to sink their roots and secondly proving that culture is 'embodied', thus supporting Werbner, 2005, p.746.

**Female Interview Narratives**

Werbner's (2005) work on 'translocation of culture' defines two cultural paradoxes (briefly mentioned above). The first is the process by which the diaspora sinks its roots into the host country by setting themselves socially and culturally apart and the second, that, within these communities culture 'can be seen as conflictual, open, hybridising and fluid, while nevertheless having a sentimental and compelling force' (Werbner, 2005, p. 745). Evidence for both paradoxes is highlighted in the narratives throughout the study but it is important to define culture from the outset. The argument supersedes previous definitions and stems from the culture being 'embodied in ritual, in social exchange and in performances, conferring agency and empowering different social actors: religious and secular, men, women and youth' (Werbner, 2005, p.745). The process of forming an encapsulated community can therefore be visualised through context by the narratives given; for example, arranging the provision of halal meat, a Pakistani barber and supporting each other emotionally and financially are a few situations. Werbner (2005, p. 750) has detailed the 'cultural practices' that created some power struggles locally in the study.

A gendered power struggle was that of married women and their spouses. This theory is applied to the Pakistani women arriving in Newcastle. In addition, I have noted there is a second major issue that gave dominance throughout these interviews and that was the communication issues, both locally and to the diasporic homeland. The communication aspect will be described through Urry's (2007) terms of network capital. Hence, Geertz (1973, cited Werbner, 2005, p. 746) defined culture as 'a system of symbols and meanings'.

Firstly, it needs to be clarified that the experiences of female interviewees have been contextually different to that of the male interviewees. From this viewpoint I have found it has been extremely beneficial and interesting to study the diaspora over the five or so decades and witness the movement of people, ideas, information and objects and the neglects and omissions and advances. An attempt has been made to implement the experiences contextually in this work e.g. mediation modes, mobile telephony, network capital and multiple mobilities (Urry, 2007, p.18). To further clarify this statement the gendered lifestyle progression issue has been shown to evolve with both the female and male interviewees but in distinct areas and with varying degrees (Werbner, 2005). In the case of females, the narratives have shown 'women struggled to recapture their control over quite a different form of social exchange', an argument made by Werbner (2005, p.749). Hence, the female situations are discussed relative to the ethnic and identity-based experiences as well as communication factors that were significant with the local to the global level.

Ms Aleya, now a widow explained how she came to London roughly forty years ago with her three children. She said she found the English people to be very helpful and pleasant. Her husband's workplace (the Hunters Bakery in Gateshead) gave her husband the supporting papers for her to come over to the UK and paid for the tickets too. Whiteness studies have revealed that although initial perceptions were of fear that the South Asian immigration would create chaos, this was not the case. She concludes in her findings that their relationships were 'multifarious and diverse' and networks were informal as friends as well as work related (Herbert, 2008, p. 47). This friendship has been further proven by the female interviewees i.e. to attend hospital appointments with English woman; but also stories of the 'local shops functioning as important sites of sociability' (Roberts, 1995, cited Herbert, 2008, p. 49). Evidently the fact that a private bakery provided tickets for the family further emphasises the fact that attempts were made by both parties to overcome 'difference' to engage as theorised by Herbert (2008, p. 55) and interact at a higher level and not only at a resident level. However, the in-depth interviews also recalled the isolation aspect and how Ms Aleya spent all of her time looking after the children and cooking. She went into a lot of detail about her daily chores and emphasised several times that there was no washing machines in those days and she had to wash all the nappies by hand. Significantly, for this study, perhaps, she also gave evidence and reflected critically about her means of communicating with her Pakistani 'home', as follows:

> …Women did not go out in those days…there were phones with batteries on and Bhatts used to have one and we used to go there to phone Pakistan because in those days there were no phones at home. There was also a man called Brother Tahir and we used to go to him and he would write letters to Pakistan for us…they were very hard times…the kids went to learn Urdu and Quran in the mosque. (Interview date: 21.11.05)

Communication methods were thus relatively limited in this period, usually restricted to air mail letters and for emergencies sending telegraphs. Telephones were around but they had to go to the local shops or call boxes to phone and this was an expensive method of communicating. This led to a fair degree of isolation for many women who had previously experienced living as part of extended families. Another interviewee, Mrs Anum stated that when two other women from Pakistan came a year later to live near her this was a relief. She described her first year of living in England as very painful due to the isolation experienced:

> ...This was very hard ...I cried for a full year as there was no-one I could talk to. It felt like Walaith was a jail because I was used to living with a family in Pakistan and when I came to England there was absolutely no-one except uncle (her husband). I had my son after seven months. An English lady who uncle knew would take me to the hospital and back. Uncle used to go to work all day and I would stay at home all day. (Interview date: 18.11.05)

Migration was thus undermining her perceptual expectations, shaped by her habitus and an unsettling experience resulted from the threat which spanned into the females ontological security. As Giddens (1984, cited in Herbert, 2008, p. 71) defines 'confidence or trust that the natural and social world are as they appear', which is maintained by predictable and consistent routines'. Importantly, she recalled going to the shops for the first time at least a year after she came to Newcastle from Pakistan. Prior to this she only had and wore the clothes that she had brought from Pakistan. Perhaps, as stated by Ahmed (1999) this can be another example of the migration process being experiences as a lived embodiment of feelings, perception and sensing in a new space as opposed to a spectacle. Indeed, at that time it was the men who did the 'grocery shopping'. Help was not always available from other Pakistani women and hence, it was usually local English women who helped them. Moreover, as women arrived interestingly, although they were streets away from each other socialising was not as easy as it has been noted in Bradford where they lived next door to each other (Watson, 1977). Hence, it can be argued that unsettlement experiences can be as follows; relational (Adey, 2010) to home (Herbert, 2008) as an effect of transnational mobility (Blunt and Dowling, 2006, p. 196). In these scenarios they are both applicable. The conceptualisation of home and home-making practice through material and symbolic practice (Tolia-Kelly, 2004) has also been evident; however, it is shown in these interviews that it is the men who came to the UK first and therefore began the home-making process (e.g. Mr Shan).

When the women and children arrived, these homes were 'houses' that were partly sub-let to tenants or the women had to share their homes with other tenants who were both English and from the diaspora group and all men (as Mrs Anum points out). Thus, the displacement of women and the experience of an 'ideal' transnational home was not the 'homing' they had experienced from their homeland (Blunt and Duncan, 2006, p.198).

The majority of women lived amongst an extended family structure in Pakistan with the female members of the house managing household affairs. As female migrants these affairs were regained from the male members over time but initially caused a lot of distress (Bhopal, 1998, cited in Herbert, 2008, p.97). One reference to this is made by Mrs Anum who went for a year without buying any new clothes for herself. Some of this isolation was developed through moral views of what respectable behaviour should be for a married Pakistani woman. As recalled by Mrs Anum, as a respectable Pakistani woman she did not allow herself to go out for a social night with her husband. She explained that:

> ...There was once when my husband asked me to go to the cinema with him on Sunday and I said I am not going to a place like this...and I was thinking that my father would say to me that now you have gone to England you have 'gone free' and probably my brother-in-law would have told my father that he saw me at the cinemas so I didn't go... (Interview date: 18.11.05)

The conflict arising as a result of ex- Mr Anum wanting to take his wife to the cinema expresses this abstract morality and Mrs Anum's refusal was an example of assertion in the home despite 'given' a room or a house by their spouses. Her role was to look after the family home while her husband went out to work (can be referred to as patrilocality, Herbert, 2008, p. 97), although she did move into another family home. Finally, separation for Mrs Anum added to her isolated experiences that were looked down upon and stigmatised (Ballard, 1994). Some of these points have also been highlighted previously in Telang's (1967) study of Newcastle (see chapter 2) and re-enforced by these findings. Modood (2006) confirms this behaviour to be in support of maintaining an identity in the host country but only assimilating where it is was necessary. This is also classed as a 'nostalgic clinging to tradition' (Werbner, 2005, p.750).

Bourdieu (1977, cited in Adey, 2010, p. 140) focussed his study on bodily mobility and theorised that the biggest 'differences in gendered mobilities were displaced through attitudinal dispositions to movement. For female centripetal disposition, their movement was very inwardly directed leading towards the house and hearth. A man knows where he is going and knows he will arrive on time, whatever the obstacles, expresses strength and resolution'. Although this embodiment is significant it is the mobilities that are reproductive of 'a series of social norms, values, and ideas about being a woman or a man, (Adey, 2010, p.141). Men identified themselves outside the home suggesting the need for reassertion because there 'ethos was threatened by migration' (Herbert, 2008, p.86) but also as Durkheim (1984 cited in Herbert, 2008, p. 86) phrases pressure to conform to 'norms and values was greatest amongst smaller groups that as social encounters increased, individualism increased and morality became more abstract'. I have found this to have been the case.

Geography historically focussed on the propinquitos communities with face-to face social interactions with those present (Urry, 2007, p.47). I argue that these social interactions were also the type Mrs Anum had prior to her migration. Hence her feelings of 'being in jail' expressed the 'boundedness' she experienced without the face-to-face contact of her close family and friends (apart from her husband) in an unfamiliar place that became her 'home'. She then explains of her attempts and the procedure she would endure to 'connect' with her family abroad. She would walk to the post office to get a 'blue airmail letter' and then go to a member in the community to have it written. If there was an emergency back home she would receive a telegram. She explained how it was months later she would receive a letter. Sometimes her family would write that they had celebrated the Eid festival but she was not aware of any Eid celebrations until having the letter read. Sometimes in an emergency if any of her family members were unwell or she had to let someone know she was going to visit Pakistan she would send a telegram or she would receive one. She described the pain of getting telegrams that a family member passed away and the agony she went through by not being able to speak to her family. There was a telephone in the local Asian grocery shop (that she discovered a year later) but this was an expensive mode of communication and therefore she did not like to ring. In agreement, Urry (2007, p.47) describes this mobility as a process defined as communicative travel. That is, through person-to-person where social life is organised across distance. Capturing this type of movement has enabled us to visualise the organisational aspect of economic, social and cultural pattern (Urry, 2007, p. 54) that paved the trans-local activity of the gendered interviewees (Herbert, 2008).

Extending Mrs Anum's experiences based on the mobilities framework it can be noted that Mrs Anum adopted her thoughts to the 'imagined presence'. This is defined in the mobilities chapter, and it is exactly 'imagined presence' occurring through objects, people and information travelling carrying connections across and into other spaces of multiple mobilities. Urry (2007, p. 47) defines this to be a social life agenda where relationships are intermittent and depending on connection and communication forms there are modes of absence. Clearly, the social practices at a global level of movement had powerful time and space consequences (Urry, 2007, p.59). It could be argued that walking was a mobility carried out by all classes with the exception of a few (Mr Yasir's Uncle had was a car owner). Bodily security, however, did not appear to be of an issue for the first-generation interviewed and it could be 'presumed that the more other people are visibly walking about the greater the bodily security afforded by that place' (Urry, 2007, p.72) and perhaps there was a feel of 'atmosphere' marked by gender, class and ethnicity etc… The pedestrian system, despite being unequal for access for people with disabilities, came up with its enemy the car (Urry, 2007, p.76) which was taken up by the diasporic group gradually and had its own implications (discussed in next chapters). The significance and implications of pedestrianism needs to be recognised apart from the statement made by several of the interviewees that they used to 'walk'. Walking is a movement that is still a component of all other modes of movement and has historically has its moments. There are four characteristics of walking. The first is that the walking body 'produces and reproduces social life' (Urry 2007, p. 64) including a sense of place. Walking involves specific 'societally variable techniques' and according to Ingold, (2004, cited in Urry, 2007, p. 64) there is nothing natural about walking. Kawada (1996, cited in Urry, 2007, p.64) has stated that there are different walking bodies 'such as Japanese and European walking bodies'. Third, there are many ways to walk; for example, walking to the shops is classified as mundane walking as well as walking for the sake of walking (a means of gathering stillness (Thrift, 2001, cited in Urry,

2007, p.65) and lastly there is walking that is 'interdependent with multiple technologies that afford different possibilities for walking and especially walking for its own sake' (Urry, 2007, p.65). In an attempt to advance this theory. I recall the issue of rules in the kinds of walking possible within the different environments. Hence, I can deduct from assessing the needs to walk within this section that there are major significances for diverse social groups. An example is of the 'flaneur' walk. Arguably the mode of walking in these findings was distinct from the modes identified by Urry (2007) and that the 'embodied' experiences of the interviewees required local knowledge of paths and pavements of the new 'home environment'. It is however, acknowledged, that walking is the most 'egalitarian' of the mobility systems and labelling the Pakistani diasporic group as 'walkers' it has been hypothesised that 'the more powerful the walking system the less social equality in the place or society' (Urry, 2007, p. 88). Alternatively, Urry (2007) argues that pedestrianism has been enhanced as a result of social inequalities and unequally available technologies. I can therefore argue that this may have been the main reason for the majority of the interviewees to walk in the initial stages of settlement. The advent of telecommunications and mobile telephony was also a significant development (see chapter on Mobility) and as mobile telephony increased so did communication possibilities for the diasporic community. With increasing prosperity and integration, it is clear from the narrative analysis that there has been 'ethnic cultural intensification' as opposed to cultural assimilation with evidence of the South Asian migrants relationship to be triadic- between production, consumption and reproduction- as discussed by Bourdieu )1984, cited in Werbner, 2005, p.751).

The sample interviewed recorded a higher percentage of first-generation women were illiterate than men, nevertheless, children attended mainstream schools during the day and after school classes and weekend classes were set up by the 'Pakistani pioneers' teaching the Quran and Urdu. A similar lifestyle was documented by Philip Lewis (cited in Watson, 1977, p58-68). He demonstrated from his study in Bradford that 'there was fear of Western influences amongst the community' and that girls were not encouraged to study. These constraints from a life-cycle dimension were, however, short-lived for many women that varied across 'class, caste and community' (Herbert, 2008, p. 84). However, I argue a similar case to represent itself in Newcastle upon Tyne albeit as theorised by Herbert (2008) short-lived.

When Mrs Riaz's mother arrived she cried and her daughter said she really felt for her:

> ...My mother hated it she had no-one...so they moved back to the west end...We then later bought a house in Heaton... (Interview date: 7.12.05)

Mrs Riaz's mother and Mrs Anum both expressed the psychological issues were far greater for them when arriving in Newcastle, thus, supporting work by Telang, (1967 and Ali et al., (2006). Mrs Riaz explained in detail how her father, another pioneer of Newcastle, would help men and families who came to Newcastle with living accommodation; filling in forms; reading letters and getting work. She clearly remembers the Uncles who would come and with whom her family are still in touch with all over the country from 'back then'. They are forever grateful to her Dad for helping them all those years ago. Her father was an example of the early pioneers helping all those who came afterwards from his homeland to settle but it is also emphasised that the networks within the Newcastle households were indispensable as the initial pioneers relied on each other heavily for support. Hence, these findings further address the issue that the Pakistanis, of both genders, adopted 'flexible and adoptive strategies' and trans-local activities 'to offer an alternative to the bottom rung of the receiving countries labour market and to bypass discrimination' (Glick Schiller et al. 1995; Portes, 2004, cited in Kim, 2009, p.683).

Many of the female interviewees expressed that communication was a major problem for them. Hence, they faced greater difficulties due to this issue compared to the experiences of the men. Mrs Anum recalled how she used to go to her local Asian grocery store to use the 'battery operated fixed telephone' and visiting the 'literate' or educated' male members of the community to have letters read and written from them to her family in her homeland (although significantly the illiterate men explained a similar set-up too); ultimately an extremely long and public process in operation for communication via post in terms of the transnational perspective and behaviour of the migrants. I therefore pursue the logic that the socio-spatial unit for the transnational activity was with the family, the kinship network and the urban network in agreement with Faist (2000). Hence, social spaces were organised locally and evidently lifestyle characteristics narrated from the interviewees. Arguably, despite distance and mobility processes relationships have always been sustained but most importantly also increased through the networks at a local and global level. This scenario can be applied to Cresswell's (2006) and Adey's (2010) conceptualisations of mobility as relational and not a movement on its own. Thus, as Smith (2003, cited in King and Christou, 2011, p.455) reinforce there is continuous dialogue or fluidity along the diasporic fields of the interviewees in Newcastle and their families in the homeland.

Unfortunately, the pathways may have been a means of a lifestyle with the local community for the able bodied but for the 'supermarket of friends available globally' it has not been an option to walk to family and friends (Wylie, 2004, cited in Adey, 2010, p.158). Thus, it is clear from this analysis that the body politic is no longer an enclosed nucleus of identity (Grosz, 1994) and from a migratory perspective I agree it is a powerful social force (Faist, 2000). This social force has been described as a social capital that is a local asset but the migrant networks enable a process of crystallisation and a process using a 'transmission belt' concept to have evolved. Hence, this work also shows the transformations in the technologies of transport and communications that have made it possible for 'transnational connections – including home visits - being sustained at a greater density and multiplicity than in the past (King and Christou, 2011, p. 455). The main themes have therefore supported the fact that mobile technologies have transformed many of the aspects of economic and social life experienced by this diasporic group where new forms of fluidity through physical travel and modes of communication and in a sense are on the 'move' or away from 'home' (as theorised by Urry, 2007, p. 5). The car and the aeroplane have been the two main transport systems identified in this research. The car known as 'monopolistic, an individualised desire for privatised flexibility and associated with comfort, pleasure, of security, emotion and dwelling' (Urry, 2007). But most significantly as reinforced in the 'travel in UK section' is another means of face-to-face-meetings except on the move. The train was minimally referred to in the results. Interestingly, the connections the interviewees possess with reference to the train system (that was a prominent tourist gaze in their homeland Pakistan and also an operational network available in the UK) may highlight the systems strengths and weaknesses and the role it has played in their lives.

A statement that can be applied to the diasporic group under research is 'certain kinds of social capital depend upon extensive long range travel or network capital, especially exploiting the opportunities provided by 'structural holes' that arise in-between different social networks (Burt, 1992, cited in Urry, 2007, p. 2000).Thus, the range, extent and modes of mobility all effect social capital in particular physical travel for the male interviewees; but also significantly later for the women that led to face-to-face-co-present conversations and facilitating in making links and social networks. I also argue that the 'post' was the most economical and main method of communicating for the diasporic families living in Pakistan. The experiences of the interviewees can be implemented into Urry's (2007, p.200) theory by researching 'community transport' and 'lift giving' that the 'means of movement are themselves places of conversation and social capital. However, it is the 'local social networks' that were maintained by the interviewees (although, evidently more applicable to the male interviewees) that played a significant part of their daily lives through regular provision of lifts. Interestingly, it has been demonstrated that this was the case despite good bus services and arguably a key element of the 'intensive' social networks and capital developing. This factor has also been significant for the chapter on travelling in the UK. Another correlation that has been made in this research compares with the 'struggles to reclaim the streets for the pedestrian system' statement by Urry, (2007, p.201). Both genders recalled and reminisced about their past histories and felt 'its all changed now, you never see anyone, nobody goes out'. Hence, the auto-mobility era may be responsible for the changes, with a culture of car ownership as evident in these empirical findings. Putnam (2000, cited in Urry, 2007, p. 204) argues on social capital that it is 'good to talk face to face; this minimizes privatisation, expands social capital, makes people live longer and promotes economic activity, in mutually self-sustaining ways'; an issue the first-generation Pakistani migrants experienced and evidently now lack.

As Alba and Nee (2003) relate to these women used these places to network and expand their experiences, i.e. sew Asian clothes, knit, go for daily walks, reminisce about the place and home they left behind. When conducting these interviews, the atmosphere could almost be sensed and felt in the era as well as the environment the group was living amongst. Thus, the pleasures and bodily security are afforded to those able to walk about and co-present with strangers. A further deduction is the way they walked also supports this notion, i.e. A leisurely walk (flaneur characteristics) or mundane walks (going to shops) thus non-representational practices (through movement and experienced in a swift method quoted, Thrift, 1996). However, this mobility system was also the main mode of movement for going to work or working that involved walking (pedlars).

The Pakistani men, in general on analysis, followed their fathers, family line of work, i.e. door to door salesmen, labourers in local factories (i.e. Reyrolles, Hunters the Bakers, Vickers). For those who worked in factories although there was a 'lift system' discussed by the interviewees they preferred to use organised lifts. As explained despite a good bus route available the migrants claimed they would get to work regardless of the weather. Snow was deep at times but they managed to walk to their jobs, hence a scenario that has not been possible for the other mobility systems the car, rail or aeroplane for example the recent 'ash cloud' experience where people were unable to meet their daily routines arguably the group may have worked at a closer vicinity to their homes as well as their social practices.

Evidently, hard work and long hours became the norm for success amongst the community. The Jesmond cinema and another in Newcastle town centre would show Indian movies on Sundays. In summary these social practices were networking places for the Asian men as well as some women but also through these practices first-generation Pakistanis was the face-to-face contact in the co-presence of the local population through walking and integration opportunities increased supporting Renshon's (2008) statement that 'access and support' aid integration. Pitchford, (2001, cited in Herbert, 2008, p.51) writes 'overall, contact did help to erode negative judgements of South Asians by prompting individuals to amend their beliefs in the context of specific experiences and therefore contributed to the construction of a more positive 'collective identity' subject area that can be pursued in other areas of study. Face-to-face contact also enabled the white population to 'grasp the internal difference and diversity often encapsulated within the single, mythical 'Asian community. The process arguably, on the other hand I believe (as an insider as well as a researcher), was accelerated through the mobility system therefore having a positive impact on society.

## Experiences of Work

The narratives throughout this section of daily working life are assessed through a reconceptualization of migration theory. A gendered critical analysis is therefore carried out below in terms of Pakistani migrants experiences of work in Newcastle upon Tyne.

### Male Interview Narratives

Mr Majid first arrived in Glasgow. His main aim was to get a better job as he was an educated young man from Pakistan. He lived there for a year working as a door-to-door salesman. He then moved to Newcastle and worked on the buses until his brother-in-law came from Rochdale to work with him and he bought a grocery shop:

> I was educated I have passed metric in Pakistan. I was educated and I wanted a better job I went to Newcastle in 1959 and there I applied for a test to Newcastle Corporation Transport test for a conductor. After half an hour they told me that I had passed (laughing). I was then working at Byker Depot for training for two months...When my brother-in-law came over from Rochdale I bought a shop in Brighton Grove. It was a small shop then... as the business grew, I gradually had my family work for me like the accountant is my wife's little brother. We bought houses next to each other but now we have a big house where we live together... and now we have the restaurant and the storage place. (Interview date: 20.11.05)

Mr Majid came to the UK as an adult. A theme that is prominent from the male narratives and especially the male 'adults' who were educated is that they were not expressing feelings of empowerment but powerlessness. A theoretical key characteristic of the diasporic consciousness has been this 'need to belong' along with the initial sense of displacement (Vertovec, 1999 cited in Herbert, 2008, p. 175) but dominated by the stories of work. In comparison to the study of Leicester (Herbert, 2008, p. 141), the male migrants visualised the UK as a place where 'success and status could be achieved. Hence, their experiences unequivocally were influenced by their former class status' (Herbert, 2008, p. 150). An education from back home thus created and demonstrated in this research an impermeable environment in the host society for work. Mr Majid was very proud of the got a job on the buses after a half an hour interview, especially as he was one of the first migrants in Newcastle (early 1960's). He was, of course, under the pressure to achieve economic success, the prime reason for his migration that was reinforced by the UK's record of it being a place where success and status could be achieved. In line with previous academic studies, he felt his loyalty to Pakistan was important too as was the need to develop a structure in the habiting area to cater for the expanding communities specialised goods and services confirming his transcending boundaries (as theorised by Kofman and Raghuram, 2006). At the same time the remittances 'may have boosted his status 'back home' by demonstrating his economic achievements'. Mr Majid was therefore an individual looking to maximise his utility and falling within the remit defined by Brettell and Hollifield (2008) that conforms to the neo-classical theory (movement from a low wage country to a higher wage earning country). In this case it is from Pakistan to Britain (Massey et al., 1994). This is also an example of the 'specialised ethnic economy' that Heisler (2000) refers to within the ethnic or immigrant model. Significantly, Mr Majid was one of the first migrants to establish the now well-known Asian food store in the heart of the 'ethnic enclave' (in the West end of Newcastle). This food store from a researchers reflexive perspective and having local knowledge of Newcastle is well known to all communities but is marking the South Asian identity as is referred to as cosmopolitan by Hannam and Knox (2010). Theories of rational choice, supply and demand, world systems and network have also a part to play in explaining the role of the 'migrant' and therefore applicable to the majority of the male interviewees. A deeper analysis extends to 'involuntary migration' surfacing. In particular, referring to the women and children who left their country to be with their husbands / families in Britain (Sirojudin, 2009, p.710). It has been noted that this may have been the case for some interviewees. However, I also recognise that this can also be disputed (as involuntary migration) and defined as gender inequalities within households (Herbert, 2008, p. 107) but an area that requires further work before attempting to theorise on this issue.

Mr Shafaq arrived as an adult. He worked for a couple of years and then returned to Pakistan by road with two friends. He added that the weather was bad; it was snowing, and it took them a month to get to Pakistan. When he came back, he bought a shop in Newbiggin Hall Estate. However, when Mr Shafaq came over, he already had three brothers in the UK but still feels all he has achieved was through his hard work and commitment.

Mr Shan's first job was in a bakery:

> My first job was in Carrick's the bakery it was night shift I use to go
> with other people. I used to do six full night shifts Monday, Tuesday,
> Wednesday, Thursday, Friday and Saturday. I used to get five pounds
> for the week. The wages were very very low across the road was a
> cigarette factory, a WH Smith and the company. There was this gaffar
> called Mr Alex and he said to me that your wages are very low and I
> said to him that before the war - half a crown, two shillings and six
> pence was our wages so I said we were well off compared to that so
> then he felt a bit better because later our wages were two shillings
> and six pence they became five shillings then ten shillings then they
> rose again and then after five years I became a bus conductor in
> transport. (Interview date: 28.11.05)

Working as a pedlar involved walking the streets and several of the
interviewees claimed to have done this when they first arrived in UK but not
in Newcastle. Mr Shan recalls visiting far away places and 'beautiful places'
accompanying his father with their suitcase of 'material stuff' notably a
romantic notion with hindsight by the interviewee. The main mobility system
to travel was the bus to get to these far-away places and then they would walk
the streets knocking on doors trying to sell their goods. This can be expressed
as diffused mobility and the expression of 'beautiful places implying the
'embodiment' and sense of place by Mr Shan while in movement during a
corporeal movement according to Urry, (2007). Adey, (2010) defines the
sensorial characteristics of this mediation as well as the emotional registers
that play a role in this mobility system. The nature of the work involved face-
to-face meetings but with people that spoke a different language and were
from a different culture to him. It could be argued that this work also
addresses and signifies the current theoretical advancements of transnational
fluidity of identities (Werbner, 2005) of the embodied person (Adey, 2010)
as well as the mobility of the skills transferred (Urry, 2007). Further work in
the homeland of this group can enhance the literature on modes of mobilities
and from a corporeal aspect to ascertain similarities and differences. For
example, the male interviewees may not have felt the isolation to the degree
females felt mainly due to the daily face-to-face-interactions they experienced

with their group members as a result of walking or car sharing regularly. Thus, this may also explain why the degree of isolation was greater for the women (who managed their homes in their home country and carried out their daily activities by walking); hence a proposal for research methods. As it was stated earlier Mr Shan's father was a seaman, and already having lived in the 'global society' before coming to the UK (Urry, 2010) his experiences proved invaluable to the process of settling. An insight into the comment about the 'beautiful places' by Mr Shan and the expression and glow on the interviewee's face during interview highlighted his thought process in, 'an imaginery way', of 'flaneur' characteristics that may have been adopted by father and son while peddling.

Mr Shan was a bus conductor before he became a bus-driver in Gateshead. He adds:

> ...I had a good record. I got a certificate for being good with customers, a good employee and timekeeper. I used to also work in Newcastle, it was called the Newcastle Corporation Stagecoach. There were some of us in Newcastle and when I passed my test it was on an old type of crash box...this meant we could drive all categories apart from motorbikes. (Interview date: 28.11.05)

Mobility systems for mobility have been significant in the roles and experiences of the group. Central to the analysis has been the recalling of social practices and corporeal travel with which walking was the main mode of mobilities. Walking, in the contemporary era is regarded as sedentary practice and an option for increasing physical activity, although all mobility involves intermittent walking (Edensor, 2001). Walkers were from all classes and historically there have been extensive struggles for the middle class to aquire rights of access to be able to walkover landlord dominated areas (Urry, 2007, p. 78). However, the railways opened a new 'imagined' countryside and people no longer had to walk out of necessity, poverty or vagrancy. The diversity of modes of transport enabled mobilities of people based on comparisons and contrasts and no longer did walkers need to wear work clothes in the 1940's and 1950's (Samuel, 1998, cited in Urry, 2007, p. 84). Walking was their main mobility system as it was the most cost effective. Although this further clarifies the issue of social inequalities post-war for the migrants, I propose this to be a power status era for the men relative to their capital status. It was a means of gaining a high social capital through face-to-face-co-present conversations making links and social connections. One interviewee did have an uncle who had a car and telephone. He was the envy of the community and the interviewee explained that it was used for familial and social obligatory reasons (as will be discussed in the next chapter). It was also recalled that as more migrants arrived in Newcastle, they travelled to work via several means i.e. the buses and in many cases had lifts by others from the same work place. The petrol costs were shared. Hence, this has been as another opportunity for face-to-face contact with friends or relatives when corporeal travel was by car with instantaneous time (Urry, 2007, p.121) as compared to presence and being in the co-presence of others when using this mobility system. Mr Ahmad said he used to 'change a few buses to get to his workplace' (British Engines). He smiled and said that he was happy when his friends got a job in the same factory and they started to get lifts. Hence, apart from the time saved through not travelling by public transport it can be argued he also enriched his quality of life by face-to-face-conversations before and after work or corporeal travel. Urry and Sheller (2000, cited in Adey, 2010, p.90) ponder over this capacity of face-to face- conversations in the car bringing people together and the automobile leading to an isolated life in the public arena as there are fewer chances of meeting each other. But I have attempted to include evidence from the results for these diasporic Pakistani migrants that there is a tendency towards Tuans (1977, cited in Adey, 2010, p.54) explanation that it is the 'not the abstract dots but the points as foci of meaning with space lying in and between'.

Further work in this area may identify the timetabling arrangements of the migrants when they were on different shifts and how they overcame these; there connections with members of the community who owned cars and the power and capital status of these men; were car owners at his time from the migrant diasporic group marginalised to those who were educated and able to pass the driving test; was it divided by class as well as gender; and the effect it had on the older migrants' daily lifestyles to date. Although this may be considered as 'an actual or a past thing' (Hall, 2005 cited in Adey 2010, p.99) it may shed some light into the slow, gradual and perhaps hidden nature of the hybridity and fluidity of identities and permeable barriers 'developing from the bounded' theories.

One characteristic to point out is the brain drain issue. Brain drain and brain gain have been linked to the country 'emigrating from' and to the 'immigrating to'. However, as the narrative above expresses poignantly and a common characteristic of reminiscing by the male interviewees identified, they all 'worked hard' irrespective of their inequalities and played a significant role in the labour market. Mr Hussain, a retired engineer, recalls how educated his father and a pioneer in Newcastle;

> ...My father helped to buy the first mosque in Cruddas Park. He was the first Asian man in Newcastle to come and preach Islam and was in the Navy....My father educated my brother and myself, we have both worked very hard I worked for 'British Engines' and saved the company millions of pounds I was a Design Engineer. I worked very hard I would go to college after work and do additional courses to help with my job...(Interview date: 15.11.05)

Mr Hussain demonstrated the extent of the mobilities practice, as an intellectual and as a diasporic migrant the relationships within which he mobilised. Hence, he has also signified his life as 'hard work', a philosophy consistently recalled by the Pakistanis arriving in UK irrespective of social status; this theme was also gendered and perhaps patriarchal as he reinforces this throughout his interview how hard his father worked. As a child he was sent to private school in Pakistan and emphasised this tradition of working hard and achieving was with him 'throughout his entire life'. Thus the 'migrants stressed the obstacles and hardships they endured', (Werbner, 1980, cited in Herbert, 2008, p. 150). As Werbner (2005, p. 758) argues this can be conceptualised as a discourse 'imaginery of selfhood, identity, subjectivity and moral virtue' moving away from the analysis of 'culture' or 'religion' and but as an 'essentialised, disembodied systems of meanings and prescribed practices to cultural performance through oratory and political argumentation'. His father was from an 'educated background' and was in the Navy in Pakistan. It was through his travel he arrived in Newcastle and began a 'homemaking process' through acts of cultural and material creativity. Interestingly, through little choice this process was gendered but it was the men who began the process. This further supports Cresswell's (2006) notion of 'mobility' not simply a movement but a movement within context and the 'former habitus' (Herbert, 2008, p. 150) requiring 'amendment' to live in their new social world. Hence, the male Pakistani migrant's experiences of disappointments, frustrations and powerlessness have been translated into 'worked very hard' as recalled by Herbert (2008, p. 150). I also support this notion but also that it justifies their movement and existence in the UK. An alternative explanation through marginalisation of mobilities can also explain the motivational factor to try 'even harder' and prove they 'have never been on the dole', perhaps a pride issue or a status preserving tactic.

### Female Interview Narratives

Mrs Sheinaz came over to England to Leeds when she was twelve years old she went to school and left school to work in a sewing factory as a machinist. She also sewed from home and did this for two years until she got married and moved to Peterborough. Eventually she moved to Newcastle. She went to school for three years and gradually moved up the ladder:

> …I could not read or write then either. I learnt my speaking English in the factory, that is what you usually do in a factory, sew and yabble…in 1977 I realised that I got paid more doing sessional work (crèches) than sewing a full jacket for one pound!… and you could barely make one or two jackets a day! (Interview date: 10.11.05)

Werbner (2005, p.749) theorises culture as a field of relatedeness, agency and power. The framework of analysis by Werbner (2005) cuts across is 'the British Muslim' diasporic struggle for recognition in the context of local racism and world international crises' and argues 'the need to theorise multiculturalism in history but rather than being fixed by liberal or socialist universal philosophical principles multi –cultural citizenship must be grasped as changing and dialogical, inventive and responsive, a negotiated political order' (Werbner, 2005, p.745). This, in principle could be classed as the overlap amongst the complexities of the mobilities paradigm (Urry, 2007) and therefore would be I feel interesting to explore gendered work experiences through this dialogue; with a consciousness of 'blurred boundaries' emerging through the text (discussed in the migration chapter).

The interviews regarding work experiences of women were not as intense and lengthy as the male interviewees. They revolved around the idea of 'production of mobilities in the home' (Cresswell, 2006) although, but they did mirror 'the hard work' philosophy. This notion of 'production of mobilities of home' has been discussed in conjunction to earlier narratives of settlement in order to perceive the progressive nature of the empowerment of the Pakistani women interviewed.

The different characteristics of body that are discussed by Ahmed (2000, cited in Jamal and Robinson, 2009, p.649) also argue the uneven access to mobility. Another theme identified from the results is that this phrase of, 'uneven access', has been proven to empower and connect for some interviewees and disconnect and socially exclude others (Sheller and Urry, 2006). The movement towards the 'mobility of empowerment' and the differentials have been shown to be embedded within the interviewees, hence the 'mobile body'. This notion has been implemented to explain the power and positioning from a structural position by gender but also by race, age, and class (as theorised by Tesfahuney, 1998). I have related this information as these connections have been pertinent markers in the mobilities of the female interviewees (in the dominant gendered cultural practices of the diasporic Pakistani groups, discussed by Herbert (2008). In the early period of migration of Pakistanis, the women revealed they did not participate in the outside / outdoor activities. The previous section linked this episode with the process of 'home-making' (Blunt and Dowling, 2006). I aim to further advance this notion in theory in this section with the 'production of mobility in the home' (Cresswell, 2006, p.115).

Cresswell (2006) summarises the accounts of Lillian and Frank Gilbreth and 'motion studies at work'. After Frank's death, Lillian was unable to find a space in the male spheres of work. This led Lillian to 'gender her work by applying motion study to the home' (Cresswell, 2006, p. 113). A speech by her in the 1930's reflected on this experience 'We consider our time too valuable to be devoted to actual labour in the home. We were executives. So, we worked out a plan for the running of our house, adopting charts and a maintenance and follow-up system as used in factories. When one of the children took a bath or brushed his teeth, we made a cross on the chart. Household tasks were divided between the children. We had three rows of hooks one marked, 'jobs to be done' one marked ' jobs being done ' and a third marked 'jobs completed' with tags which were moved from hook to hook to indicate the progress of a task' (Laurel, 1999, cited in Cresswell, 2006, p. 115). Thus, she referred to people in the home as management and labour and established herself as a leading figure in the scientific management in the home. Motion-study experiments looked at activities such as beds and setting table, to dishwashing. Significantly, she was unable to separate the manager and worker (as with production of mobility in the workplace) and therefore not possible to separate the measurement of motion from its enactment. Therefore, by providing knowledge women were given the 'power' to 'police their own motions in order to produce their perfect kitchen. I have recognised, arguably, that this process has also a 'place' within the remit of the settlement process discussed earlier in this thesis, however it has been adopted to the scenario of female work experiences for two reasons. Firstly, roles of the men and women changed from home to work with all the productions of mobility and secondly, as the 'procedures and work instructions' of the production of mobility at home improved this allowed for more space-for-time to become meaningful elsewhere, in this scenario work. Hence, new moral geographies were invented in the home as well as work (Cresswell, 2006, p. 121). Evidently, it was the men from the diasporic Pakistani who were the initial 'workers' of the production of mobility in the home. This can be argued to be a result of 'no choice and necessity' within the gendered role remit as highlighted by Cresswell (2006, p.121). Interestingly, the men continued with some of the extended mobilities for the home such as: several male interviewees as well as the women interviewees described how the men would go outside the home and get the groceries; a mobility crossing ethnic and cultural boundaries and being re-constituted in the host country. That is, until the women became efficient in their production at home by a 'new form of productive power' and also began to bring in the groceries themselves. Apart from the process of hybridisation developing the identities and roles of the male and female interviewees are expressing traits of fluidity (Urry, 2007, 2010; Adey; 2010; Papastergiadis, 2010). Thus, it has been established theoretically that identity like place, space and time are not fixed or static identities are in a 'continuous process of negotiation, re-negotiation and de-negotiation' (Ali and Holden, 2006, p. 218). The practice of 'embodiment in a place' is not discrete, and therefore the experiences create another social space with meaning (Tuan, 1989, cited in Cresswell, 2006). It can be argued from Tuan's (1989) perspective the activity mobilised knowledge and awareness of outside activities including. I have given the example of this knowledge by the narrative by Mrs Anum -

the realisation that there was a 'fixed' telephone in the local grocery shop from where she could communicate with family members', a significantly important factor and process for the diaspora. Secondly, 'the subject becomes produced from the process of hybridisation' (Mcleod, 2000, p.219) and together with the practices of the spatial imaginary concept (Adey, 2010) 'the migrant is empowered to act as an agent of change, deploying received knowledge in the present and transforming it as a consequence (Mcleod, 2000, p. 219). Finally, the prospect of 'doing the shopping' was a practice that several female interviewees confirmed to help 'overcome the problem of isolation as well as gain valuable advice and confidence through this form of social capital' (Herbert, 2008, p.164).

'Boundaries appear to have become blurred' to a greater level when women needed to attend specialist female gendered establishments for healthcare services, particularly the maternity services. The male interviewees would arrange local English women to attend such appointments with their wives. Hence, these experiences are supported by Telangs (1967) findings and it can be reasonable to conclude this to be a 'moment of history' that communication was a necessary mobility to live within the boundaries of the host society. Several female interviewees recalled 'homing' and 'child rearing' practices in the earlier years resulted in feelings of isolation with less social capital but as 'boundaries transcended' this increased. The study of Leicester city also recorded experiences, transition and settlement in UK to have 'deeply affected by the respondents ethnic origin and former economic, class and status (Herbert, 2008, p.171). Bhabha's (1994) work was influenced by the psychoanalytical work of Sigmund Freud's writings on 'unheimlich' that means 'unhomely' or 'uncanny' and is translated to bring 'trauma and anxiety' to this 'uncanny disruption'. A similar scenario presents itself in Newcastle, although empirically gendered. Work relating to former class and status before arriving in the country (mobile research methods) may enable 'distinct charateristics' of women as well as men as part of future research.

Social differences have also played a major role for 'woman in later life'. Thus, the embodied culture as performance has developed in traits as the reports progress with the significant portrayal in the culture as a discursive imaginary of the self (Werbner, 2005, p. 746) to be a progressive role. To define, the diasporic Pakistani women interviewed within the realms of 'women in later life' it is important to consider the implications of women in later life from the host society in general. Research carried out by Maynard et al., (2008, p. 8) focussed on eight major aspects of their lives to ascertain a quality of life. There were two main themes these were organised into. The first was physical and material issues. Here 'the women discussed such matters as their health and issues of embodiment. They reflected on leisure and work opportunities and activities. They also spoke about resources, for example, about money and about access to reasonable housing and transport. There was also a concern about environmental issues, for those who lived in inner cities, for instance, accumulations of rubbish, fear of crime and lack of safety. The second theme focussed on emotional issues, psychological wellbeing and social support. Here the women concentrated on the benefits of social networks of family and kin, friends and community. The minority ethnic contributors emphasised the significance of shared identities, language, culture and tradition in their lives. The women discussed the role of faith and spirituality throughout the life course, but particularly in relation to aging. They also indicated that bereavement and dying and, for those who were widows, the loss of a partner, were important influences. Income, although an issue for those who participated in this study did not emerge as the most central issue in terms of quality of life. Each mobility has a connection to the next and therefore the results of this research has followed a pattern of distinguishing experiences of genders separately hence, according to some scholars the gendered behaviour observed is an 'internalised and effectively shaped individuals' psyche' rather than an external framework (Roland, 1988, cited Herbert, 2008, p. 84). The work pursued by Mrs Shan demonstrates the 'racialised and gendered' entry into the labour market and on the trans-local level permeability of cultural boundaries (Werbner, 2005) being crossed displaying; a Pakistani woman working. Mrs Shan conferred that she would work in a factory with other Asian women so there was no real need to speak English hence women tended to cluster in occupations that were shaped by gender (Herbert, 2008, p. 161). The factory was an opportunity or place to transcend ethnic barriers. Education enabled Mrs Shan to 'mobilise upwards' hence, a sense of empowerment for women (Herbert, 2008, p. 166) of which success and identity of a Pakistani woman was based on at the time. The working women interviewed have therefore successfully expressed their role as carrying 'double the burden' (Herbert,

2008, p. 161). It has revolved around the children's schooling and management of the home and then grandchildren.

Likewise, the dominant mobility system for the diasporic women was also paths and pavements. In mobility terms this can be described as an economic component of the notion 'access' where the group were 'motoring poor' (William, 2005, cited in Urry, 2007, p. 191) at the time of settling. However, spatial geography was mapped in that Mrs Anum lived only yards away from the Asian clothes shop and the grocery shop was a couple of streets away. She was happily reminiscing about her visits to the clothes shop and how she sat there all day sometimes and met with other ladies from the community. However, it was also norm for the Mrs Anum and her friends to sit together in backyard and knit or crochet while chatting. This situation hence places enabled Mrs Anum and her friends to gain a high social capital status, thus networking gave confidence and led Mrs Anum to sell haberdashery from the small back room of her home. Thus, this social face-to-face practiced corporeal movement of Mrs Anum and her friends was intensified by walking.

Mrs Sheinaz explained how she was helped by the teachers in her children's school and for two hours work she got a cheque for five pounds. In her words ...I never stopped from there, I did crèche courses and the lot and here I am... (Interview date: 10.11.05). Mrs Sheinaz is a classic example of the route taken by several Pakistani females in the study. Hence, she holds a management position in a voluntary organisation as well as being part of executive boards in several private and public bodies.

The 'scwing' can be classed as the habitual embodied movements and power that can be broken down into 'counting motions and allowing for predictability of a motion beginning and another starting, but interestingly this also involves the motion that the head makes and the eyes. Mrs Shan recognised this process of production and at the earliest opportunity changed her work to the service sector. The decision to change her job was an economic choice. The eyes important in this line of work as they cause fatigue (Cresswell, 2006, p. 106). However, she also stated that the practice of 'ideas and decisions of the mind' were more of a challenge for her in comparison to the manufacturing industry (although cyclical) (Cresswell, 2006, p.108).

Hence Mrs Shan takes great pleasure in defining herself as a career woman of diasporic identity with her upward mobility. Her work career has enabled her to experience the production of mobilities in the workplace and 'find her feet' in the service sector (in the preceding chapters she also states that she travels to her diasporic country regularly and owns a house in Pakistan as well as other touristic global places). She has in one sense established her 'fluid identity' and recalls she can 'switch on and switch off' the identity she wants to portray or wants to be at a given time or place, an argument made by Urry, 2007). This is almost like the analogy of being 'intermittent during the life process although possessing the qualities of a whole'.

## Chapter Conclusions and Summary

The notion of 'hard-work' that was a heavily expressed theme for both genders in this research and has been further investigated through the concept of the production of mobility at work. Hence, I suggest for comparative differences work-output of the Pakistani diaspora can be compared with work-output of the people from the host society mobility in which 'counts' are recorded to ascertain any ethnic differences of the mobilities at work. Clearly, testing out this hypothesis it is difficult to control all variables between the different ethnicities. Work-output could relate to the manufacturing industry or service industry but for the latter the criterion for standards needs to be physical as well as intellectual (e.g stamina). Bhabha (1994, cited Mcleod, 2000, p.220) on the other hand argues these internal differences are displaced, existing beyond representation and hence 'incommensurable' and that we should concern ourselves 'with the understanding of human action and the social world as a moment when something is beyond control, but it is not beyond accommodation' (Bhabha, 1994, cited Mcleod, 2000, p. 220).

This notion of 'hard work' expressed leads to another challenge; the 'identification of their own ethnic group to be superior workers' (Herbert, 2008, p.153). This can arguably be explained through the production of mobility at work framework. Thus, male interviewees could have interpreted work ethics as a habit with consistent results of a certain standard. The Gilbreths (1917, cited Cresswell, 2006, p. 107) were fascinated with the automation and habits being constant and workers were taught initially to 'work as fast as possible rather than the quality of work'. An additional complexity in this mind-set of work may have included reasons such as they were economic migrants. The female interviewees who worked have highlighted their success stories too and recognition stages by their employees creating a sense of 'embodied proudness' thus both gender perspectives may prescribe to the 'editing of excessive and superfluous mobility' as defined by Cresswell (2006, p.109). These findings have therefore highlighted that in Newcastle upon Tyne when the Pakistanis first arrived there was a great amount of pressure from 'back home' and the 'host society' for them to succeed in the jobs they were in. Mr Malik, for example, even had his skin burnt by an acid in the textile company he worked for and went back to work the next day to prove he was a 'good manager' to his bosses. He wanted to prove his worth despite his health suffering as a result of the accident. The 'double burden' women experienced therefore displaying stamina relative to the experiences of the male interviewees.

A gender analysis has allowed for differences and similarities in the themes analysed to be highlighted. In particular ethnic and cultural traits as well as religious traits were identified where possible. Previous studies (Telang, 1967; Watson, 1977; Werbner, 2005, Herbert, 2008) and many more have pursued issues of 'social exclusion' (Urry, 2007, p. 191) to have been a direct or an indirect result of the cultural differences. Thus 'defined parameters' by the Pakistani men of 'appropriate behaviour' ascribed duties of women to be 'the paragons of virtue'; that is, women's ascribed role as symbolising their nation or community (Herbert, 2008, p. 87). Although, there have been elements of this research that have mirrored some of these experiences, it has been evident that the group is at the later stages of its life and hence the empirical findings have demonstrated experiences that are also applicable to the older people in the wider community (Maynard, et al., 2008) although historical findings have enabled the 'fluid identity traits develop over a period of time in a new place. However, the cultural and ethnic differences (intensified or not, Werbner, 2005); segregated lifestyles or fluid identities (Urry, 2010; Adey, 2010) have displayed exacerbated embodied feelings and needs. Hence, that is when access is not possible from an economic, physical, organisational and temporal perspective. To support this statement Maynard et al. (2008, p. 165) in their study recall 'older lives are not simply about either gender or ethnicity' but can involve complex relations between the two'. A valid scenario that I have implemented in this research on establishing differences, although existing, it has been evident that there are issues on a larger scale with ageing and access.

In summary, this chapter was an explanation of the social and obligatory practises that took place at the settlement period immediately after arriving in the UK. The aim was to implement the mobilities paradigm to the experiences of the interviewees and relate theory from the three frameworks under analysis and to make comparisons to other empirical work in the field. Evidently, cultural issues have been a significant factor in 'settling' for both genders. Fear and confidence also played a part in the earlier days of arrival. Migration, evidently, was therefore experienced at the 'level of lived embodiment; it entailed feeling, perceiving and sensing' (Ahmed, 1999 cited in Herbert, 2008, p.72).

Arguably, the experiences of the initial men and women interviewed of the 'self' and how the world was seen and felt was shaped by the 'mode of movement' (Adey, 2010). The main mode of movement for the group was walking. Hence the atmosphere was in the relationship of people and objects and as local amenities for the community were established a correlation with social capital was evident especially upward for the women, but already 'attuned to' particular places already occupied (Heidegger, 1962, cited in Urry, 2007, p. 73) by the men. Small businesses established became a vehicle for ethnicity (Dahya, 1974, cited in McLoughlin, 2006) in Newcastle upon Tyne too. Traits have been displayed through a complex system of analysis including that of the mobility system accrued by the diasporic identities maintaining a degree of 'community endogamy' but not complete 'group isolation'. An attempt has been made in this chapter to bring together the global human mobility with a more 'local' 'concern about the everyday transportation, material cultures, and spatial relations of mobility and immobility' (Urry, 2010, p.10). Arguably for these post-colonial migrants identity was not an issue in the 1960s and these findings supportive of work by Brah (2006) but once families were re-united and financial investments made citizenship and rights also became issues and thus the conflicts arising through the differences have been described by some of the interviewees in the 1970s and 1980s (Brah, 2006). Significantly, the female interviewees despite their 'education profile' have demonstrated key economic roles in their households and in the labour market. Hence, the reconstruction of cultural traditions and political dialogue has also been a part of the female interviewees' experiences opposed to a, 'passive stereotype', as argued by Puwar and Raghuram (2003, p.44). The next chapter analyses the Experiences of Public Services of the Pakistani diaspora.

# CHAPTER 4

# PAKISTANI MIGRANT'S EXPERIENCES OF PUBLIC SERVICES IN NEWCASTLE UPON TYNE

## Introduction

The aim of this chapter is to critically analyse the social practices of the Newcastle Pakistanis arrival after the Second World War. These practices are investigated through an emphasis on the access of mainstream services (health and social care) as well as their activities in the private and voluntary sector. There are two sections to this chapter, namely 'Social Services' in the context of community involvement and 'Access to Health Care Provision'. The analysis also attempts to observe 'the capacity of migrants to adapt to the new 'liquid' social structures' that commentators have commented to give the impression that they are spearheading the broader social transformation from the 'space of places' into 'spaces of flow' (Bauman, 2005), although differentiation of the experiences of gender are evident. This concept is further observed in the next chapter.

In order to develop a deeper insight into the lives, thoughts and behaviours of the first-generation the intermittent cultural traits and western values that are referred to as 'fluid identities' are investigated. Brettell and Hollified (2008) have written extensively on a migrant's lifestyle changes when leaving one country and its culture and entering into another culture. However, I argued that this group has been living in the country for an average of five decades and some traits have been intensified and others diluted. Although, all the group cannot be classed as 'ageing' that is over 65, there have been an alarmingly significant number of experiences recorded from which issues have been identified and the shortfalls of services established.

In the case of the ageing population, generally speaking, adding 25 years on to life expectancy has been a great achievement of the last century. This demographic information together with the fact that the proportion of those aged over 65 and over have increased with a percentage fall of those aged sixteen years and under (ONS, 2003, cited in Maynard et al., 2008) has 'not been greeted with unbounded enthusiasm due to the implications they are said to have for the dependency ratio' (Maynard et al., 2008, p.2). Many later life researchers have extended this case as a 'demographic time bomb' with critical situations in the welfare state and how the issue of ageing is being addressed by both politicians and media (Maynard, 2008, et al., p.2). Hence, as it has been identified in this research some issues have been overlooked such as the (potential) increased productivity of those who work, and the fact that retirement is no longer defined only by age. Other scenarios of raising taxes and national contributions and / or reducing welfare state provision and encouraging individuals to fund privately are all under debate. According to Arber and Attias-Donfut (2000, cited Maynard et al., 2008, p. 3) women's position is also excluded noting that retirement and pensions were 'developed by men with men in mind' (Hill and Tigges, 1995, cited Maynard et al., 2008, p.3). Hence there is the issue of seriously financially disadvantaged women in the UK with a greater likelihood of living in poverty due to part-time working, lower wages and reduced rate contributions (Maynard et al., 2008, p.3). Taking this information into account and Maynard et al.(2008)'s statement that 'while there is a research obligation not to minimize the real social and economic difficulties that face significant numbers of older people and older women in particular, as the sources of social policy problems, we need also to investigate the circumstances that enhance their ability to pursue their lives' (Maynard et al., 2008.p.5); hence, this is also an aim of this research.

It was by the 1960s when different paths of integration were recognised by theorists and the classical assimilation model modified (Alba and Nee, 1997). The reception from the host society together with the characteristics of the migrant were therefore reference points to develop theories from the classic model, needless to say, 'the responsibility for change was solely on the immigrant group', (Lee, 2009, p.730). It has also been well documented that the lifestyle choices of the migrants demonstrate a hybrid culture which falls into the 'third space' within the diaspora (Bhabha, 1990). Issues surrounding the 'Myth of Return' (Anwar, 1979); notion of access (Urry, 2007) and gendered studies have played a major role in developing the contemporary issues at a local, national and international level for the diasporic Pakistani migrants interviewed. Herbert (2008, p, 172) in the context of a gendered attitude of 'home' as a complete life story and 'with the understanding of the divergent experiences of migration and settlement for women and men' has 'supported previous research on gender and migration which has revealed that men tend to express a desire for eventual return to the 'homeland', whilst women favour the prospect of permanent residence in the new country of settlement' (Pessar and Mahler, 2003, cited in Herbert, 2008, p. 172). This research has also demonstrated the case for women but challenges the desire of men to achieve eventual homeland arguing they also favour the concept of permanent residence of remaining in the UK and identify with 'fluid identities' visiting the homeland but also experiencing the spectacular (discussed in next chapter) as the women interview have quoted. A gendered critical analysis is thus carried out below in terms of Pakistani migrants' experiences of Social Services.

## Experiences of Social Services

### Male Interview Narratives

When Mr Mohammed (widower) was asked about how he spent his time he also did not mention how he carried out his daily duties around his prayer times until the end of the interview. An important aspect identified in this research of the ageing Pakistani migrant in Newcastle upon Tyne. One explanation I put forward could be to explain that because the prayers are part of the lifestyle, and hence embedded within the person, they are carried out without thinking like brushing your teeth, which is second nature. This deduction is also made from the researcher's reflexive perspective. However, it is the non-relational aspect of his lifestyle that is perhaps an area to investigate in terms of quality for life. Hence, when Mr Mohammed was asked about how he spent his day he replied:

> I don't really have any fixed or regular things to do. I usually have breakfast and then sometimes go to town and sometimes the Metrocentre to kill a couple of hours…I am now 74 years old…there is loneliness if I had a partner then it would be different. (Interview date: 28.11.05)

Mr Mohammed's social capital can be referred to as 'weak'. He has felt this more since his wife has died despite living with his son's family. He described himself as a very lonely person. This issue was not pursued in the interview due to the sensitivity of the topic. There are several issues that are underlying in this narrative and have been considered through the notion of 'access'. Urry (2007) has argued that there are four components to the notion of 'access'. These are economic, physical, organisational and temporal. The examples of economic resources include the need for a taxi or a car for the motoring poor or a 'point of contact' is through the ownership or availability of a telephone, hence all mobilities require economic resources; Michael (2000) states that even walking requires a pair of good shoes. Urry (2007, p.191) has identified that those with 'most access is also those with best access to communications 'at-a-distance', although the low entry cost of the mobile phone, the minute cost of the cheapness of internet cafes is altering some of this'. It will be seen later how this may not be an option for those with low network capital or low literacy levels which relates to the next component of physical aspects of access. This is when one is unable to get in and out of car or drive a car; unable to read timetabled information, difficulties in walking or carrying large or weighty objects. Access to services and facilities has thus been identified as depending on one's ability to 'organise'. This has been illustrated by Raje (2004) in his study of Asian households, where the ability to negotiate lifts with others; a trait identified by the male interviewees in the previous section on obtaining lifts to work, was undertaken despite timetabled bus services available. But also, an issue for the travel poor who have few choices waiting in unsafe bus stops. Lastly, there is the factor of 'availability', for example there is no public transport after a certain time or where 'time sovereignty' issues and the degree to which people 'do or do not have control over or flexibility built into their temporal regime'; is defined as social exclusion (Urry, 2007, p. 192). Mr Mohammed can also be classed as someone who is social excluded despite having extensive resources of time and hence a high degree of flexibility through the timetabled availability of public transport. A significant contextual difference of 'isolation' was experienced by this interviewee. Arguably, I take the view this contests the tradition of the older generation being looked after by their families.

Mr Saleem is self-employed and owns a travel agency but plays a large role in establishing and providing social occasions for the Pakistani community including men's social evening gatherings:

> We are running an organisation called the Pakistan Cultural Society. It has been running since 1993... I am the Chair...it is voluntary and

charitable. When we started, we supported art and culture from Pakistan and South East Asia. We are linked with organisations all over the world working with organisations locally and nationally. Art is the tool to bring the communities together. It involves the Asian and local English community… Then…I will tell you, then I was PCS is now a regular funded organisation. The local council, the last five years we had five workers, we had an office and a hall and now because of 'cuts' (stressing this word) it is a very bad situation, very critical. It is nearly finished, but I am very very…all of my members and the community is very upset. We are not satisfied, because we are the only 'one organisation in Newcastle' (stressing these words) which is working in this kind of work and they are not going to support one organisation, we are very annoyed…because it has affected not just these groups but also the women's groups like the ones who go on day trips have been affected as well. (Interview date: 15.11.05)

Mr Saleem through his business expressed other needs and developed these with community involvement. It is these services that have been set up by individuals like Mr Saleem who have pioneered the final life cycle stages of the Pakistanis in Newcastle. This comment on Pakistani-ness can be compared with the results of the Parekh report (2000) on 'rethinking multiculturalism'. Mr Saleem referred to the cultural capital as Pakistani-ness and arguably this evidence displays an offshoot and has kept the independence of the community by creating their own 'strategy for survival' by 'enforced segregation'. This evidence supports Watson (1977). McLoughlin (2006) has called this a 'vehicle for ethnicity'. Mr Saleem continued:

…I will explain a little bit more, it was an Art organisation same kind we have developed a social – health and social network for the ladies. The ladies' group was called 'Sohelia' meaning 'friends'. There are about 65 or 70 members, they do art and health projects. We do that we provide a hall, and they organise a little bit from their own funding. There is another group, it is the men's group called and 'Health and Social Network' meeting…Thursday night every Thursday from all over the community… whoever they are they are all welcome. It is like a social network where they sit down have a chit chat, discuss the problems if anybody wants to read poetry, sing...They look forward to this every Thursday. That's very interesting. (Interview date: 15.11.05)

As Mr Saleem points out here funding has stopped and his service users, who are mainly pensioners, are asking him why the funding had stopped. I have referred these as 'health services' or 'voluntary services for the elderly'. According to Mr Saleem these services are mainly provided by the government to the host society and Mr Saleem is working on a voluntary basis to provide similar services. The Parekh report (2000) references equality as does Modood (2007) defining equality 'to be applied to groups and not just individuals'. This is a point that I feel needs addressing as a significant finding for health and social service planning.

I also do charity work, I raise funds...the earthquake in Pakistan...because it is cultural and art... do that kind of thing we raise money from all the communities not just Pakistan when there was an earthquake, we raised nearly £20-£24,000. I am not exactly sure, and we went and build schools. One person went and they are still working on it. It is very high area on hills called Muzaffarabad. There is also for the flood victims we raised £22,000.00.

However, it is the government funded services that are referred to here and need to be addressed i.e. the future provision or lack of mainstream entitlement in compliance with the cultural embodiment identified. (Interview date: 15.11.05).

In another interview, Mr Saleem added:

Our events are known all over the world and people wait for these events. The poetry event is very famous, and people come from all over the world. It is multi-lingual reading called 'mushaira - it is Persian - Arabic known all over the world. And the charity work covers whatever country where there is need, you know when there was an earthquake in Turkey in Afghanistan, Iran, erm Japan now. You know wherever. (Interview date: 15.11.05)

When referencing the Pakistani community, the 'blurred' boundary fits into the description given. The 'blurred' boundary as in this case can also shift or move. It is also variable depending on the reception of the host society. If it is not as receptive then only those who are similar in appearance have blurred boundaries and if it is receptive those groups who do not have similar appearances can also have a blurred boundary. This is a useful analogy especially as the interviewees experienced hostile treatment from the host society. There are also several instances where the bright and blurred boundary can be identified as an experience from the narrative in these themes.

In this context Mr Saleem added:

> ...And then I am involved in the 'Mela' in Newcastle. Asian arts and Music, there is one festival every year. It is a big two-day festival 38 to 40,000 people come, local and Asian and is very popular. I am involved in that organisation as a treasurer. And through the Pakistan Cultural Society I am involved in the radio. I do two shows in a week eight until ten and they are recorded and put on twice again in a week. My shows are also question and answers too I give information to our community about their problems related to the High Commission... I tell them about the Pakistan Cultural Society programmes and any other activities in Newcastle. People ring me live on the show and they joke, sing songs, read poetry everything. The other thing I am involved in is Asian Artist Network, the majority of the members are doctors from South East Asia and it is a family type organisation. (Interview date: 15.11.05)

Mr Saleem described processes that can be viewed under social capital within the context of migrants.

Mr Saleem is clearly carrying out several functions together of which each of the above concepts can be related and hence a cause of concern for him when the resources are removed. And as Heisler (2000, cited in Lee, 2009, p.741) writes these individuals may comply through the fear of group sanctions than from 'group loyalty which is the driving force behind bounded solidarity' This can also be compared to Fried's (2000, cited Gustafon, 2009) analysis that reduced local bonding can limit the opportunities for participation and identification in larger groups. On analysis, the opposite can be applied in this scenario too, as Mr Saleem has needed these connections to be regarded as a valued businessman. Mr Saleem describes several 'transnational social spaces, which are defined as 'combinations of ties, positions in networks and or organisations, and networks of organisations that reach across the borders of multiple states' (Faist, 2000, p.191). The variety of activities Mr Saleem is involved in as a transnational migrant and the benefits are self-evident and an important justification of identity.

Mr Saleem's experience relates to the theory similar to the one above but called ethnic or immigrant entrepreneur model. A large part of Mr Saleem's work is voluntary. Mr Saleem feels it is his 'duty' on behalf of the community to help hence taking on a greater role developing a 'specialist ethnic economy' (Heisler, 2000). His frustrations are therefore self-explanatory as the services he has worked hard on a voluntary basis can be classed as having perhaps mainstream facilities such as health and emotional well-being activities for the community and day-care services especially the first-generation. Mr Saleem believed the city council had cut his funding without any regard to how much time and effort had gone into establishing the services he talked about. Heisler (2000) has adopted the view that this stems from cultural theory where entrepreneurship comes from individual level influences or collective networks and a collective need for resources that are not being met by the host society. This has created solidarity amongst the Pakistani groups and 'vehicles of ethnicity' especially when there was no service of this type prior to the migrants arriving in the country. Hence, the analysis of migrants in Newcastle has also mirrored these previously well documented issues for South Asian migration.

### Female Interview Narratives

When Ms Zatoon a widow, was asked how she spend her time she explained: …I go to the gym twice a week and I go out for walks and shopping… (Interview date: 13.05.05). Ms Zatoon's explained how these activities revolved around her prayer times. She described going to the gym in the mornings and then arriving home in time for her afternoon prayers. She then described after her midday prayers she usually meets her friend who lives in the next street. Their priorities were visiting people who have had a death in the family to give their condolences. This is referred to as 'afsos' in the Pakistani community and ranks the highest level of social practice in the Pakistani community. This is a social obligation, and it is an important requirement to have a face to face meeting. Ms Zatoon emphasised that she needs to go to these visits because if she didn't then nobody would come to her funeral in turn. This can be seen as a 'local' mobility and behavioural pattern of the local community at which meetings communication and networks are exchanged, but also an obligatory social practice significant for the members of the family who take their elderly parents or partners to places by car. Bolognani (2007) has investigated that 'afsos' also ranks high for the Pakistani's in Bradford and in their home villages. These visits signify the social capital amongst the community the greater the turn-out the higher the social capital hence 'izzat' (respect) in the community. The study in Luton by Ali and Holden (2006) displayed similar findings. These 'ideal norms of behaviour were also reinforced through discourse of shame (sharam) and honour (izzat) which were vital mechanisms of social organisation' hence it was argued that this responsibility was not shared equally but confined to women (Herbert, 2008, p. 84). An assumption found to be the case in this study where Mrs Zatoon and her friends claim to spend a lot of their daily activities around these expectations compared to Mr Mohammed who does not have this 'burden'. Again, it is reinforced that this appears to be an issue related to the retired first-generation Pakistanis interviewed and these gendered differences need to be further investigated in terms of 'quality of life of the older persons' dilemmas in planning and developing services. Ms Zatoon added that visiting the sick is a means of gaining reward and benefitting in the life after death, a religious belief that is closely linked with philanthropic activities. Arguably, I emphasise that these findings play an important part of the lives of the older Pakistani migrants yet little theory relating to these social practices.

Of significance is the perception that older women from the Indian subcontinent although respected felt their standing was diminished by widowhood 'to an extent that most had retreated into their religions' (Maynard et al., 2008, p. 164). Thus, from my findings Mrs Zatoon's narratives can be described through the gendered expectations to uphold family values by conforming to social practices, but arguably it is the religious practice that seems to fulfil the arena. Maynard et al., (2008, p. 139) concluded that

'religion has disempowered many ... women in specific ways, for instance through isolating them from the wider community. But their isolation also stems from culture, ethnicity, racism, lack of mobility, lack of opportunity to learn English and so on. They have called upon their faith to sustain them through the difficulties. It is important then that religious aspects be taken into account in planning and policy-making when considering the current elderly generation. At times they may find themselves excluded from mainstream services due to a plethora of causes, one of which may be a lack of sensitivity on the part of providers to issues of faith'.

Ms Mumtaz also a widow when asked how she spent her time also stressed most of her time was spent indoors. However, Ms Mumtaz also explained in detail that she was previously a volunteer working with the community improving the local area and also attended a voluntary organisation that was centred on activities for Asian women:

> ...I used to go to groups regularly but then they stopped them, the worker Riaz a community worker was really good she used to do a lot with us...now there is a Bangladeshi worker, the Mill in Centre ...and they don't do much for us...she does work for the Bangladeshis...I used to enjoy going we had some fun times...but now I am in the house and ill... (Interview date: 15.11.05)

There are two issues that can be seen from this response. Firstly, it is the reliance on voluntary activities and organisations that the women attend to maintain a 'normal social life' and secondly, going to places where there are other Pakistani women of the same generation is something they enjoy and want to do on a regular basis. I note that this falls into the category highlighted in work areas of women's feelings being with others in a supported environment. Namely, that she feels safe, comfortable and enjoyable rather than adventuring on independently supporting the work by Myers, (2010).

Ms Anum had similar issues when she was asked how she spent her time:

> ...Well as you know it is a lot harder now. When I get up in the morning I stay in bed and it takes me a good 10 minutes to move, my whole body is frozen I slowly move my legs, It feels as if my whole body is asleep and I can't get up straight away then I have a stick and

I wake up move my hands and feet then I come here and I go to the bathroom etc. then I do wuzoo (wash for prayers) and change my clothes and prayer and then I read other prayers and then have breakfast. If I can then I will do a bit of housework but if I am not upto it then I won't…Sometimes… before we used to go to different places. The one who takes us for exercises now is called Freda, they don't take us to Birmingham and that; but the … group (government funded) take us to places like Bradford… They take us for shopping and now they don't get any money (funding). As you know every week, they used to cook dinner but now that has all stopped for those who live close by eat their dinner at home or you can take a packed lunch and they only give you tea. The ladies used to all cook and we paid £1. 10p and we used to eat afterwards now they give you tea and biscuits. This is 12pm till 3 pm, the ladies sit there and chit chat. I go at 12pm and stay till 2-2.30pm.

(Interview date: 18.11.05)

There are several issues within the text above. The 'encapsulation' of the lifestyle is, however, well demonstrated. Ms Anum explains her 'social exclusion' on many different levels. Access is important from the mobility aspect for which she has limited walking abilities arguably as her motility diminishes so does her mobility however economic and organisational access factors can play a part in reference to socio-economic status. Ms Anum describes her capital status as low and poor on economic resources.

It is the total reliance again on these activities Ms Anum has that is the point to note (as was with Ms Mumtaz). I suggest this evidence also supports the notion that lifestyle choices ascertain an individual's identity as conceptualised by Modood, (2006). In contrast, citizenship; that is, dual identity has also been demonstrated to increase participation in the social and political as well as collective action (Klandermans et al, 2004) as evident by Mr Saleem and Mrs Sheinaz's narratives. All the interviewees interviewed possessed dual citizenship. The fact that funding is withdrawn within the voluntary funded groups providing services to these communities highlights several issues:

a) Feeling neglect and betrayal

b) Voicing dissatisfaction.

c) Future lifestyle choices limited for the Pakistani older people

d) Quality of life affected

e) This may evolve into a larger crisis if not addressed imminently.

A gendered empirical finding, as communicated, suggests that it is mainly the women who are adventurous and like to try knew experiences and join groups and explains 'downward mobility' patterns in some of the female (and male) interviewees. As it has been mentioned in the literature review these feelings of falling are associated with passivity and the fate of oneself identifies with loss of self-determination as argued by Game, (2000). The male interviewee's have demonstrated integration or fluid identities through the banalities of work, shopping and social practices as well as voluntary and philanthropical activities. Therefore, quite understandably as motility and health factors are dominant in the group's lives a daily lifestyle or 'a removal of a service' can only be creating negative feelings of the void. As Urry (2007) describes mobility can be viewed as a social good and the opposite denotes failure, defeat and being left behind, that is, immobility.

Two interesting observations were made while interviewing took place in the homes of the Pakistani diasporic migrants. The first was that the material culture varied from home to home; there were homes that displayed a significant amount of goods from the 'homeland' as recalled by Tolia-Kelly, (2004) there was an imaginery presence of the homes they left in their homes in Newcastle. However, there was little evidence of any material capital from their homelands with a total contemporary feel to the houses. Arguably, this may also be a performance of 'fluid identities' that are only recalled through memory and imagination than material objects. Secondly, almost all of the interviewees who were interviewed at home, in the privacy of their own homes were had the TV on a 'Urdu' speaking channel; to name a few common channels observed to be watched were Geo News; Bollywood Music channels, Drama Channels; Ikra TV and Peace TV. This has been a practice that Urry (2007 p. 247) recalls as the social life being organised across distance; hence, an imaginary travel moving 'across of images, places and people appearing on visual media'. Arguably, the only option for the motility low interviewees but also alarmingly and of greater concern unable to access virtual movements through illiteracy; an area that needs further work. An important aspect to investigate is the 'access of network and virtual mobilities' by the first-generation Pakistani diaspora, the advantages and disadvantages. Lastly, it has been found that day trips are a gendered based activity that may have been a coping strategy (Herbert, 2008, p. 138) for Ms Anum and Mrs Mumtaz and this service is no longer running hence adding to a 'downward mobility'.

Mrs Anum and Mr Saleem both gave lengthy accounts of services they either have developed or use as a member of the Pakistani community in Newcastle. Mr Saleem can also be referred to as an individual where dynamics of power relations are also active in his work and social life in line with Modood, (2006). Not providing services for the groups and the group service users has deeper implications and there is a connection between these instances and the embeddedness that Heisler (2000) refers to within the social capital and the networks concept. Heisler (2000) distinguishes between 'relational' embeddedness which is the relationship between people and 'structural' embeddedness which is the mechanism required to steer the relationships between people in a group. Alba and Nee (2003, p.42) recall these conditions to be necessary 'in order for the development of conditions of a group to function appropriately'. If the group members cannot rely on these functions at a time of need then these norms are affected. Although these are positive network mechanisms by 'visualisation' the situation that these interviewees, one as a member of a group and the other middleman minority class, are facing amongst the community are not positive. Although, this theory can relate to new migrants entering the country and previously established migrants help with the process of gaining employment. This is a good example of integration as explained by Portes and Rambaut (1996, p.87). This is a necessary tool in the process of integration and can be inferred from Mr Saleem's interview. Hence Mr Saleem has proven that his feelings of efficacy and embeddness in social networks result in involvement in civil society organisations as well as meeting the criteria for collective participation argued by Klandermans et al. (2008).

Ms Sheinaz added:

> I go to work every day then in the evenings I have a busy life with my family, children and grandchildren. I socialise a lot, so I be out

every week at least once a week I go out for a meal with friends...
(Interview date: 10.11.05)

The community in Newcastle is smaller to that compared with Bradford and Birmingham, however, there is still a preference to live within an ethnic enclave (Heisler, 2000). The impact on government funding is affecting these organisations and Pakistani community in general hence displaying signs of the heavy reliance of these groups as social activities for the group. It could also be argued that this affects their well-being from a social and health point of view too. Maynard et al. (2008) has however theorised that for some women later life brings the opportunities and freedom to travel and involvement in leisure and other activities, thus an issue to investigate in the group interviewed and the role of socio-economic status.

Mrs Sheinaz is involved with a National Park organisation through work:

...from work conferences and things like that, I have done residentials with work. I am also a 'Community Champion for National Parks' and the project is called 'MOSAIC' and we do 4 residentials in a year at different places...We go ourselves and get all the training, information about how to do the walks the area the risk assessments and we come back and out that into practice in our work (Interview date: 10.11.05)

Brah (2006) explains assimilation and the 'helping to adjust to the host society' is an important dialogue to compare with the experiences of the interviewees when they have expressed the attempts made to 'mix in' inspite of the 'un-host like fashion towards the new arrivals' (p.38). However, this study has revealed the immediate arrival reception was found to be pleasant in general. As Ms Sheinaz explains once the confidence of an individual develops, they attempt to integrate but barriers prevent integration. It is argued that integration may not be an appropriate 'word' to use but visualise on the continuum of 'fluid identities'. Urry (2007) argues that the identities where fluid are a good position to mobilise from. Whereas the Pakistanis were seen as 'aliens' Ms Sheinaz highlighted the same analogy in the opposite context. Over time she recognised that the English culture was approachable and slowly started to experience the 'British way of life' as her 'comfort zone' expanded. Thus, her integration was not consciously sought at arrival.

There are notable differences between the women in terms of experience and skills. The main reason between the men is the socio-economic status of the interviewees before they arrived in the UK. Critical analysis suggests interviewees who have had some kind of education from their homeland seem to have done better and created a better lifestyle with greater expectations by living in the UK, despite integration and attachment. However, for those who were not educated or from poorer backgrounds the women have suffered to a larger extent after arriving into the UK. These women (Ms Anum, Ms Samina and Mrs Fozia) several decades later are still struggling but there issues are different; they are related to issues in women in later life (Maynard et al., 2008). Changes have included enduring the loss of the social support system they had when their children were younger or single adults. And nor do they have the health. Some of the women interviewed have forged social networks while pursuing a career in the labour market enhancing their power within the home, while other have become socially excluded and isolated (Mrs Sheinaz). Arguably, Ahmad and Modood, (2003) call for interpretative approaches moving beyond these monocasual and culturalist explanations applicable to younger South Asian women expressing their identities through facilitative and dynamic frameworks can also be applied with the first-generation women. The men display similar characteristics except they are contemplating their identities as they spend more of their time at home (Mr Maqsood and Mr Mohammed) while some of the men working are disillusioned with their future prospects at the wider systems level (Mr Saleem). Next, a gendered critical analysis is carried out below in terms of Pakistani migrant's experiences of access to healthcare in Newcastle upon Tyne.

## Experiences of Access to Healthcare

### Male Interview Narratives

Mr and Mrs Azaad were both ill. Mr Azaad had been in hospital for a long time and Mrs Azaad takes cares of him as well as coping with her own health issues. Mr Azaad was slow to speak but he did make some comments: '...we don't go anywhere we don't have the strength anymore' (Interview date: 7.4.11). Their lives can be related to Game's (2000) views that there is a kind of passivity and loss of self-determination because of the motility aspect of their lives hence falling or downward mobility resulting.

Mr Hussain (retired engineer) had suffered a major attack and has dementia since our last interview. His family are his main carers and his daughter (Ms Hussain) agreed to be interviewed on behalf of her father.

>...Since my father has become ill he has required 24 hour, 7 days a week care. My mother does the majority of the care, he is only able to look after himself if someone prompts him. If he needs to eat, he needs someone to prompt him to eat, you have to prompt him to go to the toilet, you have to prompt him to remind him because the brain has been damaged he needs prompting... (Interview date: 18.4.11)

With the interview with Mr Hussain's daughter, it was felt the field text should remain in its length in order to perceive the total daily dialogue the family and external agents endure to obtain optimum benefit for their father. Here the car, or 'physical access' Urry, 2007, p. 191) was explained in detail surrounding issues of concern:

>...First of all, at home, in home they have provided some provision, such as help to get on and off the toilet or he has got a banister to hold and help him to be more mobile. Luckily, he can walk so he does walk but gets tired quickly, so he needs more mobility support for that em if he wants to go for a walk my mother does go for a walk as well, she's got back problems, they do go for short walks but there aren't very many chairs to sit down on. There used to be lots of park benches and things; there is less now cos they need to stop and start erm to do that. The caring service erm do also Take him for a walk as well although the caring service is .... I don't feel are very specialised in what they provide him and they did provide a Pakistani carer to look after him but because he's so familiar with the culture he took a lot for granted. He used to come late and go quickly; he wouldn't adhere to the rules correctly. He would say things that he thinks he would get away with it and he probably wouldn't say to somebody who was (unclear here). They did try to find someone who spoke the same language, but my father could obviously speak fluently in Urdu and English both. But it is sometimes useful to have

someone who understands the culture sometimes is quite helpful, but it didn't relay work out, but it helped my mother in terms of language and if they come, they could talk to her. We did have a Sikh women who came she was really lovely, and they would talk about food and when she had to look after my father and my mother wasn't there, they could make roti's or something so that support was nice. Erm I think it would be much nicer to have somebody who has more culture and speak the same language if they take him out. But it is a sitting in service, and they might take him to the park or somewhere. I think it would be nice for him to have somebody who was part of the community I think is nice to have. But we compromise on what we get and that is somebody who has an outgoing personality to take him for a walk.

Yeah, the NHS caring service has not been good at all. The support has been very poor, and it has been about searching and finding and chasing, it is very hard to do for someone who is a 24-hour carer so if I've got to do it my mother can't do it cos she's looking after him. It is a needle in a haystack and there are lots of facilities to help him, but it is a case of sourcing them and finding them and getting people to do things for you. If we want to travel out, we can do it but you can do it through the day centre he goes to. The daycentres more orientated towards different tastes and things? There are only a couple of Asians who go there. There isn't anyone of an Asian background and when my father comes back saying he is bored...
(Interview date: 18.4.11)

In the case for Mr Hussain although family are helping 'around the clock', his daughter who works full time and her elderly mother care for Mr Hussain daily. Despite this they have needed to access social services for care and health as well as for respite. Distress and frustration have been an experience for the family when accessing these services. Mr Hussain on his first interview was fit and well and was proud to talk of his career achievements by working in a high rank of the engineering firms he worked for designing on projects that made his 'company make millions!'. His wife and daughter are now struggling to find care that is 'appropriate for his needs'. Mr Hussain 'needs a service that is culturally sensitive'. He has attended day care services which

Mr Hussain's family believe are inappropriate for his needs. Again, this is further evidence to suggest that an additional service provision requirement is needed.

### Female Interview Narratives

Ms Mumtaz explained what her experience was like in hospital and how she finds it difficult to get appointments with the doctors:

> I have diabetes, heart problem…I had the heart problem and stayed in hospital for a month, at that time I went through hell. My god it was terrible. They gave me one wrong tablet and I went through all of this. That tablet was wrong. The doctor was good there though and I said to him "I know you when you are talking quietly amongst yourselves about me you know you have given me the wrong tablet and just admit it". They did say that you can complain if you want to, we have no problem with that …Anyway, I can't remember the doctors name, he was a really good doctor but Ozzy said, "no just leave it is not nice". There used to be this nurse and she was a right one, whenever she used to come, she always used to say something. I was a bit ill and really couldn't be bothered. But one day there was an Indian lady next to me and the poor thing was in a lot of pain and the had like a heart machine (monitor) on her and she couldn't walk and the nurse said to her you get up and go to the toilet yourself. She didn't really understand English very well and she got up and when she got up she said she couldn't walk because I have the machine on and that. She used to have a stick, the nurse smacked her on her back here (showed side of bottom), anyway she went to the toilet. When she came back from the toilet, she got really bad there and then and I thought there is no way she is going to survive everyone made a racket and the doctors and that came. I told them all that she did that. But as you know they don't listen to you because that is their own, as you know. (Interview date: 7.4.11)

Ms Mumtaz's conversation started of quite light-heartedly but as the interview progressed a deeper sense of awareness and political issues arose. Ms Mumtaz had been attending voluntary meetings that were designed to improve community relations and the inner-city area that she lives in. Despite knowing her rights she feels she has been demoralised by the lack of co-operation and response that she has experienced by her local councillors and the police as well as the voluntary organisations she was representing. These findings display the 'grievances' are examples of dissatisfaction from a British Pakistani who feels she is not heard or listened too. On the other hand, she is also poor in capital and financially less well off by becoming a widow when her only son was seven years old. She claims she has struggled always and despite her list of illnesses is not eligible to any disability benefits. Thus, Ms Mumtaz is an example of an immigrant settling into Britain trying her best to be among the culture and improve her area and community living in the area.

Ms Anum, meanwhile, struggles with her mobility, housework and cooking on a daily basis and had to pay back money for home help she had received and commented:

> …Like people go on holidays I have never been, you know I am by myself and I get scared. I don't even go to town even though I know the way. People say you have a pass and go in the mornings, but my legs hurt and my feet and I get dizzy and I get scared I don't get that much help I have to pay £10 an hour for home help and I can't afford that. I am already paying back £100 they have said they have given me. (Interview date: 28.3.11)

Ms Anum talks about her health here but finds her motility situation is causing mobility issues although evidently lives in an 'imagined presence' as discussed by Buscher and Urry, (2009) by maintaining contact with her family by telephone.

Mrs Riaz's narratives are a classic example of the racial inequalities and conflicts that have led migration theorists 'to go back to the drawing board after the realisation of the failure of the assimilation model. Mrs Riaz' describes her family experiences in Britain with sadness and rejects the notion of 'being in a better place' as researched by Brah in 1996. She also claims coming to 'Vilayath' has split her family and her parent's expectations and ambitions were never fulfilled in the UK who' father is now deceased and mother has multiple health care needs and 24 hour care whom she cares for. Hence a notion that has been expresses several times to me in this fieldwork.

Mrs Riaz explained:

…Sometimes I think my father would have been happier not coming to England, he has paid a large price for coming to England. He used to say it's not been worth him coming over, his sons married English women, they are both divorced now and one left leaving two young sons for my brother to bring up. His family has just fell apart… (Interview date: 7.12.05)

This scenario reflects the perceptions of older women indicating that interdependence and close contact between family members is expected and a norm. hence 'a strong sense of obligation, duty and reciprocity leads us to talk of the moral economy of kin, with older women playing a pivotal role, through childcare and doing other domestic tasks…the women from ethnic groups clearly also expected to receive reciprocal help from children and grandchildren in the future' (Maynard et al, 2008, p. 94-95). An argument I agree that is perhaps relevant to all walks in the ageing society but an area that was touched by one or two interviewees and requiring further research on hopes and expectations by kin.

It is not the 'myth of return' which may have been an issue five decades or so ago but the age at which health issues are prominent amongst the 'first-generation' especially those either living alone or widowed. More than half of the interviewees from this generation were living alone; an issue that is highlighted by Sirojudin (2009) struggling, to find a balance between the social needs and effects of isolation and loneliness as well as managing health and social needs. This is an area that Sirojudin (2009) states to be lacking in meeting the specific needs of 'older persons' of the Pakistani community and there is a 'need to strengthen' that has also been highlighted in these findings.

These themes and examples demonstrate the point that Brettell and Hollifield (2008) are attempting to make regarding assimilation with examples from the strong ethnic practices embedded into the Pakistani / Muslim culture. Hence the classic assimilation theory is no longer an outcome of integration but deviations from the linear assimilation model – segmented assimilation theory (Brettell and Hollifield, 2008). It is thus a recognition that cultural practices and religions are distinctive for individuals to this right. Ultimately a responsibility and need that requires further research to pursue Werbner's (2001) argument that these individuals should be able to retain their practice.

## Chapter Conclusions and Summary

Social services and community involvement and access to healthcare provision have been evaluated from a social and cultural perspective. A significant finding relates to the ageing of the Newcastle Pakistanis. This critical analysis has demonstrated that the majority of the older persons from the first-generation who are retired or over the age of sixty are living lonelier lives and in some cases in isolation with several interviewees living on their own. An issue not previously heard of for this community. Hence, it can be deduced that once these Pakistani people may have been strong in social capital in the early years of settling. However, a culture change amongst the community and as the second and third-generation lead their own lives and the extended structure has become minimum e.g., go to work; take children to school etc. This leaves little time in today's busy and stressful lives to spend time with the Pakistani older person. A relative difference to the ageing English population who migrating to Spain as they feel they have 'earned' this leisure, there is no comparison to be made apart from the Pakistanis have worked hard and have not displayed a desire to move anywhere else. This area needs further work to establish if this is a trait amongst the diaspora communities.

Through the analysis of the themes, it is apparent that health deterioration relative to motility therefore limits mobility at home, locally, nationally and internationally of all corporeal travel. Thus, the social differentiations and mobility constraints are effected and 'are intimately related to one another in the way they have effects and exert force. There is considerable tension along the geometry as these forces push, pull and flex producing unequal and uneven consequences' (Adey, 2010, p. 102). Evidently there are degrees of motility that have been demonstrated to display some unusual mobilities. Hence Urry (2007, p. 208) has described a 'socially inclusive' society as minimising 'coerced immobility' and if all else were equal 'a good society would not limit travel, co-presence and resulting good conversations' and initiatives in transport, planning and communications should promote networking and meetingness (and limit missingness). This is a dynamic notion of citizenship that values 'freedom to' rather than 'freedom from'. Such a notion means that zero friction, the death of distance and the untrammelled pursuit of movement are undesirable goals' (Sager, 2006, cited

Urry, 2007, p. 208). Likewise, Urry (2007, p. 208) describes these 'capabilities agenda for mobilities is of course massively difficult to implement' and; the 'prima facie starting point would be that all social groups should have similar rights of co-presence'.

The results for many Newcastle Pakistanis demonstrate deteriorating health and immobility issues and additional 'weak ties' exacerbate isolation by losing touch with their friends or neighbourhood (e.g., through spatial assimilation or death). It has resulted in 'weak' social capital (Urry 2007) and the notion of access and services has become central to their daily activities and significantly religion at the forefront as argued by Maynard et al, (2008). Experiences have been similar for both the men and women. Hence, it has been empirically shown that those with the highest motility traits are the most mobile of people (Adey, 2010).

In summary as empirical evidence also suggests mobility and motility patterns this century will be changed by 'networked computers' and 'mobile telephony'. However, 'lack of accesses for the illiterate or the 'socially distinct' groups who arguably prefer the 'powerful force' or 'rush of energy' (Urry, 2007) although the benefits for the motility low (also referred to as poor access) may be greater; another area of work, especially the imagined presence carrying images of travel and carrying connections across and into, multiple and other social spaces (Urry, 2007).

The Parekh report (2000) highlighted culturally sensitive practices that may have been developed in the past. However, empirical evidence has demonstrated the 'lack off' facilities to meet the health, religious and social care needs of many of the interviewees. This need can be explained by through work carried out by Finney and Simpson (2009) that describe the processes that led to funding cuts of services provide to the minority groups. Interestingly, it has been demonstrated that those interviewees who have access to network capital (in most cases this means the use of the telephone either fixed or mobile but for the purposes of definition the term network capital is used) and claim to keep in touch with friends and family through this means as a substitution of face-to face conversations (complimentary substitution discussed earlier) have been identified to have low motility. However, despite maintaining several identities it is the social and care needs that are dominant across the debates of 'social cohesiveness and social inclusion' for the older Pakistani community into the mainstream services rather than intermittent voluntary projects providing these necessary services.

The next chapter considers leisure and tourism aspect of the Pakistani population. This will be analysed from a local, national and international level. However, the religious aspect is also analysed further with the obligatory requirements shown to be a global requirement such as visiting Saudi Arabia for a pilgrimage.

# CHAPTER 5

# PAKISTANI MIGRANT'S EXPERIENCES OF LEISURE AND TOURISM

## Introduction

This chapter critically analyses the leisure and tourism mobilities of the Pakistani diaspora in Newcastle upon Tyne. There are four sections in this chapter, travelling experiences in the UK; experiences of returning to Pakistan; visiting other places outside the UK other than Pakistan; religion and visiting Saudi Arabia. An attempt is made to differentiate between gender experiences in each section. A significant finding that has been identified in this research is that Pakistanis travel extensively in the UK. The travel habits, however, also vary significantly amongst the generations and genders.

## Travelling in the UK

### Male Interview Narratives

The purposes of these visits on a local and national level conform to Urry's (2007) proposal of the mobility framework. There are several categories of which the obligatory requirements can be defined under this umbrella. A question that has arisen is the frequency of visits that take place especially on a national level but to places of close vicinity. Visits from Newcastle go as far as Yorkshire regularly - a daily trip with the Pakistanis interviewed. The Pakistani generation have thus kept up with these visits. One explanation I put forward is that it could be as a result of more disposable income and car ownership and improved infra-structure or perhaps by keeping 'in touch' there is contentment and reassurance and support amongst family, friends and the community from 'back home'. Arguably this reduces the need for the 'myth of return' Ali and Holden (2006, p.235) expand on and explain how the first-generation have found themselves in a 'three-fold predicament'. This stems from the settlement experiences of racism, creating a sense of 'unbelonging' or better known in South Asian terms as 'a pardesi'. These feelings grow with living in the UK and having relatives and friends in Pakistan and the inability to have a close network of family and friends outside their homeland.

Mr Yasir stated a process within social networks that involves travel, meeting and a lot of talking. Thus, he feels the need to perform duties for 'waada qaata' purposes. Hence, in my view addressing the mobilities paradigm as Mr Yasir states an obligation to sustain relations. All interviewees travelled for 'waada qaata' reasons unless they could not travel because of ill-health. Thus, to keep the 'myth of return' alive' it is re-lived by compromising and pursuing obligatory and social visits 'in excess' to that expected it is creating social capital high for the mobile and network capital high for the less mobile persons. From the three obligatory practices this one is defined as a 'familial obligation' as theorised by Urry, (2007) and as expressed by Mr Yasir can be classed as a 'mobility burden' especially when the need is to travel at specific times and specific reasons because of 'expectations of presence and of attention' (Urry, 2004, cited Jamal and Robinson, 2009, p.649). Arguably, this may be an extension of the 'home-making' or as Urry (2007) theorises 'to cement the weak ties'. This can be supported by the theory from Hetherington (2000) that the Pakistani diaspora in Newcastle want to be part of something but most significantly it is because they want to be part of something larger and take these obligatory face-to-face visits as part of the process for them to fit into this larger 'something' and emotionally anchoring themselves for meaning and feeling as concluded by Tuan (1978).

> ...As you know our networks are looking after the whole network... the extended family you sort of say hello to everyone by telephone or by visiting them at home... Err going to the deaths and marriages that's the important bit and going to see people when they are ill and thirdly just casual visiting that gets left out quite a lot because you are so busy you haven't got time to do a casual visit. Err going to the deaths and marriages that's the important bit and going to see people when they are ill and thirdly just casual visiting that gets left out quite a lot because you are so busy you haven't got time to do a casual visit...So the majority of occasions we visit...Middlesboro... that town more than the others because there is always a marriage or death or someone coming from Pakistan and those type of times you give more credence to, cos it is close family you have to physically show your face... Then their children then the network breaks down as it

gets lower and lower and that.

It is usually a family event and because they are within like that 150-mile zone, you go there early morning and come back in the evening. We have never had the occasion where we've stayed overnight. Middlesboro…if there is a death in the family you stay for one or two days. Even the weddings you know you go early in the morning and come back and go the following day again. (Interview date: 6.4.11)

This narrative illustrates Werbner's (2005) statement that diasporic activities including those of culture and lifestyle are essential ingredients of diasporic activities to live in a safe and harmonious environment. There is also increasing evidence from this information that a paved journey and network is the result of these diasporic activities that demonstrates the sedimented aspect of mobilities as argued by Urry, (2007). In addition, attempts are made by the Pakistani community to 'keep in touch' and therefore maintain a strong social network although it is also recognised that life is busier now than it has ever been and therefore the 'communicative' travel is adopted where it is felt necessary (Urry, 2007). These points are significant in terms of social practices and culture and expressed by the narratives in this section. Mr Yasir has experienced that these meetings involve some kind of movement, and the better the technology, and motility the greater are the obligations to meet. Hence, the social obligation refers to quality of time being spent with the other face-to-face (family, friend or colleague). Thus, these presences enable weak networks to gain strength and trust members being able to 'read' what the other is thinking and observe the body language; but also, an opportunity to hear first-hand what they have to say, to sense a response and to observe emotions. A classic scenario is that of the journey made by an interviewee who had a remarkable story to tell of his journey by road that took months and involved a car crash, but he eventually got to meet his father 'in such a messy state'. In his words he recalled his father's words 'I thought people who went to England came back in suits, what has happened to you'. Urry (2007, p. 234) expresses this to 'create a temporal feel for the moment, separate from and at odds with 'normal' life. This is arguably either returning to the homeland or in this case, national mobilities.

In addition, the non-localised network proves to be useful in the case of

Newcastle. That is, many of the interviewees that settled in Newcastle did so because of the contacts they had sustained from the initial onset after leaving their home country. Werbner (2005) has identified this to be the case in South Manchester but significantly negating the class differences as well as the type of biradari one belongs to and social relations. Whilst results have demonstrated these activities link Britain to their homeland, casual visiting has been the first activity that has 'been dropped' from this perspective which has led to 'weak social ties'. It is left to the individual to choose visits 'for and not' and with whom they sustain social and obligatory links and or communicative movement. This is also known as mobility substitution (Adey, 2010). The face-to-faceness is considered to 'incur a powerful force or a rush of energy' that is believed to be the core of social life (Urry, 2007). But also, to 'cement' the weak ties face-to-face or even body-to body (Urry, 2004, cited Jamal and Robinson, 2009). Hence, as Urry, (2007) identifies from the mobility paradigm it is the first three that are 'mobility burdens' because as Urry defines expectations of presence and of attention (Urry 2004). These issues have been significant in interviewing the older generation and empirically justified. In addition, Urry, (2007) also states that increasing motility increases the obligations for meeting that exacerbates the 'capital poor' from the 'capital rich', thus highlighting the inequalities of power.

The term 'waada qaata' has been exposed many times under this category and can be interpreted as a 'face-to-face' mobility requirement by the group. This can be from one or more of either familial, social or an obligation although legal and economic reasoning is not out of the question. There are also types of mobility empowerments with different types of human mobilities. Arguably, the statement by Hannam et al, (2006) 'places, technologies and gates enhance tourist mobilities of some while reinforcing the immobilities (or demobilisation) of others' is evident through the empirical findings in this chapter. For example, those interviewees rich in social capital travel more from an enclave in one city to another enclave in another city e.g. Bradford, Birmingham and Middlesbrough and consume tourism achieving a higher level of cultural capital and hence reasserting the banal as Hannam and Knox (2010, p.103) define as, 'accruing cultural capital for public display among other members of their home communities'.

The term known as 'waada qaata' is literally translated 'for some reason or loss', in practice, this refers to visits and the fact there is a reason to travel e.g.travelling to a wedding to visit family because of a death in the family. As a member of the community in Newcastle I can also argue from a reflexive position that the depth of the relationship determines the need to travel which can extend to births, celebrations, religious ceremonies or someone going or returning from Pakistan. This is a factor subtly evident empirically, with significant behavioural traits between the men and the women at the local level but an issue that requires prior insider knowledge to decipher the networks in play. Social capital is higher for the women than men, but the opposite is true for national travel. That is obligatory travel and familial is a gendered trait but on an international level woman are travelling to explore the world with their partners and also on their own. However, this is a generalisation and further work is needed re-hypothesis the changing behavioural patterns. In summary both genders place priorities on extending relationships under this term 'waada qaata'. Thus, it includes the wider network of the community friends, colleagues and associated members of the community (people with position or power in the community are sometimes identified by their social capital status). Telephony, however, still has been noted to be to most common form of communication at a distance, and obligatory visits are deemed obligatory for the mobile person. Repercussions of not meeting social or obligatory practices because of 'motility issues' travelling locally, nationally or internationally have ties sustained through the telephone. It would be interesting to note what 'economic considerations' are implemented when using the telephone, i.e., internet phoning or buying pay-as-you go cards.

As Mr Yasir stated relationships sustained by performing obligatory and social meetings are by car. Mr Yasir also explains this is complimentary to the use of telephones, for travel in the UK. Cyber mobilities or aeromobilities is discussed in the section for travelling to Pakistan in this chapter. Social mobilities reflects a local asset based on this analysis but as it will be demonstrated in the later sub section it can 'turn into a transmission belt when it crystallises in migrant networks' (Papastergiadis, 2010, p.347). Apart from visiting for familial obligations travel has been minimal for Mr Yasir in the UK:

Well as you know we very rarely go on holidays and I have taken kids out my kids when they were younger to the Lake District and Scotland like a day out thing but it's not a holiday holiday…you know you feel guilty you know the other children come back to school after the summer holidays and they say we have been there and we 've been there…our kids miss out so I used to try my level best and say alright we'll go to the Lakes or Scotland these were just day trips rather than overnight. (Interview date: 6.4.11)

Mr Yasir has attempted to integrate into the host society 'to stop his children from being discriminated against' by trying to take them to day trips to the Lake District etc. He has felt that children in school talk of the 'Disneytization' places and his children need to be introduced to this culture in order to 'mix in' and feel left out hence from the western perspective culturally poor.

Mr Ayaz has a lot of connections nationally and travels extensively:

…Regular I go to Leeds, Middlesbrough, Bradford, Sheffield and I go to Birmingham sometimes…Most of the time I go to visit somebody died (like a funeral) or if anybody dies I go to the funeral and if anyone gets married I go…for parties… Wherever there is a 'waada qata' I must go there, this week I was three times in Leeds…I have been three times Leeds and Sunday I was in Sheffield, somebody died in Sheffield and I was in a funeral. Three times there was a funeral… in a week. (Interview date: 19.4.11)

When Mr Ayaz was asked about any other reasons to travel in the UK he said:

I have been to Blackpool with a community trip. It was a community trip I have been many times with them Blackpool to see the lighting with a couple of English friends…we just take the car in the morning and come back in the car…I went three times with the Muslim Association and people who come to see us to Bradford. (Interview date: 19.4.11).

It is clear that this interviewee has links that are rich in social capital, but he has also proven as a first-generation male that he is also rich in cultural capital and enjoys visiting 'spectacular events'. I relate this to 'ethno-cultural units' and 'social networks' that capture the 'dynamics of power' but as lengthy details demonstrate above and below, it is the 'transnational social field' which as Kim (2009, p.683) states 'signifies different perspectives of the nature and role of the nation-state under globalisation'; Nash (2000) argues identities although fluid are also non-representational behaviours representing a part of the whole process; an aspect that is relational on this thematic analysis. Although these scenarios have demonstrated the physical travel, it would be significant to establish the correlation of telephone communication alongside the travelling. Mr Ayaz has also engaged in a different form of tourism that can be regarded as an upward social mobility but also taking visitors from Pakistan on heritage visits.

### Female Interview Narratives

Ms Anum from Newcastle, despite her ill health has already mentioned she travelled alone by train to her grand-daughter's wedding in Sheffield but does not like to travel alone at a local level in case she falls or gets lost but visits family for special occasions when she can:

> ...Before we used to go on trips to different places the one takes us for exercises Freda and them they don't take us to Birmingham and that but the Roshni group take us to places to like Bradford...I have a daughter who lives in Sheffield and she is always saying come come! Before her husband used to come and pick me up, he had passed his taxi test, but he has a had a heart attack and he has not got the permission to drive. I went last year as my granddaughter (daughters' daughter) got married. (Interview date: 28.3.11)

From this narrative I reinforce that 'access' to social provision and healthcare or the 'organisational' structure (Urry 2007) is an important 'potential' (Kaufmann, 2002). Hence, motility is an issue for her abilities in communication and for the potential to display her determination and will to pursue social and obligatory practices despite 'changing from the fast lane (when she was more mobile and was walking was not an issue for her) to the slow lane' (Hannam et al, 2006). This can also be interpreted as 'diasporic tourism' which Adey (2010) believes to be in search of their roots, hence self-discovery and identity affirmation. A significant part of the interviewee's narratives on reminiscence areas. The majority are illiterate and do not drive themselves. When they were younger, they were part of an enclave who supported such activities and as the Bradford study noted there would be a group who travelled in a car for 'lena dena' (McLoughlin, 2006). However, the interviewees lifestyles over time were 'constitutive of a mobility system' (driver) and have broken or fragmented due to several reasons. The first-generation is now part of the 'ageing population' and family members who can drive either do not have cars or are 'too busy' for the traditional 'lena dena' aspect of the culture. Therefore, the social life is minimised to the level of relying on others when and if they are 'taken' to pursue the 'lena dena'. The main worry that has been established of the Pakistanis in Newcastle is that if they do not attend other people's weddings and funerals then no-one will attend theirs...this is given high precedence in the culture as low social capital is a sign of 'no izzath (respect)' amongst the community. This aspect was originally discussed by Zelinsky (1973) where immobility is exhibiting a defeated position of being left behind and failure. In summary the interviewees have stated they have a higher use of network capital which is due to three main reasons:

a) Time factor;

b) Immobility (age, health deterioration, loss of community culture);

c) Identity affirmation (by engaging in everyday tourism (Adey, 2010).

Several reasons have been noted for the gendered differences. Some of the female interviewees are working women and have their own disposable income and therefore have more choice on how to spend. On the other axis there are also some women who do not work and need to 'organise lifts' locally and nationally in order to carry out social and obligatory practices but feel frustrated as they end up staying at home as there is no-one available to take them to these places. Hence, their social life revolved around attending activities arranged through voluntary organisations and social services.

An important observation made during interviews was that the majority of homes visited for interview the televisions were on and tuned into playing the channels from their home countries either news or entertainment. This demonstrates the 'imaginative' travel effect from the mobilities paradigm where images of people and places are formed and reformed across media (Urry, 2007). Buscher and Urry (2009) have defined this scenario to take place when there is a physical absence there may be an imagined presence through the multiple of technologies of travel and communications across a range of media. There are definitions for film-induced tourism (Beeton, 2005), however, it would be valuable to measure the effects of this activity from home (in the 1960's and 1970's Asian men would go to the Asian cinemas to watch a Bollywood film). To clarify this point Ms Anum's quote can be referred to where she wouldn't go to the cinemas as it was against her cultural belief. Nevertheless, watching the same movie from her living room is culturally acceptable. She has, however, claimed to have sustained her links with family and relatives in Pakistan through using telephony as a means of communication. This is an important concept that requires theorising for the motility low as argued by Urry, (2007).

Ms Anum struggled unless someone else takes her locally or nationally:

> ...I usually go to the fruit shop with my trolley when I feel up to it...but unless my son takes me, I cannot go anywhere else. The last time I had to go to my granddaughter's wedding in Manchester I had to go in the train by myself...that was scary, but I got there... (Interview date: 28.3.11)

Ms Samina also added ...I only go anywhere if my sons take me, but they are always busy... (Interview date: 20.4.11). Thus, there has been recognition from the theoretical perspective of these qualities and features identified of the distinctive Newcastle Pakistanis (Scheffer, 2006). Evidently 'everything seems to be in perpetual movement throughout the world' and as Hannam (2006, p246) writes 'there are new forms of mobility which were unimaginable a generation earlier'

### Returning to Pakistan

The majority of interviewees in this research are according to Heisler's definitions migrants (those who permanently stay in the host country) as well as from the anthropological field known as migrants who travel backwards and forwards (Horevits, 2009). It is also acknowledged that there is an 'imagined presence' (Buscher and Urry, 2009) as described above.

### Male Interview Narratives

Mr Ayaz is self-employed and claimed:

...I have visited Pakistan at least twenty times ...I go to visit family and I have got my own house. I go and visit places when I go the last time I went all over Pakistan. (Interview date: 19.4.11)

Mr Malik's experience was more of an adventure it took him thirteen days to get to Pakistan. In total he said he has been back three times:

...I went by road; it took thirteen days...it was the summer in 1965 that there was a fight in Lahore that India did. On that day we were on way in car there was so many things that happened on the way. I was with five friends...I went by road because I don't have the money and secondly there were friends to go with...25 Kilometres from Turkey, we had an accident. We were taken to hospital, then an Arab they took us to an American hospital base In those days Pakistan Iraq and Turkey were quite good with each other they took a lot a care of us there. Especially the girls when they see Pakistanis. I am truly saying this they were very good we were in hospital for eight days. Me and this other man; this is a long story...we crossed Dover then Belgium, Germany, we stayed there eight days because there was one person with us (he was a good guy) and he was driving a big colonel car and he couldn't control it and he crashed it. It took a while to repair it. Then we went to Austria. Austria, then Bulgaria Yugoslavia, Turkey, Iran and Pakistan...You get an A membership they do insurance of car etc and you get a booklet with it which tells you every detail of what water is like etc although we didn't use many of them you get every inch of roads. I had a bandage and leg was broken and we got a place to stay in. It had nothing in and in the night three men came in we had already received tickets to go in the morning and he was saying come and have a look at my car it was a Volkswagon -Toyota then you believe me whatever was with us our pockets were cleared...I didn't mention I had money with me though.

It was not just mine the person whose car it was and the other person with us. So, from here we got to Iran. The person whose car it was had a brother who worked as a Principal in Sindh. His Ambassador at the time in Iran was his friend, anyway we stayed in a hotel and got washed and bathed. I couldn't do anything at the time because of my leg, but we went to the airport and you wouldn't believe our bad luck we were giving the money and the ticket got booked we went home then and went home and the next day; Irans other border joins with Pakistan and there my Uncle was there (working on railways). He was a driver, when we got there. We were going along the Black sea, it was a very dangerous way, we went about 400 miles and a few times I we stopped off and washed our feet and that in the Black Sea. After that when we got to my Uncles- we parked our car at customs I went to the railways and asked about my Uncle. They said that he has gone to Quwaita. Anyway, we went through customs etc and then eventually got to camp. We stayed the night and the next day (as it was late when we got there) and set off again in the evening for Quwaita (in Pakistan). We stopped off at another place further on and has some food at this place was my wife's uncle. We were not on good terms, but we talked a little. He insisted that we stay the night. But we set off and in the morning about three o' clock we reached Quwaita. I phoned from hotel. We still never met my Uncle. So, we went back as we left two of the people at the place we stayed at. We then met with the Turkey Embassy and arranged for some money to come through. The money came through and the next day…when we eventually got to Wazirabad my father was there waiting… that is Gujrawala, there is a big station there…

Any way I was saying my father was there and I had all my injuries on my head and that when I arrived there, and he said to me 'people come from England and do they come like this!' (laughing) and then I had a bath and that. This is my 'by road' story. (Interview date: 3.12.05)

The significant factor here is that despite the absence of today's communications technology network capital was present and sufficient to meet the needs of Mr Malik and his friends who eventually arrived in Pakistan. Finally, it was the determination and courage of these men that was present to go and see their families. In mobility terms this journey can be described as an act from 'access and potential motility' hence at the time Mr Malik and his friends were at the peak of health although capital was not very high, the body was able to function in the 'fast lane' and supporting Hannam et al. (2006) theory. This journey by road cannot be compared to the embodied experiences that have remained with this interviewee but aeromobility has significantly reduced time and place or mass space travel has transformed the futures of travelling at a global level (Urry, 2007, p. 155).

Visiting for the purposes to see family and friends is one reason to go to the diasporic homeland. Another relates to Bourdieu terms, cultural, social and economic capital. The economic capital is investment, property, home ownership, etc. It is the 'volume and composition' of the capital over a time in social space that determine the differences in a society. Hence, well over half of the interviewees owned a property in Pakistan. This is also a means of tallying the 'volume of capital' amongst each other, i.e., one person has built a house in Pakistan and another is inspired. This concept is also applicable from the social aspect as well as cultural as discussed in the earlier section (travelling in the UK). From Thieme's work this illustrates the how the multi-local dynamics benefits using Bourdieu's theory (2008) - the habitus is not forgotten by the migrant, but the social field is adapted creating a new social space (Thieme, 2008). This has been termed as 'transnational habitus' (Kelly and Lusis, 2006) where the background of the migrant can be an indicator of advantages or disadvantages for the individual. Thus these findings highlight it is the 'fluidity' of interviewees to adopt one lifestyle to another in both Britain and Pakistan that is the key and determines the individual's 'power relations' as described by Ellis (2003, cited Thieme, 2008, p.67) and as demonstrated becoming rich in cultural capital at the same time.

I also argue that this generation has an advantage of transnational family formation, but it can be denoted that as time passes and there is an accumulation of mobility capital the migrants also feel removed from the homeland. This facet has been theorised by Scott and Cartledge (2009) and descriptions of this nature has been evident in the narratives. For example, it was noted throughout the interview that Mr Maqsood did not express a preference or a need to return to Pakistan, but unspoken statements such as smiles as he talked of Pakistan and his family re-unions expressed his attachment. He explained how trips used to be made to Pakistan but not anymore as he has no kin relations left in the country. Hence, he has not made visits to re-live past memories as argued by Ali and Holden (2006). In addition, he was clear his link to Pakistan was 'only his roots'. His children have all settled in Britain, both husband and wife's parents and immediate family either live in the UK or have passed away. Another marker to note is the remittances that were once linked to maintenance and supporting families (Blunt and Dowling, 2006, p. 204) have not been included as significant expectations by the first-generation interviewees. Assumptions can be made that they have stopped, or the next generation has taken over or quite simply as Mr Maqsood quotes 'I have no family in Pakistan and therefore no links apart from my roots'. Interestingly, Mr Maqsood added he now travelled to America to visit his daughter who moved there after marriage. He claimed it was a long journey 'by plane'. Of significance is the relationship with the new country, a different arena and additional tourist complexities; this is an important issue especially for members of the first-generation diaspora travelling as a 'migrant' turning 'tourist'. Visiting their extended families and children who live locally, nationally and those who live abroad therefore enable more mobilities and worthy of research from the point of view of this group being more mobile. Questions, such as the elements of requirement for national attachment can be pursued and priorities debated especially in relation to culture and identity in a global world. Thus, summarising it was the roots that belonged in Pakistan and nothing else.

This shift in identity association has connotations that lead to the homeland regarded as challenging one's sense of place (lessness). Hence a visit 'back home' can be regarded as a mobility experience that modifies a migrant's capital accumulation and ontological security associated with 'home' that is not grounded within one's home. Thus, an analysis in this research has demonstrated that visits to the homeland Pakistan by those interviewees who attend regularly also have tourism interests and may only use the term 'homeland' as an excuse to travel.

This highlights the multitude of reasons for the diaspora retaining links as well as the revival of the 'myth of return' which could in part explain one reason for this. Another factor that has been significant in the return journeys is the types of mobility systems, namely the car, trains and aeroplanes (Adey, 2010). This, a super advancement but has especially provided the journeys 'back home'; a form of touristic travel as well as meeting the familial obligation. When a diasporic Pakistani arrives in Pakistan, they have noted that they also visit many sites once in their homeland to visit family friends and their home. They have also stated that the main form of mediation is trains, buses and cars in Pakistan. The majority of interviewees talked in detail of their 'doing mobility' experiences in Pakistan and the significance of each act, i.e., sensing, seeing etc (see mobilities section) (Urry, 2007). As an interviewee pointed out earlier when she sees melons, she can smell her melons from back home almost 50 years ago. I argue these experiences have significantly added to the field of Pakistani migration experiences as well as a critical analysis of the practicalities of the mobilities paradigm in practice.

Mr Maqsood as already stated did not mention any desire to go back to Pakistan. He was clear about his position in definition to his transnational identity. He had no family left in Pakistan and also no connection left with the country, his only connection to the land was his roots belonging to Pakistan. Both Mr Maqsood and his wife agreed that their priorities were to visit their daughter and grandchildren as often as they can who lives in America. Hence arguably 'complete integration' developed (Renshon, 2008) in the UK but with a new set of 'mobilities' developing in the US. Hence, transnational identities appear to be becoming a norm for this group. In summary, with a reduced diasporic travel and increasing tourism travel; an area to pursue theory and descriptions, meanings and habits are continuously changing in the global arena.

### Female Interview Narratives

Ms Zatoon a widow was asked why she visits Pakistan: 'for my house...to see my family... and my house' (Interview date: 13.5.05). Ms Zatoon states that she has a house in Pakistan just in case she is asked to leave England at least she will have a house to live in, in Pakistan. Thus, the concept of home discussed earlier for settlement is applicable for this female interviewee. Together with the memories and 'imaginary culture' Ali and Holden's (2006, p.232) meaning of homeland can be supported in that 'homeland' takes on a new meaning of 'heartlands'. She explains in detail of her parents work in Pakistan of how her family grew fruit by season and then went and sold it in the local bazaar on a donkey's back. She recalls the fruit melons a lot and the smells they gave off when they were ripe in their agricultural land. She said she could visualise the fields with melons and taste their sweetness to date hence whenever she sees melons this brings back memories of her days in Pakistan as a child. The research on material cultures researched by Tolia-

Kelly, (2004) can thus be identified amongst the community with the interviewee's personal stories and belongings at home. As as example, going to the cinema which is mentioned in the earlier theme of 'arrival' by Ms Anum; it could be argued that this is a western practice that Ms Anum was not happy to go with her husband but from a gender perspective was a normal practice for the Pakistani men to go to on a Sunday, yet Tolia-Kelly (2006) refers to this activity as a cultural magnet for the Asian community (Tolia-Kelly, 2006). In the study by Telang (1967) and provides significant evidence that 'home' is complex and multi-dimensional (Armbruster, 2002) and ownership of a home is a tool to negotiate identities (Salih, 2002). Evidence of gendered perceptions of the 'home' and the 'myth' are noted but assumptions are not made due to the relatively small number of participants. It is therefore argued that these stories of an identity from the interviewees have become blurred through assimilation and integration and shows Tolia-Kelly's (2004) work that the notion of 'land' and 'nation' is an essential part of the diasporic individual for survival.

It is significantly viable to say that the majority interviewees have maintained a connection with their home country Pakistan. As was cited in Hannam and Knox (2010) several theorists have linked this travel to a form called 'ethnic tourism' and more importantly these creolised or hybridised identities may or may not visit family but a desire to travel to the home country and visit friends and relative too. Mr Ayaz has certainly proved this point and having travelled from to and back from Pakistan at least 20 times! It is also Urry's (2007) mobilities paradigm that has incorporated this 'face to face' contact. Mr Ayaz has pursued with this trait over the years without it diffusing. This is in addition to the new technologies for the migrant 'pass in and out of intellectual and political borders as never before' (Kearney, 2004, p.549). Ms Fozia explained how she visited Pakistan when she was younger but now can't go over to visit her family parents, brothers and sisters. When Mr Azaad and Mrs Azaad were asked if they went on holiday he replied: '...No no, we have never been on holidays, never' (Interview date: 24.3.11). Mrs Azaad agreed with her husband and both replied:

> No, no, no ...dear... never, we have definitely not been on any holidays...I used to go to Pakistan but now I am too ill and can't travel...when I used to go it was something we saved up for and it

took years ...ten or fifteen years to save for the ticket...unlike today where people go every year... (Interview date: 24.3.11)

Mrs Azaad and her husband went and intended to stay longer on their recent visit this year but had to cut it short and only stayed for five days due to Mr Azaad's health deteriorating. They had also gone to sign some land over. Motility determinants play a role in this scenario and it could be argued that Kaufmann's theory (2002) on actual movement and potential movement has validity. Especially when the ageing Pakistani population can 'access' movement but it is an 'empty category' as described when physical movement is not possible negating the fluidity facet of mobilities. Ill health prevents long distance travel and complications for airlines and insurances as well as the individuals and their families. Therefore, as Kaufmann (2002) points out a distinction is necessary between the potential of movement and actual movement. It is, of course, an ideal situation for the diasporic individuals to maintain a family life from a distance and connecting through 'weak ties' and maintain a high network capital as argued by Hannam and Knox (2010) other than actual movement. This continual reference is discussed in the 'mobilities' and termed 'trans-locality' (Appadurai, 1995).

It is also necessary to point out that a few of the interviewees despite ill-health maintain a longing to go back to Pakistan. Mr Azaad only stayed for a few days and had to return home. This was an expensive trip for them but proves Brahs (1996) concept that the interviewees hold and ideology of return. The extremes behaviour of trying to go back home had proven to be difficult for a number of interviewees, but their immobility has not allowed this. This may not be possible for them again which Hall (1996) also theorises arguing that the diasporas will never return to their roots. But as Mrs Azaad states she uses the telephone and keeps in touch with her family by this method. A developmental generalisation from this work (has also been discussed in earlier findings).

Extending the above theory to belonging, it is also evident from the empirical data that Pakistan is a place the majority of interviewees long to be and travel to when they can. As Tolia-Kelly (2004) writes they create an environment from home to home with traditional home decorations and materials from Pakistan. This is consistent with Gustafon's (2009) outlook that mobile people tend to have a greater sense of belonging. Castles and

Miller (1998) suggest this to be common with both the sending and receiving country over a period of time (may be lengthy) which has also been evident from the information. Interestingly it is the 'cultural sites' that are referred to when the interviewees have been talking about their home country such as their land or house. It can also be argued that there is an element of an 'emblem' that the group identifies with its diasporic national identity and pursues with these return visits interwined with the 'myth of return' (Ali and Holden, 2011). To advance the social identification as Mr Ayaaz and Mrs Sheinaz have shown that mobilities or a high capital network can be a tool to validate one's social status within the community. For example, Adey (2010) refers diffused mediation or diffused mobility (Urry, 2007) that is the aeroplane and cars that have enabled greater freedom and flexibility. However, they also promoted the social status of an individual with a larger disposable income (higher socio-economic status). It is therefore viable to use this argument for the diasporic Pakistani community in Newcastle.

### Visiting Places Outside of the UK (other than Pakistan)

#### Male Interview Narratives

Although from the interviews it has been established that travelling forms a significant part of the Pakistani diaspora lifestyle, it is important to clarify from the outset that the majority of interviewees discussed issues relating to Pakistan naming it as their 'original homeland' through the lens of their latest visit or their latest planned visit. Hence the 'imaginary homeland' was always present along with the ideas of when they were last there or going to go. For example, interviewees have mentioned that they have been two years ago but still talk about the visit to Pakistan as if it were 'yesterday'. Others plan to go 'next year' but are preparing to go now in terms of saving for the spending money, buying gifts for relatives etc. The inherent theme that 'going back to Pakistan' is a widely accepted phenomena of the diaspora, however when it comes to 'visiting other places or tourism' there is a wider gap of perceptions. Mrs Madia went to France. When she was asked about her holiday to France, she was very shy and timid in speaking about her visit to a country other than her homeland, France, and when she did she was very quiet when she spoke of the visit. There are two possibilities for the reason behind this timid-ness. One is that Mrs Madia regards herself as ranking higher within the local community in 'cultural capital' and within her mind-set the Pakistani diaspora should only travel to and from the homeland. She could be displaying characteristics of a bounded, person, that lives amongst a hybrid community as discussed by Herbert (2008) with 'little' fluidity of identity and any other travelling was viewed as 'a waste of time and money'; apart from this visit that was solely a social and obligatory visit to France. She did not participate in any activities in France apart from stay in her niece's home that in reality translates as 'being forced to travel outside of her diasporic expectations. Hence, bordering and assimilating into 'tourism capital' together with excitement and reluctance perhaps a category in the vertical differential feelings (Bachelard, 1988, cited in Adey, 2010, p.162); she did not want to openly express this aspect; suggesting a blurred identity which is in compliance with work by Ali and Holden (2006, p. 220). Although, the visit was only to see a relative, the fact that she agreed to go to France was a huge milestone from the cultural and touristic aspect and although cannot be classed as ethnic tourism that Hannam and Knox (2010) define this interviewee kept within her dietary and religious requirements (ate halal food, prayed en route). On the other hand, there have been interviewees who have openly and happily expressing touristic activities regardless of rankings of the cultural capital (this term has been translated as izzath that means respect or honour and sharaam means discourses of shame that have also been highlighted by Herbert, (2008, p. 84).

Mr Saleem, (a travel agent) said '…Last year we went to Holland for the flowers – tulips…Yes they have a flower show, always have in March/April…' (Interview date: 5.4.11). Mr Saleem illustrates that tourism is not only within the home country but also on an international level (Adey, 2010). Arguably with reference to Mr Saleem's travel to countries abroad, that is, to see the tulips in Holland. Arguably this does not fall within the boundaries of trans local activities. However, in comparison to theories on mobilities of earlier settlements (Turner, 2010) and accessing movement through paths and pavements; whether segregated or not (Finney and Simpson, 2009) ; my findings have demonstrated a major network amongst the first-generation diasporic Pakistani migrants travels. The notion of diaspora tourism seen as voyages of self-discovery and identity affirmation 'in search of their roots' (Hannam and Knox, 2010, p. 163) is shown but from a completely different (touristic) perspective in this situation.

**Female Interview Narratives**

Mrs Madia is first-generation she does not have a sense of pride in saying she went to France. Infact is 'trying to play down' the fact that she went here. In fact, she went to visit her niece. This is an area where further work may identify cultural religious or economic barriers to travel and advance access to holiday destinations with prospects of a business boost for the travel industry by this group.

> …Went to France…My niece lives there, it was for a holiday we went for four days…didn't go anywhere… (laughing- and embarrassed) we didn't have the time to go anywhere, we just went to close places but never went anywhere far. (Interview date: 1.4.11)

Some of first-generation seem to view holidays other than Pakistan and Haj to be 'a waste of money' and do not value travel as a worthwhile activity. Money in their opinion can be best spent in better places.

Mrs Sheinaz

> Pakistan to start off with, Dubai every year I go…Yeah, we have been to Turkey a few times, Florida and Spain, Egypt, last year I went to Egypt mmmm that's in Spain to…Pakistan is a holiday and to visit family…that is both… (Interview date: 11.3.11)

Mrs Sheinaz described in lengthy detail how they used to spend time in Dubai airport whole on their way to Pakistan. Urry (2007) describes Dubai airport as an immobility and Mrs Sheinaz staying their classed as the temporary immobility. This affordance has enabled Mrs Sheinaz to extend her 'stop gap' time from eighteen hours to three to four days and sometimes a week.

Mrs Sheinaz also adds:

> …I have in the last…I have truthfully I think up to about seventeen ,eighteen years ago I would go every few years and I think that was more about not being able to afford it em whom you have got kids you know growing up, and you have their future to think about and stuff like that, I couldn't afford it seventeen, eighteen years ago even though I have worked myself and my husband working, we both worked but there is no way we could have afforded a holiday like you

know so to have a holiday or even you know to go and visit family in Pakistan. It meant we had to save quite hard for a few years before being able to go. You know you just can't just go. Because even when you are there you need to think how much you need for the few weeks you are there to spend. So, for example if we go for four weeks, we need to have spending money for four weeks and the money for the food because nobody there can give you money, you know, So for us it was like every few years. Then after that the kids grew up and started to do their own things, we've started to go every year...I go for three weeks ...I would say it is for both visiting family and a holiday because I would find it kind of if I was just going to see the family the way I am I would find it stressful! But it is nice...I have a house there... (Interview date: 11.3.11)

Mrs Sheinaz is one of the several interviewees who travel to and back from Pakistan as part of their lifestyle; social and obligatory basis that can also be termed a banality (Hannam and Knox, 2010) that I also argue to be the case in this scenario. This is a major topic and needs to be expanded on from the tourists' point of view and the host. Factors such as cultural sensitivity are thus prominent in the minds of the Pakistani tourist i.e., halal food availability, no alcohol etc. Hence it is the spectacular that is being viewed and an area for development by the tourist boards especially with this activity increasing. Mr Saleem has identified this need but can only have his passengers stop off in Dubai and has yet to develop links with the agents there to direct the 'journey breakers' places to stay and visit in Dubai. This Pakistani woman arrived as a child from Pakistan went to school in Leeds before getting married and moved away from Leeds to Newcastle, she has worked her way up the ladder, so to speak, from being dinner a lady and then into community work helping members of the community especially the rights of women. As Nadje and Khalid (2002) point out it is the 'capital rich' who have the ability to mobilise themselves as in the New Orleans disaster. Despite such mobilities as Friedman (1999) argues the boundaries from the initial onset of migrating have remained for Mrs Sheinaz although she has not been explicit continues to visit Pakistan her home country. She also hopes to work towards her duties as a Muslim (e.g., go to Haj). Thus, despite attachment (Alba, 1990) taking place of the host country it is evident that individualisation is taking precedence with a fluid, mobile and liquid diasporic identity. Arguably, it can be deducted that Mrs Sheinaz is capital rich and has means to 'access' to go on a pilgrimage to Saudi Arabia, but arguably she has not reached the peak of her religion (praying five times a day) compared to some of the interviewees (notably those who are not working) and therefore can be defined to be amongst the continuum of Muslims by identity but not practicing. Thus, this can be viewed as another major factor in the portrayal and display of fluid identities and transnational citizenship 'opportunity participation'.

Mrs Madia (a pensioner) was married in Pakistan and came to join her husband in 1970's. She has been to France to visit her niece on a social basis. Whereas, at one point in time it was unheard of visiting relatives abroad other than the UK this case demonstrates the first-generation are now moving the goal posts and consider visiting other places apart from Pakistan and Saudi Arabia; a cultural development. These findings can be explained within the broader context of human mobility; 'Those who first experience tourism and travel as children, are probably more than likely to become independent youth travellers, and then to take their own children on holiday, and finally to become well-travelled elderly people. Each round of tourism and travel, at different points in the life course, extends direct experience of particular places and general familiarity with tourism. Williams and Hall (2002) summarise this in turn establishes the knowledge base and the expectations that will sustain high levels of mobility in later stages of the life course. Another observation, although not part of the remit of the study made while interviewing was that interviewees who went to Haj, had pictures and artefacts displayed on walls and shelves with images of the Kaaba and Mosques in Mecca and Medina; one or two houses were totally floral in decoration (a 1970s fashion) and other houses (living rooms mainly) had some if not very little material cultures (Tolia-Kelly, 2004) from Pakistan; but most had material cultures of the contemporary era another marker to employ for further research to establish reduced cultural and ethnic practices.

To conclude, 'the connections between power and knowledge that need to be explored' (Hannam, 2002, p.231) amongst the community and between generations, as the generations evolve tourism discourses will also escalate and tourism development scrutinisation in parallel to the contemporary global issues discussed in migration section. In particular reference made to

Shurmer-Smith and Hannam (1994) can relate with the diasporic Pakistani migrants interviewed, thus empirically identified, it is clear that human beings differ between needs and wants and desires in contemporary tourism the needs are food and shelter but the desires are more problematic, in that they reach prominence as needs and wants become satisfied and tourist experiences become hyper-valued. Arguably it would be interesting to pursue these aspects of the group; that is, do they put themselves and their cultures up for sale (Hannam and Knox, 2010, p. 55).

Arguably as Bauman, (2000, cited in Urry, 2007, p. 201) explains there is a result of the network capital society, the interviewees have subconsciously agreed a key element of a stratification order of 'exit'. As interviewees from the Luton study (Ali and Holden, 2006) revealed discussed in the literature review they felt that they were unable to travel anywhere else as their relatives in Pakistan as this would impinge on their social 'ties'. This 'exit' strategy is primarily a technique of power that has shown to be displayed by the interviewees, such as Mrs Madia, although it appears, she is going through the 'grievance process' of acceptance of her decision. That is; normally she visits her family in Pakistan and used to see her niece when she visited Pakistan. Her niece married and moved to France and on this visit to France she only saw her niece and not the rest of her family; arguably a decision based on the desire to visit the spectacular (as defined by Hannam and Knox, 2010). Hence 'escape, slippage, elision and avoidance, the effective rejection of any territorial confinement' and the possibility of escape sheer 'inaccessibility' (Bauman, 2000, cited in Urry, 2007, p. 201). Bauman (2000, cited in Urry, 2007, p. 201) states that a high level of network capital 'enable smooth and painless exiting from where their obligatory practices involved. There are in this case, however, the interviewees who perhaps 'have an 'understanding and trust' with their diasporic families abroad that they also carry out touristic holidays as well as maintain links with then for obligatory and social visits. Interestingly, the Emirates airlines have allowed free stopovers in Dubai when travelling to Pakistan and this is now a standard destination. This has been made possible by the risk free and predictable movements within mobility systems (Urry, 2007). A reason for this can be explained within the context of 'escapism from the corporeal movement' (Urry, 2007) and the banalities (Hannam and Knox, 2010) expected at home and from the hybrid structure they live amongst. The future domain I argue, despite logical reasoning of these activities amounts to the realisation that challenges exist within the 'social scientific methods of inquiry and units of analysis by destabilising the embeddedness of social relation in particular communities and places' (Gille and Riain, 2002, p.271), namely the Pakistani diaspora. An example of this scenario is Mrs Sheinaz. Hence, material mobilities also playing a significant role in this activity by 'gift buying' from other holiday destinations for the families in Pakistan. Hence, there are several theories that have been identified and have been supported by the narratives that are briefly mentioned. Although gendered in theory (Tolia-Kelly, 2004), it refers to the physical movement of objects (Urry 2007) and it has been outlined that the traffic of clothing and fashion goods has acted as a significant brigde (Werbner, 1999).

### Religion and Visiting Saudi Arabia

### Male Interview Narratives

Mr Ayaz stated:

> ...Each male member of the community gave £500 towards the purchase of Elswick mosque...we did a lot... The current president of the mosque is more interested in getting the award by the Queen than listening to what the community wants...I was really really hurt when one of our friends passed away. He gave a lot of money to Elswick mosque and when he passed away the Mosque members made a fuss about his family not keeping up with the committee membership payments and his ceremony was held in a mosque in Heaton... (Interview date: 11.11.05)

Mr Yasir added:

> There has been this thing with Punjabis and Mirpuris. In the religion there are divisions between the Wahabis and the Sunnis. There is the Sunath Ul Janah too their belief is different. The Wahabis originate from Abdul Wahab in India.

> From a historical point of view there was a mosque in East Parade. This was a Sunni mosque and had a lot of uneducated members. They take things for granted and carry-on tradition and also work on emotional blackmail from generations ago. They do Khatums and

remember God through Prophet Mohammed (PBUH) and believe that on the day of judgement will be gate keeper who will let into heaven. There was also the Wahabi mosque in Westmorland Rd. next to St. Mary's church. These people were educated and questioned everything. Haji Majid is Wahabi. Wingrove mosque is a Wahabi mosque too. My belief is that you should be a good Muslim and your own good deeds will take you to heaven. Anyway, these two groups came together and in 1970 purchased Elswick mosque. The more affluent people moved to Heaton Jesmond and Gosforth. (Interview date: 6.4.11)

Saifullah Khan (1977) refers to 'fragmentation, fission and segmentation' that describes the group deviations based on biradari, caste, regional or other reasons that have impacted on the community. Since then, several mosques have emerged in Newcastle. The theme in Islam is not homogenous and less static (Saifullah Khan, 1977). This is also an example of what Lewis (cited Ballard, 1994) explains as differences exaggerated by personalities and egos of individual Muslims in the community. These differences between sects have also failed to connect with the youth. This is what Mrs Sheinaz stated earlier and confirms work by Saifullah Khan (1977), hence associated with 'isolationists'. In summary it is meaningful to conclude that the definitive means for the community as a whole was sects of the religion not ethnic labels (Herbert, 2008, p. 18).

### Female Interview Narratives

Ms Samina has her daily routine mapped out with prayer times as central times of the day:

'in the mornings I pray and then make breakfast and tidy around, then it is time for lunch I have that and then read the midday prayer after that I usually sit and watch the drama's, then after that I go out sometimes to my friend's houses like you're in the next street and Aunty Rehmatha further up my street. I sit with Hajra or Rehma and then I come home again, and it is time for the next namaz (prayers). And after that prayer I sit and watch the dramas again until the next prayer time. I also sit with these two grown up granddaughters for whom I'm responsible for wait for the nighttime prayer watching dramas and talking with these until bedtime. I then go to sleep and wake up in the morning for morning prayers and start the whole thing again. (Interview date: 13.5.05)

The intensity of religious activity is demonstrated in this narrative but also the process of change has correlated on a smaller scale to that experienced by Bradford. The initial pioneers who came to Newcastle actually worked together to provide a service for the local Muslims. The fragmentation, fissions and segmentation that Khan (1974) noted in Bradford a similar outlook appears to have evolved in Newcastle. The pan- Islamic productions of culture can be expressed in this scenario and 'the changing same' further reinforcing the Pakistani culture and traditions in Newcastle as explained by Gilroy (1993).There was efforts by the first pioneers such as Mr Maqsood's father, Mr Shan's and Mr Hussain's father who set up a mosque in the Cruddas Park then as Mr Ayaz explained how each individual Pakistani gave £500.00 each from their wages. The contested assimilation expectations thus led to integration strategies and adjustments took place to accommodate the cultural and identity issues such as building mosques in the 1970s. From one main mosque in Newcastle (Elswick), there are now several mosques of different sects that are attended by individuals on a basis of religious sect although other factors such as distance and access have also been noted to be decisive in which mosque to attend. It is however also an issue of politics and personality egos that have in slowed the progression of the community as a whole compared to other cities and towns. This has been an important marker that has created a 'generation of youth' without the commitment the early pioneers showed to their community. As a double disadvantage both groups have voiced grievances in terms of the framework and structure of the educational needs of Muslim's, especially children but a negativity observed by the interviewees from the host population since September 11th 2001.

## Haj

Haj is a pilgrimage for Muslims in Saudi Arabia and is one of the five pillars of Islam. Most of the interviewees had been to Haj. This is perceived as a need and obligation to visit to fulfil an expectation of the religion. However, there is also the element of going to Haj no longer a once in a lifetime dream but fast becoming a global Muslim expectation that is wanted on a regular basis. Although, the context of the need wants and desires that Hannam and Knox (2010) outline can also be applied to this situation. There is a need to go on the pilgrimage to Mecca and Medina, but overtime wants, and desires have led the Saudi Arabian government to carry out major changes and improvements on a large scale basis. Hence, visiting Saudi Arabia for Haj is an extension to the religion as opposed to a travel experience or a desire to visit another country.

The host country has attempted to cope with these demands and expectations. Thus, government officials have regulated and are continuously improving the country. There are currently several programmes to expand under development. The main factor is that Saudi Arabia wants a certain type of guest (and at certain times) that can be hosted but as Hannam and Knox (2010, p.11) summarise 'they both might have to settle for what they can get in a particular type of context' and issues of non-conformity arising for the guest and hosts in today's global environment. Future changes into the way Haj is and can be performed may change due to the sheer volume attending at one time in one place especially in for those Muslims who are capital rich and can attend more than once. Questions are revolving around expansion at the cost of losing historical places (but good for the economy from a touristic point of view) or capping from an international level. There is the political instability in neighbouring regions with Orientalism issues (Bhabha, 1994) and contemporary tourism advancement in this region 'in search of experiencing the Other' (Hannam and Knox, 2010). In particular, Hannam aand Knox (2010) references made to the mediatised representations and experiences the travel agents have on offer; competing against touring opportunities and journeys, hence the commodification can be argued as an element of these findings.

Carrying out religious activities and social gatherings on a religious level has been interpreted as extremism especially after September 11 and 7 July bombings. Since the death of Osama bin Laden in April 2011 the threats have remained leaving the world in as much chaos regarding terrorism prior to Osama bin Laden's death. It can be seen from the quotes that the lifestyle of the majority of interviewees, revolves around religious activity. This maybe a celebration of Eid or a Friday prayer or it may be reading five prayers a day, waking up at dawn going to the mosque to prayer and reading the Quran on a daily basis for two to three hours. Watching Islamic channels and preaching the religion to the wider community. It seems that the word 'extremism' is too harsh for those people who live a genuine life based around Islam, a better way to describe these Muslims could be that they rank high in religious capital. There are also those Muslims who rank low in religious capital hence such as Mrs Sheinaz who consciously wants to pray five times a day and would like to go to Haj but hasn't got round to it.

### Male Interview Narratives

Mr Yasir prayers when he can and attends mosque on Fridays and when he was asked if he had been anywhere outside the UK apart from Pakistan he said:

> ...No, I haven't been...well I have been to Haj but that's not a holiday that is erm compulsory...Because of religious...it is one of the pillars that if you can afford it you have to go there once in your lifetime ...so I have been... (Interview date: 6.4.11)

It almost seems that Mr Yasir has 'ticked a box' as a practising Muslim is required to pray five times a day and Haj is the final journey. Mr Majid said he did not go anywhere outside the UK apart from Haj: '...We go to Haj...four times' (Interview date: 4.4.11). In many cases unless asked directly the interviewees did not mention visiting Saudi Arabia when asked where they travelled to outside UK. This may be because it is embedded in their lives as a requirement and do not see it as a visit outside the UK.

Mr Shan (pensioner) has been to Haj:

> I have been to Saudi Arabia. Err twice, I have taken my mother and performed Haj of my father, my deceased father. I went to Haj first in 1970...it was by air and also, I went in 1984 to take my mother to perform haj of... (Interview date: 18.4.11)

Mr Majid said he didn't go anywhere for holiday but when asked if he had been to Haj, he said he had:

> We go to Haj...four times ...the last time was...about four or five years ago... I just go to Saudi Arabia. I am going this month on the 16th of April. I am doing a collection for my mosque... Grainger Park Road. Mostly the Saudi Arabians, from the Mosque in Saudi Arabia

and from very rich persons; rich like you…. (Laughing).Write it down there now 'rich like you'. (Interview date: 4.4.11)

It is the ontology of this process that is important but also the embodied experiences that are non-representational that is the signifying reasons for re-visiting. Also Lash and Urry (1994) explain to construct the identity forming, it is the identity one wants to display to the outside world in addition to the self-identity one wants to portray. Importantly, it is the 'differential mobility empowerments' (Hannam and Knox, 2010) that have been significant in going to Haj at all in comparison to how many times an interviewee has been; likewise, the same scenario is applicable to travelling to other destinations abroad to Pakistan and beyond. Mr Mohammed said:

> …The next generations are changing things now they go on holidays to other countries like Spain and that and not much emphasis is on religious activity. (Interview date: 4.4.11)

As interviews progressed it was interesting to observe how many of the interviewees when asked if they had been on holiday gave a complete answer and said no but when probed later and even when they were asked had they been out the country said apart from Pakistan nowhere. I argue this to be a significant perception by the group for whom these practices are embedded rather than a spectacle. When these interviewees were asked if they have been to Haj, alarmingly, the majority said yes. This could be another inherent duty as a Muslim that is not regarded as a separate action but acknowledged only when prompted a -contradiction in itself arguably a difficult distinction to make unless there is prior knowledge of the groups personality traits.

> I don't go anywhere I just pray at home in the mornings…Have been to Haj and Mrs Azaad is preparing to go to Umra… (Interview date: 24.3.11)

### Female Interview Narratives

An important pont at this stage is to relate the fact that Mr Azaad and Mrs Azaad live in the 'West-end of Newcastle (living in an enclave) as they feel immobile as a result of hostility from the host community yet they have travelled to Haj in Saudi Arabia displaying the significance of their religion, despite the local immobility felt. Mrs Nighath gave a similar response when she was asked if she had been anywhere outside of England and only when prompted. And it was her niece who reminded her, and she acknowledged it:

> Nowhere!! Just Pakistan that's the only place we go to. (Granddaughter answers) Yes she has (chit chat), she has been to Haj... she doesn't like going on holiday. (Interview date: 7.4.11)

Mrs Madia also commented:

> ...We have been to Haj and Umra in Saudi Arabia...About nine or ten years ago...I have done Haj too; we did that after Umra. (Interview date: 1.4.11).

There is an overwhelming majority of interviewees who have been to Saudi Arabia for Haj but a greater number returning more than once within their lifetime. From a religious stance it is recommended that a Muslim travel at least once in their life time for the pilgrimage to Mecca but there is also concessions for those who are unable to afford the trip or are in ill – health. Interviewees have demonstrated that they have been once apart from one interviewee Ms Mumtaz who is a widow with one son and aspires to visit Saudi Arabia. This can be interpreted to mean that the interviewees are capital rich according to Urry's (2007) explanation of individuals mobilities and Ms Mumtaz is capital poor hence unable to go. Saudi Arabia has also expanded and transformed Makkah where Muslims go for Haj along with Riyadh and Jeddah. It has been from the late 1950's that Saudi Arabia decided to carry out a large expansion to accommodate the increased number of pilgrimages. There are more than two million worshippers who attend prayers with this number presently increasing. It has actually led to further development with the government building high rised buildings hoping to integrate the sacred with the secular but at the same time to preserve 'in coexistence' (Shuaibi, 2001).

It is evident from the narratives that Muslims loyalty to the faith and its belief is a priority for the majority of Muslims. The interviewees who have not been to Haj all have an intention to go. The interviewees all Muslims although not attending mosque regularly prayer on a Friday as a minimum. This has been well documented by Ali et al. (2006): what is present amongst these Muslims is a 'main thread' and presents the notion of the 'Ummah' Hussain (2005 cited in Mc Ghee, 2008, p.135) views this as 'Muslim loyalty discourses'. It is these discourses that can or cannot personalise an identity. For example, according to Parekh (2006 cited in McGhee, 2008, p.134) those Muslims who prioritise their loyalty to the 'Ummah' over to the country are described as Muslim Britains.

As Peach (2006, p.181) has identified from his data analysis of the South Asian population in Britain there is the political/economic integration but as far as the social integration is seen there is a 'distinct separate civil society' amongst the host society. Evidence suggests that although the economic framework maybe a mirror image, social assimilation is also evident from the lifestyle and touristic expectations and experiences. There also appears to be residential diffusion where interviewees have moved from the inner-city environment into suburban areas. Hence, the hypothesised American model may have a base in Newcastle where economic success is linked to residential diffusion and intermarriage not decoupling from social assimilation as suggested by Peach (2006, p.181). There are significant social relationships that are diverse amongst the Pakistani diaspora (Urry, 2007) and there are distinct socio-spatial patterns of mobility (Urry, 2007) and for this category the social form is also distinct.

Visiting Saudi Arabia is a soul-searching process and it has been concluded that praying five times a day also gives this peace and therefore the generations who practice feel they have completed their religious obligations. These obligations have been a theme throughout each section in this report and the interviewees may have displayed fluid identities' but have 'intensified' their religious activities as they have become older. The issues of 'Modernity and Islam' are not the remit of this research however it is valid to conclude that there are significant contemporary cultural religious tensions as well as identity politics within the global arena (Tibi, 2009) that have impacted at a local level, hence the perceptions of the Pakistani diaspora concluding to have disillusion with terrorism activities affecting their daily activities in terms of safety and the boundaries are blurred within the context of citizenship and Islam as a transnational political force as defined by Portes and De Wind, (2008), also arguably can be described as ethnic tourism (Hannam and Knox, 2010). The behavioural aspect can be evaluated through Duval's (2006) work by the grid group theory that relates to the concept of migration and the concept of temporary mobilities Many visits have been made by the Pakistani community as a whole signifying that the socio-economic status may have increased (capital high) to fulfil this religious requirement at least once. But also, the religious embeddedness amongst the Pakistani diaspora where extremes have also been noted and 'bordering isolationist' existing. Whatever, Shaibi (2001) concludes these tourists have obviously changed Saudi Arabia enormously with major developments and scope for business. A fact that has been exposed from this thematic analysis.

Haj is a pilgrimage that Muslims have endeavoured to carry out from the conception of the religion. Hence, as it has been discussed the 'Muslim Ummah' have carried out this religious activity worldwide. The special fact, however, has been noted by Saudi Arabian officials that the visits have increased significantly which is also evident from this empirical analysis. However, arguably as Maynard et al. (2008) have demonstrated in their study on older women religious activities are intensified with age, and hence access and potential motility is pushed by the older generation who practice conforming to their religious duties including travelling to Haj despite the odds against them. The expression of identity of 'gender being mediated through religion' is however demonstrated and arguably with persistence in this group of women (Ahmad and Modood, 2003). Further work in this area is, however, needed to establish the activities of both genders that occur when arriving in Saudi Arabia. This includes business activities, shopping, eating and visiting other sites. Also, business in the locality includes local travel agents acting as representatives and adopting other agency functions.

## Chapter Conclusions and Summary

So far, it has been established that the Pakistani diaspora travel extensively, or in Urry's (2007) terms 'social capital' is high. Although, the Pakistani men carry out social and obligatory practices locally they travel more nationally for both familial obligations and as tourists and the women interviewees carry out social and obligatory practices more at a local level and are more adventurous in their travel internationally. On the other hand, the motility low (poor health) interviewees exhibited low social capital traits with a greater reliance on telephones as a means of communication at a distance. The women have experienced a two-fold barrier, the first, is ill-health leading to reduced motility and the second that it prevents mobilities. Thus, is an area of work to pursue in terms of access and motility and how to overcome these barriers, for example, the development of services that are culturally sensitive aiming to increase mobility (Maynard et al. 2008).

All of the interviewees had re-visited Pakistan and, in many cases, more than once. This may be a 'revival' situation or the fact that their socio-economic status has improved. However, it can be concluded that diasporic links are sustained, for some interviewees. Thieme's (2008) work on habitus can be applied in this scenario, that is, the transnational habitus is never forgotten even though there is no kinship left in the home country. However, owning a house in Pakistan (capital rich) has been identified to be an important part of the diasporic lifestyle and defined as core transnationalism (Portes et al., 1999). This adoption of both cultures also demonstrates the fluidity of the identities (Ellis 2003, cited in Thieme, 2008). On the other hand, the immobile Pakistani diaspora or those in the slow lane (Hannam et al, 2006) have accepted they will never again be able to visit their home country.

Visiting other places other than the Pakistan was also notably an increasing touristic activity. There were a number of countries visited with the popular destinations being Dubai, Egypt, France and Turkey. However, a characteristic displayed with a small minority of first-generation was that there was reluctance to admit they went on holiday and were not comfortable about the fact they were carrying out touristic activities, perhaps a cultural issue and ethnicity being a liability (Modood, 1997, cited in Gardner, 2002). This can also be a lifestyle change; a marker of the 'volatile' identities and interesting to observe how this volatility becomes 'stable' and 'fluid identities' are clearly and confidently defined and 'diasporic tourism' (defined as touristic activities with tourists visiting co-diaspora's, Hannam and Knox, 2010) forming a major part of the Newcastle Pakistanis travelling habits.

The Pakistani diaspora practice the religion of Islam and state they find peace and tranquillity through the religious practices and daily practices are carried out no matter where in the world the interviewees travel to. This has been demonstrated to take centre stage and has become a way of life for the majority of the Pakistani diaspora of both genders, an issue that Maynard et al (2008) have researched and this study supports. In the religion Islam the last pillar requires going on a pilgrimage in Saudi Arabia and most of the first-generation have been at least once.

In conclusion the Muslims have prioritised their loyalties to the Ummah (Parekh report). But further work on the mobile methodologies (Fincham et al.,2009), examining and understanding these religious experiences as well as the second and third-generation mobilities and integration levels will determine future tourism in light of the contemporary distillation dynamics globally between generations of the Pakistani diaspora.

# CHAPTER 6

# CONCLUSIONS

The analysis and results presented in chapters three, four and five have attempted to meet the aims and objectives of the research and challenged the diverse experiences and differences within the realms of 'a fluid identity' through the lens of the mobilities paradigm (Urry, 2007). It is argued that the opportunities for mobilities increases for people who are on the move and hence the diasporic Pakistani migrant group can be assessed by identifying 'markers' for an upward or a downward mobility (Urry, 2007). The biographical information and critical analysis of the diverse mobilities in relation to socio-economic status has provided a pattern of mobilities that has changed over time and the impact and influences of the dominant mobility systems are demonstrated on the social practices. The three main themes identified in the research are concluded separately in order to highlight the overlap as well as the diversities.

The settlement in the UK from the 1940's main mobility system was walking. This enabled greater face to face interaction in particular for the men who usually walked to work and also socialised with the community living in close proximity of housing. Arguably, some of these social and obligatory activities were based around the desire for 'the imaginary homeland' connected with 'belonging and longing' (Ali and Holden, 2006, p. 235) at which the practices and predicaments of seeking the 'myth of return' (Anwar, 1979) as central topics of conversation evolved, hence defined as 'primary socialisations' by Ali and Holden, (2006, p.237). The Pakistani migrants have recorded this era as being an enjoyable period in their lives.

Identities are in a 'continuous process of negotiation, re-negotiation and de-negotiation' (Ali and Holden, (2006, p.218), albeit 'uneven access to mobility' (Sheller and Urry, 2006). Hence, analysis showed that the current motility low or mobility poor Pakistani migrants implemented other communicative means to carry out social and obligatory practices. This was mainly by the use of a telephone. Little evidence of using any other networking facility (e.g. Internet) was recorded, although was not a primary remit of this study. This group is can now also be identifiable as 'older people' and traits of this group are similar to the study by Maynard et al., (2008) as its results correlate to the findings in this research. Maynard et al. (2008) highlighted signs of the fragmentation of the joint family and as 'women and men live through' and 'with' aging there is a developing need to explore and identify needs and requirements on this basis.

Mobility or the lack off, is the main determinant of future 'revival' as social capital is 'funnelling' and raises issues with access to network capital is limiting social networks. The groups cultural and lifestyle choices are that mirrored of the Pakistani diaspora in other parts of UK, namely Luton (Ali and Holden., 2006), Bradford (Watson 1977) and Sparkbrook (Rex and Moore, 1971). In particular, the lived experiences of the domestic home 'are reproduced and recast' (Blunt and Dowling, 2006, p.167). Thus, transnational identities (Vertovec, 1999) have been sustained but transnational livelihood studies need addressing in greater detail to posit the advantages and disadvantages (Levitt and Jarwosky, 2007) of international migration (Snel, et al., 2006).

In terms of access to Public and Social Services that were considered the central theme was that of the withdrawal of funding and lack of facilities to access. Hence, philanthropic related work (Najam, 2006) played a major part in the provision of services for the community. The diverse experiences however have been linked to the socio-economic status of the Pakistani migrants and Maynard et al. (2008) have noted deficiencies of the concepts of ageing and ethnicities that are unavailable and suggest a framework of study other than criticising the health and social services provisions.

The definition 'as a post-gerontological stance would explore difference and the ways in which different cultures and systems of belief give meaning to stages and conditions of life and how these meanings might contribute to well-being in old age' (Maynard et al., 2008, p.41). This research has revealed some of the 'ageing groups' social practices and outlines a picture of the embodied diasporic Pakistani migrant experiencing stages through their life course through the diasporic lens, an argument Smith, (2005 cited in Adey, 2010, p. 78) urges; 'researchers to engage methodologically more fully in the 'emplacement' of mobile subjects as 'the actors are still classed, raced and gendered. Observing this as a whole De Haas, (2010) views the 'end of identity' with 'fluidity' that has been identified throughout the themes analysed; this is a means of explaining the layered and multi-functional role of an individual or changing people. It is not a case of adding issues of ethnicity and ageing to existing gerontology theories, but there is a need to expand and develop new concepts and views of the ageing process and what constitutes being old within the remit of the diasporic Pakistani migrants (Maynard et al. 2008. p.41). Empirical evidence suggests a shortfall amongst the older generation (Maynard et al., 2008, p.40) and the argument extends by stating this is not so surprising given that, 'until recently as has already been seen, the ethnic minority populations in the UK have tended to have a younger demographic profile than the rest of the population, although this is changing. Where there is research on ethnic minority people in later life, this has tended to focus largely on health and social care'. Nazroo et al. (2004, cited Maynard et al. 2008, p. 40) further stress the lack of theorising and what this means having termed this to be a 'double or triple jeopardy' as a consequence of their age, the fact that they are from an ethnic minority, as well as status and gender stereotypes.

Tourism has been identified by Urry (2007) to be seen as a 'modern' experience. Some interviewees socio-economic status has enabled them to carry out 'modern' tourism. Arguably, the definition for a tourist may apply to the social obligations despite the intention or purpose of a visit; hence altering the features of tourism (Ali and Holden, 2006, p. 230). For example, a Pakistani family may visit Middlesbrough for 'waada kaata' (to give condolensces) and go for a meal on the way back home. These identities are 'spilling out' into mass tourist operations (Hannam and Knox, 2010) and the daily rituals of life are being viewed as 'mini daily holidays' hence the behavioural patterns are transposed as tourist practices (Hannam and Knox, 2010, p. 91).

Initial visits to the homeland were expensive and time consuming with no direct flights to Pakistan but it has been demonstrated how some of these visits develop a transnational habitus (Thieme, 2008). The search for the 'spectacular' also seems to be a 'sought out' experience for the Pakistani diaspora and this search has been extended to other destinations and also increasingly Saudi Arabia.

Blurring or fluid identities was a characteristic displayed by the Pakistani migrants although there was a resistance displayed in the acceptance of the term tourism activities as part of their lifestyle, arguably a cultural issue (Herbert, 2008). There was further evidence of visits to commodified and hyper-real commodified places from which an interesting debate can result of whether these are ostensible practices (Hannam and Knox, 2010) and the extent to which these are performed and the intensification of the cultural practices (Werbner, 2005) at a global and gendered level (Urry, 2010).

Another significant issue in this research has been the religious element. The religious requirements of praying on a daily basis, giving charity (for Muslims) and going on the pilgrimage for Haj in Saudi Arabia have been prominent. From the outset houses were being converted into mosques in Newcastle (Telang, 1967). Arguably as Maynard et al. (2008) argues religious activities are intensified with age as was evident also the case in this study. Gendered differences were shown, however, in that the women stated they usually prayed at home, but the men not only prayed in the mosques but also helped in the building of them.

The mobility system namely transport has played a significant part of the daily practices of the diaspora when they initially settled. The mobility system of walking was a significant factor in their corporeal practices. With the access of cars their social capital was reduced but enabled movement further away. Automobility, also allowed greater flexibility and practices of car-sharing that is still evident in local and national travel for social and obligatory activities.

Although capital has been a significant factor as well as status and education (socio-economic status) of the migrants interviewed many have travelled back to Pakistan, leading to more mobility. In addition, the tourist activities of these appear to have increased through the mediation of aeromobility. Questions on the ostensible cultural and ethnic practices need to be explored on a broader 'hybridity' level.

I have conducted in-depth biographies of 28 first-generation Pakistani migrants arriving in the UK up to the 1970's in Newcastle upon Tyne. A snowballing technique was implemented to recruit interviewees and lengthy narratives were obtained. There were two main stages of the information collated. The first demonstrated the experiences of settlement in Newcastle upon Tyne of which to which there has been a significant relationship with other existing literature in the field. The second stage elaborated previous theoretical and empirical evidence specific to migration theories, diaspora and the mobilities paradigm. Hence, a practical account has been established of the current state of play with this now 'ageing group' and the implications and challenges this presents as shown below.

I have critically examined the initial settlement period and the contemporary lifestyles of the respondents mobilities. Results have demonstrated that complex mobility systems have enabled the sustenance of relationships and networks on a social and obligatory basis at the local, national and international levels. Hence, specific cultural traits that conform to corporeal activities have enabled the diasporic links to the homeland albeit in some cases weak ties. Transnational activities have thus emerged to be a part of the Pakistani migrants' lifestyles displaying fluid identities whilst maintaining values and solidarity.

In addition socio-economic status and motility issues play a significant role in the access of the mobility systems for corporeal activities. For example, walking was not an issue when the diasporic Pakistani migrants arrived in early adulthood life, but reduced motility and health problems have not allowed transnational social and obligatory practices to be performed. In comparison a Pakistani migrant that is capital rich and mobile considers visits to the homeland a normal occurrence and pursues other forms of tourism. A significant number of interviewees were also in the 'slow lane' and have used mobility substitution through the use of the telephone to pursue social and obligatory requirements.

Familial obligatory practices were prominent during the settlement period and although still an activity at a local and national level it has been evident that tourism is on the increase for some capital rich Pakistani migrants and transnational identities are being pursued. These social and obligatory practices have been addressed as tourism activities which meet the criterion for the definition. There is notably a non-localised network marked by class divisions and social relations linking the homeland to the UK (Wernber, 2005). Visits to the homeland are continuous and in some cases a banality and as part of the larger picture of human mobilities in line with globalisation hence referred to as translocality (Appadurai, 1995). An intensification of religious activities has also been evident as part of daily practices as well a carrying out once in a lifetime pilgrimage to Haj becoming a regular or more frequent trip to Saudi Arabia; a trait Maynard et al (2008) argues to be more likely at an older age.

Critically analysis of the extent to which 'access' plays in the public and social practices of the Pakistani diaspora in Newcastle upon Tyne was carried out through the research into the lifestyles and activities the group participates in on a daily basis. The majority of the Pakistani migrants can now be classed as 'older persons' and a downward mobility pattern has been evident for the relatively immobile. A lack of provision of both social and health services has been stressed by both genders. The greatest barrier has been varying degrees of access and motility exacerbated through being capital poor. Finally, as has been the case for the objectives above socio-economic status plays a significant role in the experiences of access to public and social services for the respondents too. For the motility and capital high Pakistani migrants there is an increase in travel and uptake of leisure activities, in particular for the older women who have expressed greater freedom and travel adventurously.

There has been a significant theorisation of the experiences of the Pakistani migrants through the use of the mobilities paradigm. Additionally, the thesis has developed the contemporary empirical work with the first-generation Pakistani migrants' experiences in Newcastle upon Tyne. An example is the settlement experiences of the embodied practices (Adey, 2010) and the significance of face-to-face meetings for Pakistani migrants. Current issues of concern for the group have been presented and the needs to strengthen and encourage further work in the area highlighted. There is a growing issue of the 'mobility burdens' placed on the group and their families through the natural ageing and cultural practices and how mobility substitution (by network capital) is being utilised to maintain social capital. The research has also highlighted the maintenance of the diasporic links both weak and strong ties to the homeland by the first-generation Pakistani migrants but also how inequalities amongst the diaspora between the 'capital rich' and 'capital poor' affects the lifestyle including religion and leisure and tourism activities.

The transnational perspective is also clear in that the research has further advanced knowledge in the group adopting 'fluid identities' (Werbner, 2005).

It dissolves the discrete visits to the homeland as a specific and isolated category to an ongoing process of global mobility (King and Christou, 2011, p.460) with emphasis on transnational social fields that are multi-sited and multi-layered (Levitt and Jarwosky, 2007). It argues that the Pakistani diaspora carry out social and obligatory practices globally but again, socio-economic factors play a significant role in the networks and connections sustained. New research initiatives through the use of mobile methods (Buscher and Urry, 2009) for understanding the connections of these diverse mobilities and interdependencies especially the physical changes and in electronic communications and the challenges to the group with new forms of 'virtual' and 'imaginative' mobilities are however suggested.

The limits of this research are affected by the scope, design, and conduct of the investigation. This research originally began as a historical investigation with an overall aim to record the settlement experiences and experiences of their contemporary lifestyles. The remit was later developed by utilising mobilities theory in the study, and this enriched the research but as with all these time constraints have been a strain. Fortunately, re-visits to interview the same individuals enabled the leisure and tourism enquiry.

Although, links were made to other research it was felt that the interviewees were now 'older age people' and the roles they were compared with were either from historical studies or from a different cohort or generation. A comparative gendered analysis was therefore limited due to the level of socio-economic variables of the already small group interviewed.

There is potential in examining the differences amongst generational cohorts (Scott and Cartledge, 2009) and their interdependencies at a global level. It can be hypothesised that the first-generation are relatively well travelled people because of their travelling experiences (William and Hall, 2002) and further generational cohorts may be even more mobile. There is also further potential in examining and developing the 'access' and 'motility' factors within the realms of mobilities (Urry, 2007; Adey, 2010) in connection to the aging first-generation of transnational migrant communities. In addition, a gendered approach may highlight needs relative to service provision. This may cover network capital, social capital and mediations of mobility suitability and need for 'equal access.' Work can be differentiated by gender to include the perceptions of 'older people' and the cultural and behavioural patterns at the social and religious level (Ahmad and Modood, 2003).

# APPENDIX

## Ward Map of Newcastle upon Tyne

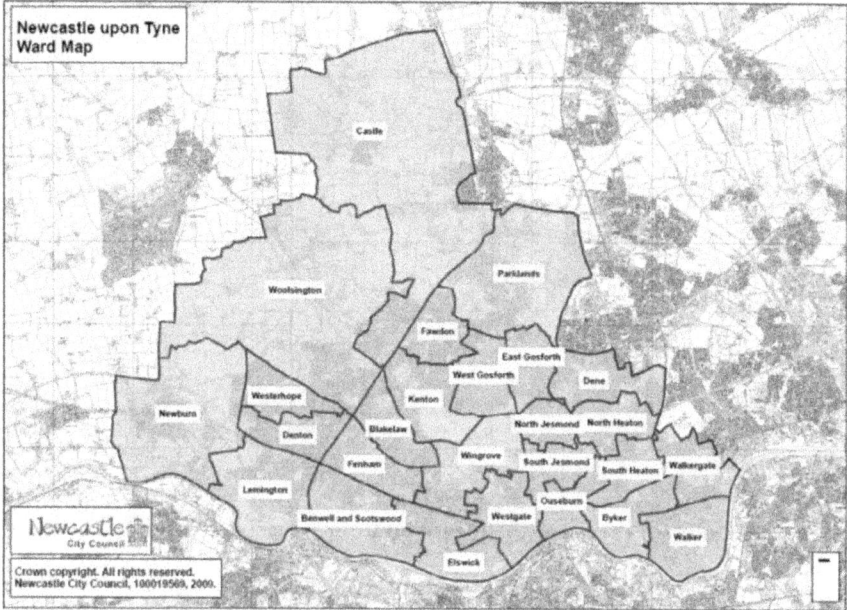

http://www.newcastle.gov.uk/wwwfileroot/legacy/cxo/instantatlas/WardMap.pdf

## Map of West End of Newcastle upon Tyne

(The five wards in West end of Newcastle are Wingrove, Elswick, Benwell and Scotswood, Fenham and Westgate)

Streets as in the 1960/1970's reproduced from the Ordnance Survey Map, (cited Taylor, 1976, insert between pages 32-33)

Demographic Profile Female Interviewees

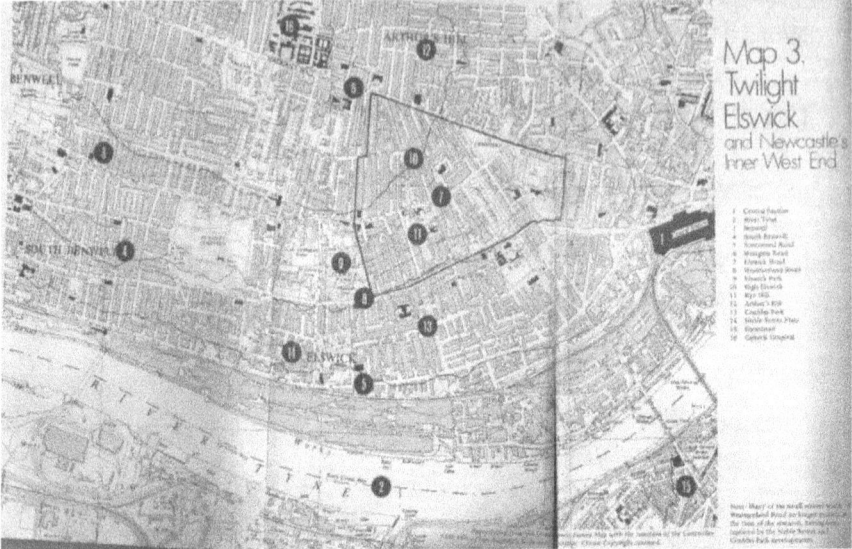

Map 3.
Twilight
Elswick
and Newcastle's
Inner West End

| Name | Age | Migrated from | Interview Dates | Interview1 Interview 2 |
|------|-----|---------------|-----------------|------------------------|
| Mrs Aleya | over 60 | Chakswari | 21.11.05 | 2011 |
| Mrs Anum | 22.2.42 | Mirpur, Jhelum | 18.11.05 | 28.3.11 |
| Mrs Fozia | over 60 | Azaad Kashmir | 18.11.05 | 24.3.11 |
| Mrs Madia | over 60 | Azaad Kashmir | 10.11.05 | 2011 |
| Mrs Manzoor | over 55 | Azaad Kashmir | 12.05.05 | N/A |
| Mrs Zatoon | 5.5.41 | Azaad Kashmir | 13.05.05 | 21.3.11 |
| Mrs Sheinaz | 53 | Mirpur | 10.11.05 | April 11 |
| Mrs Noreen | over 60 | Punjab District | 16.11.05 | Hospital |
| Mrs Nighath | over 60 | Barban | 10.11.05 | April 11 |
| Mrs Samina | over 70 | Azaad Kashmir | 13.05.05 | 23.3.11 |
| Mrs Mumtaz | over 70 | Azaad Kashmir | 30.11.05 | 31.3.11 |
| Mrs Riaz | 27.7.51 | Punjab District | 7.12.05 | Stroke |
| **Total interviewed 12** | **9** | | | |

## Demographic Profile of Male Interviewees

| Name | Age | Migrated from | Interview Dates | |
|------|-----|---------------|-----------------|---|
| | | | Interview 1 | Interview 2 |
| Mr Ayaz | 65 | Mirpur | 11.11.05 | 30.3.11 |
| Mr Zaid | 48 | Azaad Kashmir | 17.11.05 | Declined |
| Mr Hussain | over 60 | Azaad Kashmir | 15.11.05 | April 11 |
| Mr Fiaz | 2.5.56 | Barban | 17.11.05 | 29.3.11 |
| Mr Rehmath | 1.2.38 | Jhelam | 18.11.05 | 23.3.11 |
| Mr Azad | 20.11.41 | Azaad Kashmir | 18.11.05 | 24.3.11 |
| Mr Saleem | 5.5.48 | Saiwal | 15.11.05 | 5.4.11 |
| Mr Majid | 9.6.35 | Punjab District | 20.11.05 | 4.4.11 |
| Mr Ahmad | 69 | Gujrath | 20.11.05 | N/A |
| Mr Shafaq | 4.12.43 | Faislabad | 21.11.05 | N/A |
| Mr Mohammed | over 60 | Azaad Kashmir | 28.11.05 | 28.3.11 |
| Mr Shan | 76 | Dadyal | 28.11.05 | April 11 |
| Mr Usman | 18.4.44 | Azaad Kashmir | 1.12.05 | Deceased |
| Mr Malik | 2.2.38 | Punjab District | 3.12.05 | N/A |
| Mr Maqsood | 15.7.48 | Punjab District | 5.12.05 | N/A |
| Mr Yasir | 4.1.54 | Azaad Kashmir | 21.12.05 | 11.4.11 |

**Total Interviewed    16    10**

## Note

1.  All interviewees were British citizens 2). The age is from taken from
    the first set of interviews in 2004/2005 3). 'N/A' refers to 'not
    available' or 'no answer' or 'whereabouts not known.

    Transcription of Interviewee     Sample 1

Interview 1

Name: Mrs Anum (Pseudo name)
    Ref N/A

Address: Deleted for confidentiality

Age: 63 (D.O.B.: 22.2.1942)

Nationality: British

Home Country: Pakistan

Mother Tongue: Mirpuri

Home Province: Jhelum Village

Q. How long have you lived in the UK?

A. Approximately 40 years.

Q. What was the main reason that you came to UK?

A. Because my husband was here six or seven years before me then he came over and married me and then we came here together I came here six months after the marriage.

Q. Do you remember where your first home was?

A. Do you know where the church is next to St Pauls… no, no, it was just before Halal meat shop it was 40 Havelock Street.

Q. Oh yes, I think my mother lived there too

A. Yes… she moved in a few years later.

Q. Did you know anybody at that time then?

A. There was this aunty called Sat and another aunty called Maria (she is related to Aunty Sophia) these came one year later.

Q. This must have hard for you?

A. This was *very very* hard… I cried for one full year as there was no-one that I could talk to. It felt like Valaiyath was a jail because I was used to living with a family in Pakistan and when I came here there was absolutely no-one accept Uncle; I had my son after seven months. An English lady who Uncle knew would take me to the hospital and back Uncle used to go to work all day… and I used to stay in the house all day.

Q. Where did you have your son?

A. My son was born in Princess Mary hospital and this English lady could collect me for my appointments and then bring me back again. The hospital was next to the town moor area, my eldest son Shams was born there and all the rest in the General Hospital.

Q. How did you live and what did you do on a daily basis when you came?

A. We used to live with other relatives; they were all men, and I was the only woman. We had two rooms in the house and all the rest the men were living in, although we owned the house.

Q. Do you remember who those people were?

A. We used to rent out the rooms to English people there used to be another friend called Master Razaq he now lives in Whitley Bay (he was also from Ghelum) and also there was Rahmid he was our cousin ( Kamil's husband) there was also my brother in law Mohammed Yasir, he was Bobby's daddy.

Q. Were there family's not here at the time?

A. No... they were not. There was also brother Hanif he was my husband's friend there was one kitchen in the house, and I used to cook for all of them and they used to come and help themselves when he wanted.

Q. Did you used to go to the meat shops?

A. No Uncle used to go to get the groceries and do the weekly shopping. It was after one year that I went out to the town; I only used to go to hospital appointments, Uncle did not used to take me neither.

Q. So where did you used to get your clothes from (Asian dresses)?

A. I only wore the ones that I came with from Pakistan and the person who used to live here Mohammed Rafith used to sew clothes. He used to sew clothes for women; there were some ladies who used to come and get their clothes sewn from Rabia she was called Bari. She got me a suite and invited me to a dinner once. After one year... later... Aunty Mukht took me to the Asian clothes shop called Asian clothes she was the very first Asian clothes shop lady then and I bought some clothes from there then.

Q. Is Uncle Rafith still around?

A. Yes, at the time there was no Pakistani ladies mainly Indian and that was only a few they used to go to him to get the clothes sewn.

Q. Did you used to go walking to the clothes shop? ... the Asian clothes shop?

A. Yes, my son was born then and the snow was very deep.

Q. Oh yes it used to snow alot then didn't it?

A. Yes, my son used to be bigger then but even though he had high boots on(wellingtons) his clothes still used to get snow on! My son was born in December.

Q. Who did you first go to town with the?

A. I went with Aunty Mukhtyar.

Q. What do you remember about the town?

A. There were shops then that are no longer exist now. There was a small Woolworths and a large Woolworths; it was nicer then… there were lots of shops.

Q. So if you did not know English did you just give some money and expect change?

A. Because there used to be English people living in my house I could get by. There was Auntie Mukhtayar's sisters-in-law son who was about 10 years old. I used to give him a hand full of change… at that time the money was different. Half a crone used to be two and a half shillings and I used to give a hand full of this change to him and he used to get my shopping. He used to give me change and he used to say that this is your shopping, and this is what they gave back to me. Things used to be very cheap then you could get a really big bag of fruit for one or two pounds and now you get absolutely nothing we used to go to town with two or three pounds and get loads of shopping and still have change! Now you go to a fruit shop and we pay five pounds and you get a small bag of fruit. There used to be markets selling clothes, lots of clothes and fabric.

Q. How many children do you have again?

A. I have three daughters and two sons. I have two daughters that are twins it was only the biggest son that was born in St Mary's all the rest were born in General Hospital.

Q. How long did you live in Havelock Street then?

A. No, first I stayed in Campbell Street and then we moved to 40 Sceptre Street.

Q. Is that where your older son lives now?

A. Yes, that is where he lives now. from the beginning we lived in Sceptre Street... for a long time.

Q. That means that the Asian fabric shop called Asian clothes was very near you.

A. Yes then I could go by myself and there was lots of nice Asian ladies who moved in the area and we used to go to shopping together they used to come and get me sometimes. And after this more Pakistani ladies began to come, for example, Auntie Sabi and your mam and a few other people and when we met each other we became friends. We used to sit in the backyard and knit together... and go for walks in the night.

Q. You do not do this now do you?

A. No people do not have the time now a days. The men used to go to work during the day and the women used to sit together in the backyards and get their chairs... talk and knit together.

Q. That must have been a nice environment.

A. I used to go with Aunty Sabar Darnie for a walk around the block she used to come over after dinner and say come and let us digest our food by going on a walk. She used to go with her daughter and a few of her grandchildren; the kids used to enjoy it too or sometimes the kids used to stay with their father.

Q. Did you used to sew clothes aswell?

A. No I did not I used to do the crochet and knitting with needles a lot.

Q. There must not have been any fear of going for a walk in the evening then?

A. No there was not.

Q. Do you remember anything else that you used to do then e.g. happy memories or sad memories?

A. There was happy memories and sad memories. For example, the happy memories that I have were when my son was born and there were only Indians living around and there was only one other Pakistani called Fozia who lived near me then. When my first son was being born her husband Sadid sent his wife Fozia to me and asked if I needed help because I used to live on my own.

There was once when my husband asked me to go to the cinema with him on a Sunday and I used to say 'I'm not going to places like this' and I was thinking that my father would say to me that 'now you have gone to England you have gone very free' and probably my brother –in - law would have told my father that he saw me at the cinemas so I did not go. Once there was this lady who sat with me and told me to get ready and go with them (my husband's friends)… I even got slapped a few times by my husband, but I did not go. They used to say come to town but I said no… it was only after that I realized Fozia and her husband used to go to the cinema. Once I asked her that I might have the baby without knowing at night… while asleep... and she said 'no it is not like that, you will definately know. I used to ask silly things like this! that was very funny (laughing).

Q. You must have been 16 or 17 years then?

A. I was about 18 years old then.

Q. Do you remember what you used to do in Pakistan when you were little… like go to school?

A. No, we were not allowed to go to school. They used to say that girls get bad if they go to school but we used to read the Quran in our village. We used to roast seeds and our Patee ladies use to come and take full dishes of these seeds. They used to put them in the bottom of their dresses (like and envelope) and with the ones left over… we used to get de-grained and all the local friends used to come together and eat them.

Q. What kind of seeds?

A. They may be chana daal, chickpeas or other kinds.

Q. What is a patee?

A. It was like going to a place where they had a big dish like a wok; they used to roast the seeds for use and also make tandoori roti's too.

Q. Did you use to put salt on the seeds too?

A. No, just plain.

Q. Did you use to go during the day?

A. More around tea time..ish. The seeds use to have grain on the outside and we used to use a sieve to remove these and take them to the patee. They used to have a book and fill them in. The ones left over we use to bring back home and eat. It was nice because we use to play on the way there and back, girls and boys sometimes even until midnight because it was just in front of the house. In those they did not ask us young ones to work but say to us to go out and play.

Q. Were there any dolls etc. toys then?

A. Yes there was, we use to make them out of left-over clothes and sticks. We used to play with them and get the dolls to get married! We used to make dishes from clay and make small fires and get matches and pretend to make the curry over the heat. We used to have some plastic dishes and some from clay and we made pots and pans from the clay. We pretended to wash them and dry them in the sun… we used to do a lot of these things it is easier now to buy toys, plastic dishes etc. but back then we use to make our own dishes.

Q. Yes

A. Our parents used to buy us things to put the dishes in and we use to say we are learning?

Q. So you had enough to play with and kept yourself busy.

A. Yes, we were busy because there used to be the neighbours girls and boys and the village children, it is not like today when you have to keep them separate big boys and girls used to play together…there were no worries, we used to go and call on each other to come and play. We used to also play like a chasing game with the girls where two girls used to hold hands and run after the others… our games were really silly and when we use to catch the others we use to say that we won!

Q. Did you use to play with sticks for example, a game called eetee taala?

A. Yes, we did but we played mainly with the dolls.

Q. Are your parents alive?

A. No they are not.

Q. When did they pass away?

A. My father passed away seven years after I came here. I went back after they died because my baby was not six weeks yet and I could not go.

Q. Was he ill?

A. Yes, he was ill... he had cancer... he use to write letters and send telegrams asking my in- laws to send me to Pakistan while he was ill but they did not.

Q. How many brothers and sisters are you?

A. We were four brothers and three sisters, we are now... I have two brothers and two sisters left.

Q. Are you the only one from your family to come to England?

A. Yes I still am, there is no-one else but cousins and distant relatives like my cha cha's sons (dad's brothers sons). My in-laws said that when my other cousin who was written down on paper was my son would come over from Pakistan, then I could go over to Pakistan and visit my father. But my father died first and I went over later.

Q. That is sad.

A. I have never been allowed to go to any of my brothers and sisters' weddings or anything else. If you go to these occasions you meet a lot of your relatives which would be nice these are happy occasions and I have not been to any. When my two big brothers got married, I was too small and when I got married my other two brothers got married afterwards. One brother has gone to Dubai.

Q. How long?

A. It has been 24 years, when he was single. He went over and I saw him for two nights in those days there use to only be one person in the house earning and the rest of the food came from the land thay were very poor days... my father really wanted me to come and he died. And now there is money, but you cannot forget how hard it has been, my dad used to say I will pay one way and you can pay the other way but they never sent me (in-laws). They used to say the kids will die etc. etc. It is not up to human beings; I am very very upset about this. And you also now that I have lived here for 20 years (in this house) infact, it has been nearly 23 years I separated from husband. My son has got married to who he wants. You have to live and pass time don't you my daughters are also far far away... one of my daughters has not come to see me for seven years, she lives in France. When she comes here, she has to stay with her in-laws first I have twin girls one is in France and one is in Germany.

Q. Are they both married to relatives?

A. They are both with uncle's sons. My husband's family have created alot of problems my eldest daughter has been separated now with two children and lives alone in Manchester. She married into family as well; her first husband died he had a heart attack and was my nephew. It was my daughter's second husband, and they had a daughter together she now has three daughters and one son and lives alone.

Q. Is her name Pari?

A. They did something to her...black magic... they use to hit her and be horrible to her when she was married to her dad's nephew. My daughters are all far away they are not happy in their houses. My son also lives far away he used to live with an English woman and now with someone else I am ill myself I have diabetes and high blood pressure and sometimes I cannot feel my body... for quite a few days I could not feel this arm.

Q. I am just going to ask you a few more questions is that okay?

A. Yes

Q. Do you consider yourself to be a Geordie?

A. No

Q. Have you ever worked in Newcastle?

A. Yes, I have worked for 1 or 2 years in a sewing factory.

Q. Did you use to go to work or did they use to bring it home?

A. First I went to work at Sheel's road factory and then for 3-4 years i got work at home from a person called Kurshed it was making anoracks.

Q. Were your kids small then?

A. I only had 1 son then I had moved here it was here that i moved to Tamwick road( council house) 23 years ago when i seperated from my husband then i started to keep threads and material at home.

Q. Did this help you meet other people?

A. Yes ladies use to come amd I would have a chat with them.

(Part Sample Interview)

Note: N/A - refers to either not asked;not available; anot applicable; and also this question was answered elsewhere during interview.

Trancsription of Interviewee          Sample 2

2005 Interview

Interview with Mr Yasir          Male
      Ref N/A

Date of interview: 21.12. 2005

Brief Introduction to study explained

Name: Yasir Mohammed

Age: 51 years old ; DOB: 4.1.54

Nationality: British

Home Country: Chakswari, Azad Kashmir Mirpur

Mother Tongue: Mirpuri

Q. How long have you lived in the UK          About 45 years

A. I was born in Pakistan and was 6 years old when I came over. I lived with my Aunty and was aware of my surroundings. My Dad came over when... in the 50's, 60's, 1961. He worked in the shipyards and then he worked in aeroplanes in Middlesboro. He went to Middlesboro and stayed there for one week with his son. In 1961 my father lived with Uncle Maroo and Aunty. This was in Hawthorn Street, the next street to Park road. Uncle Maroo came here in 1939 and Uncle Nadin in 1940's. There were one or two other families living in Hawthorn Street and Warrington Road. I remember in 1 room lived my granddad, dad and uncle and one other person. There were at least four people in one room. The Mallik lived here too. Their nephews and I went to school together.

I went to Cambridge Street School and was there until I was 11 years old. I picked up stuff at school and mixed with the other white children. The comprehensive school I went to was Slatyford. I stayed dinners and used to play sports like hockey, football and did athletics. I nearly got picked by the Northumberland Hockey Team and for the England boys.

The first telly I remember was in 1968 and also used to go to cinemas on Sundays. There was a cinema in Big Lamp there was an Asian owner (Gem not sure what this means) called Bogan and his big brother was a pharmacist.

I stayed on at school and did my 'A' levels. I did chemistry in Newcastle Poly in 1974. My mam came over in 1968 and we got our own house in Ashfield Terrace. There was no central heating at the time, but we had an inside boiler and toilet and hot water. We had an open fire at first and used to store hot water in a big pan then and there was a back boiler and water was hot in the taps. Then there was a Geezer and there were gas fires. For the people who didn't have gas there was emersion heaters. These were then followed by Combis and gas central heating in the 80's and 90's. My Uncle Mac however was a carpet trader but had carpets in the 1960s and also had a telephone too!

Q. What is the main reason why you came to the UK

A. To earn money

Q. Why did you settle in Newcastle Upon Tyne?

N/A

Q. Do you consider yourself to be a Geordie?

A. Yes

Q. Did you ever work in Pakistan?

N/A

Q. What is your occupation?

N/A

Q. Have you had help in finding work i.e., local authorities etc.

N/A

Q. Are you married and if so when did you get married?

A. I had an arranged marriage in 1972.

Q. Did your wife and children come over to the UK with you?

N/A

Q.If they came over later did you have any problems getting them over?

N/A

Q.Do you own a house?

N/A

Q. What are most of the residents in your neighbourhood on your street from. What percentage are Muslims?

N/A

Q. Have you had any problems with racism in your neighbourhood?

N/A

Q. How often do you visit the Mosque?

A. For Friday mosque, weddings and funerals.

Q. Is there a mosque in Newcastle that you can get to easily?

A. Yes

Q. What religious functions do you carry out at home?

N/A

Q. Are you a member of a religious association in Newcastle?

A.There has been this thing with Punjabis and Mirpuris. In the religion there are divisions between the Wahabis and the Sunnis. There is the Sunath Ul Janah too their belief is different. The Wahabis originate from Abdul Wahab in India.

From a historical point of view there was a mosque in East Parade. This was a Sunni mosque and had a lot of uneducated members. They take things for granted and carry-on tradition and also work on emotional blackmail from generations ago. They do Khatums and remember God through Prophet Mohammed (PBUH) and believe that on the day of judgement will be gate keeper who will let into heaven. There was also the Wahabi mosque in Westmorland Rd. next to St. Mary's church. These people were educated and questioned everything. Haji Mavi is Wahabi. Wingrove mosque is a Wahabi mosque too. My belief is that you should be a good muslim and your own good deeds will take you to heaven. Anyway theser two groups came together and in 1970 purchased Elswick mosque. The more affluent people moved to Heaton Jesmond and Gosforth.

Q. Since you left Pakistan have you been back to visit?

N/A

Q. What places do you attend for recreational purposes and how often?

a) Cinema

b) Sporting events

c) Public Dance hall

d) Bingo sessions

e) Casino

f) Evening classes

g) Pubs/ Bars

h) Restaurants

i) Theatre

N/A

Q. Do you vote?

N/A

Q. Do you feel there is a political party that adequately represents Muslims as a minority group?

A.Could do more… Each and every party hasn't done enough.

Q. Do you feel the attitude of people in Newcastle has changed towards mulims since 7/7 and 9/11

A. Yes

Q. Have you experienced any racial abuse on the streets of Newcastle?

A. You always do but you accept it to a point.

Q. Do you think you will ever return to Pakistan?

A. Doubt it…

Q. Do you think you are happier living in Newcastle than you would be in Pakistan

A. Yes

Q. What do you think of the social and personal life of the English people

A. N/A

Q. Do you feel the local council has done enough to assist you with assimilation into society

A. No my own hard work.

Q. Have you seen any change in the way that the city council has treated immigrants over the years.

A. Very tolerant. Always work towards equality.

Q. Have you lived elsewhere in the UK besides in Newcastle?

A. …Newcastle is better. We best have of both worlds. It is not overcrowded and you have better chances here. Although… I have very few English best friends.

Q. Is there anything else you would like to add to your experiences of being a Muslim in the west end of Newcastle?

I just want to say that English is the main language and spoken for over 200years, so the perception is to go with the English and it is true to mix and learn from one another. However there is the 'coconuts' where most people have got on… I believe the socioeconomic background does affect moving up the ladder. My experience is that there is a dividing role in the system on the one hand it is segregation and on the other it is integration. The English say equal opportunities, for example, the 'hijab approach' it is a physical appearance and it does affect getting jobs. And integration what is this? The country is small but there is a huge network and everyone depends on each other otherwise are isolated as our own lives are busy.

Thank you very much for your time

Interview end

**Note:** N/A - refers to either not asked; not available; not applicable; and also this question was answered elsewhere during interview.

Transcription of Interviewee    Sample 3

Interview 2011

Name ; Mr Ayaz
    Ref A10: 10.52

Date : 30.3.2011

Interview :10

## Introduction

Q. In Newcastle on a daily basis how do you spend your time?

A. In Newcastle I have a lot of friends, I have Indian friends Pakistani friends I was involved in community work and plus I have my own business and I always have a busy life always.

Q. A busy life! Ok... Outside of Newcastle what towns do you go to?

A. Regular I go to Leeds, Middlesboro, Bradford, Sheffield... and I go to Birmingham sometimes.

Q. Ok.. And do you go to Leeds on holiday or to visit family

A. Most of the time I go to visit somebody died (like a funeral) or if anybody dies I go to the funeral and if anyone gets married I go, em..

Q. Yes like go for parties ..

A. Yes parties

Q .You mean 'Waada Kata'?

A. Yes wherever there is a 'waada qata' I MUST go there, this week I was three times in Leeds

Q. Three times… Leeds?

A. Three times to Leeds and on Sunday I was in Sheffield, somebody died in Sheffield and I was in a funeral.

Q. And why did you go to Leeds three times?

A. Three times there was a funeral.

Q. Three times… vow… that is a lot isn't it?

A. In a week!

Q. You know a lot of people?

A. I know a lot of company… and I like to show my face in these things.

Q. Yes I know… it is good. And Middlesboro is the same? Do you have family there and you go for?…

A. Yes I have family there. If anything happens I must go to Middlesboro. Same things holidays; I sometimes go for holiday for just a social visit, I meet the lads in Middlesboro and go for dinner and they come over here and they invite us.

Q. Yes and this is with your family?

A. Yes Middlesboro, Sheffield…

Q. Birmingham?

A. Birmingham, I only go for a wedding or funeral… mostly.

Q. And you know when you go to Middlesboro for a holiday do you go for a day?

A. I just go for one evening.

Q. And do you know how the English people go on holiday to Blackpool or wherever, have you been anywhere for a week or weekend?

A. I have been to Blackpool with a community trip.

Q. Oh yes… with the Muslim Association?

A. It was a community trip I have been many times with them Blackpool to see the lighting with a couple of English friends.

Q. And these are day trips?

A. Yes we just take the car in the morning and come back in the car.

Q. And is this with the Muslim Association?

A. I went three times with the Muslim Association to Bradford

Q. And what about outside of England have you been anywhere?

A. I have been to France

Q. How long was that for?

A. It was for one week

Q. And that was for a holiday?

A.That was a really...it was the FIRST holiday I have (laughing).

Q. Really and how long ago was that?

A. It was four years ago

Q. Four years ago?

A. Yes four or five years ago

Q. Did you enjoy it?

A.      Oh      yes...      I      saw      many      places...
Q. Eiffal Tower

A. I... I seen the Tower, museums and many churches. I seen the big churches you know where there is a film made of guy (doing hunchback action) (both tried to remember his name but couldn't).Plus I like the architecture.

Q. Yes the buildings are really nice...

A. The buildings are really nice honestly, we have been there for a week but it is not enough time to see. I liked the underground system.

Q.Yes...yes...

A. When we went to France because one lad he knew Paris, he knew Paris and we got off Easyjet and went to the railway station and he got a 5 day pass. He bought a 5 day ticket.

Q. Oh yes… a 5 day pass?

A. Yes a 5 day pass for 30 quid, we went to Disneyland and we been all over. We never sat down. When I came back I was more tired.

Q. Yes that's what happens when we go on holiday as well.

A. I was more tired!

Q. Yes I can understand. Did you go in the summer or the winter?

A. I went in the summer

Q. Yes cos we went to Disneyland in the Winter and it was raining, so that was no good.

A. Oh summer is better, we had a one day trip in Disneyland.

Q. Ok so you went once on holiday to France and what about Pakistan or any other place?

A. I have been to Pakistan 20 times

Q. Since you have come here?

A. Yes

Q. Probably more I think?…

A. Probably more?

Q. You've lost count?

A. Yes. I have lost count!

Q. You know when you go to Pakistan, do you go to visit family or holiday?

A. I go ALL OVER, I have been to Islamabad, Rawalpindi, Islamabad, I have been to Lahore I have got a couple of good friends in Lahore… Mostly I have been to Islamabad and Lahore… I have been to Gujarwala and em… Jhelum and I have been to Sirgoda.

Q. So when you go do you go to visit family or just a holiday?

A. I go to visit family and I have got my own house there

Q. You,ve got your own house there?

A. Yes, I have got my own house there. I have visited Azad Kashmir and I have been right out to Muzafarabad and once I went to visit the area you know where there was an earthquake.

Q. Yes I remember.

A. Yes I went to take the funds, I went all over the area.

Q. That was a few years ago wasn't it?

A.Yes, it was a few years ago…oh I.

Q. Did you go yourself or with other people?

A. I went with a group of people, there was about 6 people. We took about £95,000.00 FUNDS.

Q. And you gave it directly?

A. Oh we gave it directly to the people.

Q. You got it from charity?

A. Yes… we collected it from the people in Newcastle.

Q. That is a lot of hard work. May Allah reward you. What about Dubai or anywhere else?

A. No I haven't been to Dubai. I have been to Saudi for Haj?

Q. You have been to Saudi?

A. I have been to Saudi from England, I have been to Mecca, Medina. We flew from here to Medina then went by bus to Mecca and flew from Jeddah. We stayed in Italy a couple of hours it was em Turkish airlines.

Q. Do you have a wish to go anywhere else or travelling wish any holiday?

A. I have been to see Castle a couple of times. We have been to the Lake District a few times too when I was working in a factory they took me.

Q. What was the name of factory?

A. It was British Engine, I went on couple of times with them then I went with local Pakistani people, A couple of Politicians came over and I took them and showed them the Lake District.

...

Thank you

Part Interview


**Note:** N/A - refers to either not asked;not available; anot applicable; and also this question was answered elsewhere during interview.

## CONSENT FORM

Due to human ethics requirement, I am required to gain consent from all of those who assist in the completion of the study. To do this there is a requirement to gain the participants' written consent. The content of the questionnaire is not design to ask any intrusive questions.

It must be pointed out that participation is totally on a voluntary basis and all participants are free to withdraw consent and discontinue participation at any time. With respect to confidentiality, the only people to see the questionnaire will be the

If you are happy to assist me in the completion of the project, I would be grateful if you would complete the form below, before filling in the questionnaire.

---

( Delete, sign and date where appropriate)

I have read the information regarding the aims and objectives of the study and the information regarding my rights as a participant in the study. After reading this, I am / I am not willing to complete the Questionnaire.

Signed____                    _____ Date _____

# References

Adey P. 2010. *Mobility*, London: Routledge

Ahmad F. 2003. Still 'In Progress?' Methodological Dilemmas, Tensions and Contradictions in Theorising South Asian Muslim Women in N. Puwar and P.Raghuram. Reprinted 2004, *South Asian Women in Diaspora*, Oxford: Berg

Ahmad F. 2006. The Scandal of 'Arranged Marriages' in Ali N. Kalra V.S. Sayyid S. (eds.) *A Postcolonial People: South Asians in Britain*, London: C.Hurst and Co. pp.272-288

Ahmad F. and Modood T. 2003. *South Asian Women and Employment in Britain the Interaction of Gender and Ethnicity*, University of Westminster: Policy Studies Institute

Ahmed S. 1999. Home and Away: Narratives of Migration and Estrangement, *International Journal of Cultural Studies*, 2 (3) pp. 330-347

Ahmed S. 2000. *Strange Encounters: Embodied Others in Postcoloniality*, London: Routledge

Alba R. 1990. *Ethnic Identity: The Transformation of White America*, Yale University Press.

Alba R. and Nee V. 1997. Rethinking Assimilation Theory for a New Era of Immigration, *International Migration Review*, 31 (4), pp.826-874

Alba R. and Nee V. 2003. *Remaking the American Mainstream: Assimilation and Contemporary Immigration*, United States of America: Harvard University Press

Alexander C. 2006. Imagining the Politics of BrAsian Youth in Ali N. Kalra V.S. Sayyid S. (eds.) *A Postcolonial People: South Asians in Britain*, London: C.Hurst and Co. pp.258-271

Ali D. 2006. Arrival in Ali N. Kalra V.S. Sayyid S. (eds.) *A Postcolonial People: South Asians in Britain*, London: C.Hurst and Co. pp.32-34

Ali N. 2006. Imperial Implosions: Postcoloniality and the Orbits of Migration in Ali N, Kalra V. Sayyid S. (eds.) *A Postcolonial People: South Asians in Britain*, London: C.Hurst and Co. pp.158-167

Ali N. 2012. Researcher Reflexivity in Tourism Studies Research Dynamic Dances with emotions in Ateljevic I. Morgan N. and Pritchard A (eds) *The Critical Turn in Tourism Studies Creating an Academy of Hope*, London: Routledge

Ali N. and Holden A. 2011. Tourism's Role in the National Identity Formulation of the United Kingdom's Pakistani Diaspora in E Frew and L. White (eds) *Tourism and National Identities an International Perspective*, London: Routledge

Ali N. and Holden A. 2006. Postcolonial Pakistani Mobilities: Embodiment of the 'Myth of Return' in Tourism, *Mobilities*, 1(2) pp. 217-242

Ali N. Kalra V. Sayyid S. 2006. *A Postcolonial People: South Asians in Britain*, London: C.Hurst and Co.

Ali-Al, N. and Koser, K. 2002. *New Approaches to Migration? Transnational Communities and the Transformation of Home*, London: Routledge

Alwin D. and Mc Cammon R. 2003. Generations, Cohorts and Social Change in T. Mortimer and M. Shanahan (eds.) *Handbook of the Life Course*, New York: Kluwer Academic Publishers

Anwar M. 1979. *The Myth of Return. Pakistanis in Britain*, London: Heinemann

Appadurai A. 1995. The Productionof Locality, in Fardon R. (ed.) *Counterworks: Managing the Diversity of Knowledge*, London: Routledge

Armbruster H. and Nadje al-A. 2002. *New Approaches to Migration*, London: Routledge

Atkin K. 2006. Health Care and BrAsians: Making Sense of Policy and Practice in Ali N, Kalra V. Sayyid S. (eds.) *A Postcolonial in People: South Asians in Britain*, London: C. Hurst and Co. pp.244-255

Axhausen K.W. 2002. *A Dynamic Understanding of Travel Demand*, A Skrtich, Zurich: Institut fur Verehrsplannung und Transportsysteme, ETH, Switzerland

Bachelard G. 1988. *Air and Dreams: An Essay on the Imagination of Movement*, Dallas Institute of Humanities and Culture: Dallas Institute Publications

Ballard R. 1990. Migration and Kinship in Colin Clarke (ed.) *South Asians Overseas*, Cambridge

University Press

Ballard R. 1994. *Desh Pardesh: The South Asian Presence in Britain,* London: C. Hurst and Co.

Ballard R. and Ballard C. 1977. The Sikhs: The Development of South Asian Settlements in Britain in Watson (ed.) *Between Two Cultures,* Oxford: Basil Blackwell

Benson M. and O'Reilly K. 2009. Migration and the Search for a Better Way of Life: a Critical Exploration of Lifestyle Migration, *Sociological Review,* 57 (4) pp.608-625

Bhabha H. 1990. *Nation and Narration,* London: Routledge

Bhabha H. 1994. *The Location of Culture,* London: Routledge

Blunt A. and Dowling R. 2006. *Home,* London: Routledge

Bolognani M. 2007. The Myth of Return: Dismissal, Survival or Revival? A Bradford Example of Transnationalism as a Political Instrument, *Journal of Ethnic and Migration Studies,* 33(1) pp.59-76

Bonacich P. 1987. Power and Centrality: A Family of Measures, *American Journal of Sociology,* 92(5) pp.1117-1182

Boswell C. 2007. Theorising Migration Policy: Is There a Third Way? *International Migration Reveiew,* 41(1) pp.75-100

Brah A. 1996. *Cartographies of Diaspora,* London: Routledge

Brah A. 2006. The 'Asian' in Britain in Ali N, Kalra V. Sayyid S. (eds.) *The Postcolonial in People: South Asians in Britain,* London: C.Hurst and Co. pp.35-61

Brettel C. and Hollified J. 2008. *Migration Theory Talking Across Disciplines,* Second Edition. United States of America: Taylor and Francis Group

Bryman A. 2008. *Social Research Methods,* Third Edition. Oxford University Press

Buscher M. and Urry J. 2009. Mobile Methods and the Empirical, *European Journal of Social Theory* 12 (1) pp.99-116

Castles S. 2009. Development and Migration or Migration and Development: What Comes First? *Asian and Pacific Migration Journal,* Vol.18 pp. 441-471

Castles S. and Miller M. 1998. *The Age of Migration,* London: The MacMillan Press Ltd.

Home Office, *Census 2001,* Office of National Statistics

Cockburn C. 1998. *The Space Between Us,* London: Zed Books

Coles T. and Timothy D. 2004. (eds), *Tourism, Diasporas and Space,* London: Routledge

Cohen R. 2002. *Global Diasporas,* London: UCL Press.

Cohen R. 2004. '*The free Movement of Money and People: Old Arguments; new Dangers',* Paper given to the ESRC/SSRC Colloqium on Money and Migration 2004, Oxford

Cohen S. 2004. Social Relationships and Health, *American Psychologist* 59 (8), pp.676-684

Cresswell J. 2007. *Qualitative Enquiry and Research Design, Choosing Among Five Approaches,* London: Sage Publishing

Cresswell T. 2006. *On the Move: Mobility in the Modern Western World,* London: Routledge

Cresswell T. 2009. Place in *International Encyclopedia of Human Geography* Thrift N. and Kitchen R. (eds.) Oxford: Elselvier, Vol. 8 pp.169-177

Crook I. and Crang M. 1995 *Doing Ethnographies: Concepts and Techniques in Modern Geography,* University of Durham

Dahya B. 1974. The Nature of Pakistani Ethnicity in Industrial Cities in Britain' in A. Cohen. (ed.) *Urban Ethnicity,* London: Tavistock pp.77-118

Denzin N. 2009. *Qualitative Enquiry Under Fire: Toward a New Paradigm Dialogue,* USA: Left Coast Press

Diken B. and Lausten C. 2005. *The Culture of Exception. Sociology Facing the Camp,* London: Routledge

Duval. D.T. 2006. Grid / Group Theory and its Applicability to Tourism and Migration. *Tourism Geographies,* 8 (1) pp.1-14

Ellerman D. 2003. Policy Research on Migration and Development, *Policy Research Working Paper Series 3117,* Washington DC: The World Bank

Ellis P. and Khan Z. 2002. The Kashmiri diaspora in N. Ali andK. Koser (eds.) *New Approaches to Migration? Transnational Communities and the Transformation of Home* London: Routledge pp.

169-185

Edensor T. 2001. Walking in the Countryside in P.Macnaghten and J. Urry (eds.) *Bodies of Nature*, London: Sage Publishing

Fabos A. 2002. Sudanese Identity in Diaspora and the Meaning of Home: the Transformative Role of Sudanese NGOs in Cairo in A. Ali and K. Khalid (eds.) *New Approaches to Migration: Transnational Communities and the Transformation of Home*, London: Routledge, pp. 34-50

Faist T. 2000. Transnationalism in International Migration: 'Implications for the Study of Citizenship and Culture', *Ethnic and Racial Studies*, Vol 23, pp.188-222

Friedmann J. 1999. The Hybridisation of Roots and the Abhorrence of the Bush in M.

Fincham B., Mc Guinness M.and Murray L. 2009. *Mobile Methodologies*, London: Wiley

Finney N. and Simpson L. 2009. *Sleepwalking to Segregation? Challenging Myths about Race and Migration*, Bristol: Policy Press

Fog-Olwig K. 1999. Travelling Makes A Home: Mobility and Identity Amongst West Indians in T.Chapman and J. Lorna (eds.) *Homes? : Social Change and Domestic Life*, London: Routledge

Friedmann J. 1999. The Hybridisation of Roots and the Abhorrence of the Bush in M. Featherstone and S. Lash (eds.), *Spaces and Culture*, London: Sage Publishing

Game A. 2000. Falling, *Journal for Cultural and Religious Theory*, Vol 1 pp.1-41

Gardner K. 2002. *Age, Narrative and Migration: The Life Course and Life Histories of Bengali Elders in London*, Oxford: Berg

du-Gay P., Hall S., Janes L., Mackay H. and Negus K. 1997. *Doing Cultural Studies, The Story of the Sony Walkman*, London: Sage Publishing

Geddes, A. 2008. *Immigration and European Integration: Beyond Fortress Europe*, Manchester University Press

Giddens A. 1997. Sociology in *Sociological Research on Line*, Cambridge: Polity Press

Gille Z. and Riain S. 2002. Global Ethnography, *Annual Review of Sociology*, Vol 28 pp.271-295

Gilroy P. 1993. *The Black Atlantic: Modernity and Double Consciousness*, London: Verso

Gogia N. 2006. 'Unpacking Corporeal Mobilities: The Global Voyages of Labour and Leisure', *Environment and Planning A*, 38 (3) pp.59-75

Grosz E. 1994. *Volatile Bodies*, Sydney: Allen and Urwin

Gray D. 2010. *Doing Research in the Real World*, Second Edition. London: Sage Publishing

Grbich C. 2004. *Researching Research and Ethnicity: Methods, Knowledge and Power*, London: Sage Publishing

Guarnizo L. 2003. The Economics of Transnational Living, *International Migration Review*, 373 (3) pp.700-723

Gunaratnam Y. 2003. *Researching Race and Ethnicity: Methods, Knowledge and Power*, London: Sage Publishing

Gustafson P. 2002. Globalisation, Multiculturalism and Individualism: The Swedish Debate on Dual Citezenship, *Journal of Ethnic and Migration Studies*, 28 (3) pp.463-481

Gustafson P. 2002b. Tourism and Seasonal Retirement, *Annals of Tourism Research*, 29 (4), pp. 899-918

Gustafson P. 2009. Mobility and Territorial Belonging, *Environment and Behavior*, 41 (4) pp.490-508

de Haas H. 2010. Migration and Development: A theoretical Perspective. *International Migration Review*, 44 (1) pp.227-264

Hall S. 1992. *The Question of Cultural Identity. In Modernity and its Futures* in S. Hall, D. Held and A. Mc Grew (eds.) Cambridge: Polity Press pp.273-316

Hall S. 1996. 'Introduction: Who Needs Identity?' in S. Hall and P. du Gay (eds) *Questions of Cultural Identity*, London: Sage Publishing

Hannam K. 2002. Tourism and Development 1: Globalisation and Power, *Progress in Development Studies* Vol 2 pp. 227-234

Hannam K. 2005.Tourism Management Issues in Indias National Park's, *Current Issues in Tourism*, 8 (2/3) pp.165-180

Hannam K. 2006. Tourism and Development 111: Performances, Performativities and Mobilities, *Progress in Development Studies* 6 (3) pp.243-249

Hannam K. and Knox D. 2010. *Understanding Tourism: A Critical Introduction,* London: Sage Publishing

Hannam K., Sheller M. and Urry J. 2006. Editorial: Mobilities, immobilites, and Moorings, *Mobilities* Vol 1 pp.1-22

Hayles K. 1999. *How We Became Post-Human – Virtual Bodies in Cybernetics, Literature, and Informatics,* University of Chicago

Heisler B. 2000. The Sociology of Immigration: From Assimilation to Segmented Integration, from the American Experience to the Global Arena in C. Brettel and J. Hollifield (eds.) *Migration Theory: Talking Across Disciplines,* Routledge: New York pp.77-96

Herbert J. 2008. *Negotiating Boundaries in the City,* London: Ashgate Publishing

Horevits E. 2009. Understanding the Anthropolgy of Immigration and Migration Sociological, *Journal of Human Behavior in the Social Environment* Vol 19: pp.745-758.

Howard M. 2005. Variation in Dual Citizenship Policies in the Countries of the EU, *International Migration Review* Vol 39, pp. 697-720

Ignatieff M. 1991. Citizenship and Moral Narcissism in G. Andrewsin (ed.) *Citizenship,* London: Lawrence and Wishart pp. 26-36

Jamal T. and Robinson M. 2009. *Tourism Studies,* London: Sage publications

Kaufmann V. 2002. *Re-Thinking Mobility: Contemporary Sociology,* London: Ashgate Publishing

Kearney M. 2004. *Changing Fields of Anthropology from Local to Global,* USA: Rowman & Littlefield Publishers Inc.

Khalid R. 2011. Changes in Perception of Gender Roles: Returned Migrants, *Pakistan Journal of Social and Clinical Psychology,* Vol 9 pp.16-20

Khan S. 1977. The Pakistanis: Mirpuri Villagers at Home and in Bradford in Watson J. *Between Two Cultures,* Oxford: Basil Blackwell pp.57-89

Kim M. 2009. The Political Economy of Immigration and the Emergence of Transnationalism, *Journal of Human Behaviour in the Social Environment,* Vol 19 pp.675-689

King R. and Christou A. 2011. Of Counter-Diaspora and Reverse Transnationalism: Return Mobilities To and From the Ancestral Homeland in *Mobilities,* 6 (4) pp. 451-466

King R. and Vullnetri J. 2006. Orphan Pensioners and Migrating Grandparents: The Impact of Mass Migration on Older People in Rural Albania, *Ageing and Society,* Vol 26, pp. 783-816

Klandermans B., van Stekelenburg J., Sabucedo J. and Olivier J. 2004. Multiple Identities Among Farmer's Protest in the Netherlands and Spain in *Political Psychology,* Vol 23 pp. 235-252

Klandermans B., van Stekelenburg J. and van der Toorn J. 2008. Embeddedness and Identity: How immigrants turn grievances into action, *American Sociological Review* 73 (6) pp.992-1012

Kofman E. and Raghuram P. 2006. *Reproducing Cities, Reconfiguring Class: An Analysis of Contemporary Female Migration* Paper in Royal Geographical Society Annual International Conference in London

Lash S. and Urry J. 1994. *Economies of Signs and Space,* London: Sage Publishing

Lassen C. 2006. Aeromobility and Work, *Environment and Planning A,* Vol 38 pp.301-312

Lee C. 2009. Sociological Theories of Immigration: Pathways to Integration for U.S. immigrants in *Journal of Human Behavior in the Social Environment,* Vol 19 pp.730-744

Levitt P. and Jaworsky N. 2007. Transnational Migration Studies|: Past Developments and Future Trends, *Annual Review of Sociology* Vol 33, pp.129-156

Marcus G. 1995. Ethnography in / of the World System: the Emergence of Multisited Ethnography, *Annual Review of Anthropology,* Vol 24

Marfleet P. 2006. *Refugees in a Global Era,* Basingstoke: Palgrave Macmillan

Marshall C. and Rossman G. 1989. *Designing Qualitative Research,* London: Sage Publishing

Mason D. 2000. *Race and Ethnicity in Modern Britain,* Second Edition. Oxford University Press

Massey D. 1995. Space-Time and the Politics of Location, Transactions, *Institute of British*

*Geographers,* 20 (4) pp.487-499

Maynard M., Haleh A., Myfawny F. and Wray S. 2008. *Women in Later Life: Exploring 'Race' and Ethnicity,* London: Open University Press

McLoughlin S. 2006. Writing a BrAsian City: 'Race', Culture and Religion in Accounts of Postcolonial Bradford in Ali N., Kalra V. and Sayyid S. (eds.) *A Postcolonial People: South Asians in Britain,* C.Hurst and Co. pp.110-140

Mc Ghee D. 2008. *The End of Multi Culturalism,* Berkshire: Open University Press

Mc Leod J. 2000. *Beginning Postcolonialism,* Glasgow: Bell and Pain Ltd

McLuhan M. 1964. *Understanding Media: the extensions of man,* London: Routledge and Kegan Paul

Michael M. 2000. These Boots are made for Walking….Mundane Technology, the Body and Human-Environment Relations, *Body and Society,* Vol 6 pp.107-126

Modood T. 2007. *Multiculturalism,* Bristol: Polity Press

Mohammed A. 1998. *Between Cultures Continuity and Change in the Lives of Young Asians,* London: Routledge

Myers L. 2010. *Women Independent Traveller's to New Zealand.* Phd Thesis, University of Sunderland

Nadje A. and Khalid K. 2002. *New Approaches to Migration: Transnational Communities and the Transformation of Home,* London: Routledge

Najam A. 2006. *Portrait of a Giving Community: Philanthropy by the Pakistani – American Diaspora,* Harvard University Press

Nash C. 2002. *Genealogical Identities. Environment and Planning D: Society and Space,* Vol 20 pp. 27-52

Newcastle upon Tyne Ward Map. 2012. Online available on http://www.newcastle.gov.uk/wwwfileroot/legacy/cxo/instantatlas/WardMap.pdf. Last accessed 11.09.2012.

Newland K. 2007. *A New Surge of Interest in Migration and Development* Washington DC: Migration Information Source

Nyers P. 2003. Abject Cosmopolitanism: The Politics of Protection in the Anti-Deportation Movement, *Third World Quarterly,* Vol 24 pp. 1069-1093

Ong A. 1999. *Flexible Citizenship: the Cultural Logics of Transnationality,* Durham, NC: Duke University Press

Panayi P. 2000. *Ethnic Minorities in Nineteenth and Twentieth Century Germany: Jews, Gypsies, Poles, Turks and Others,* Essex: Pearson Education

Papadopoulos I. and Lees S. 2002.Promoting Cultural Competence in Healthcare through a research-based intervention in the UK, *Diversity in Health and Social Care,* 1 (2) pp.107-116

Papastergiadis N. 2010. Wars of Mobility. *European Journal of Social Theory,* Vol 13(3) pp.343 361

Parekh Report 2000. *The Future of Multi-Ethnic Britain* Runnymede Trust London: Profile Books Ltd

Peach C. 2006. Demographics of Br Asian Settlement, 1951-2001 in Ali N., Kalra V. and Sayyid S. (eds.) *A Postcolonial People: South Asians in Britain,* London C. Hurst and Co. pp.168-181

Plaut P. 1997. Transportation-Communications Relationships in Industry, *Transportation Research Part A Policy and Practice,* Vol 31, pp.419-429

Portes A., Guarnizo A. and Landit P. 1999. Introduction: Pitfalls and Promise of an Emergent Research Field, *Ethnic and Racial Studies* Vol 22, pp. 463-478

Portes A. and Rambaut R. 1996. Making it in America: Occupational and Economic Adaptation in A. Portes & R. Rambaut (eds.) *Legacies: The Story of Immigrant Second Generation,* London: University of California Press pp. 44-69

Portes A. and Zhou M. 1993 The New Second Generation: Segmented Assimilation and its Variants Among Post Immigrant Youth, *Annals of the American Academy of Political and Social Science,* pp.174-196

Probyn E. 1996. Queer Belongings: The Politics of Departure in Grosz E. and Probyn E (eds.) *Teaching Bodies: Affects in the Classroom, Body and Society,* New York: Basic Books

Putnam R. 2000. *Bowling Alone, The Collapse and Revival of the American Community,* New York: Simon and Schuster

Raje F. 2004. *Transport Demand Management and Social Inclusion: The Need for Ethnic Perspectives,* Aldershot: Ashgate Publishing

Rapport N. and Dawson A. 1998. *Migrants of Identity: Perceptions of Home in a World of Movement,* Oxford, New York: Berg

Renshon S. 2008. *Immigrant Attachment and Community Integration: A Psychological Theory of Facilitating New Membership, Migration and Identities* 1 (1)

Rex J. 1991. *Ethnic Identity and Ethnic mobilisation in Britain, Monographs in Ethnic Relations,* University of Warwick, No. 5 New Series

Rex, J. and Moore, R. 1971. (Reprinted). *Race, Community and Conflict: A Study of Sparkbrook.* London: Oxfrod University Press

Said E. 1993. *Culture and Imperialism,* London: Chatto and Windus

Salih R. 2002. Shifting Meanings of Home: Consumption and Identity in Moroccan Women's Transnational Practices Between Italy and Morocco in A. Ali and K. Koser (eds.) *New Approaches to Migration: Transnational Communities and Transformation of Home,* London: Routledge pp.51-67

Schivelbuch W. 1986. *The Railway Journey: the Industrialisation of Time and Space in the 19th Century,* Berkeley: University of California Press

Scott S. and Cartledge R. 2009. Migrant Assimilation in Europe: A transnational Family Affair. *International Migration Review,* 43, (1) pp.60-89

Serjersen T. B. 2008. "I Vow to Thee My Countries" – The Expansion of Dual Citizenship in the 21st Century. Visiting Scholar ACSPRI Centre for Social Research, Australian National University. *Centre for Migration Studies of New York,* 42 (3), pp.523-549

Shaw A. 1994. The Pakistani Community in Oxford in R. Ballard, *Desh Pardesh: The South Asian Presence in Britain.* London: C. Hurst & Co.

Shaw A. 2001. Kinship, Cultural Preference and Immigration: Consanguineous Marriage among British Pakistanis, *The Journal of the Royal Anthropological Institute,* 7(2) pp.315-334.

Sheller M. and Urry J. 2006 'The New Mobilities Paradigm', *Environment and Planning A,* 38 (2) pp.207-226

Shuabi P. 2001. Models of Transformation in Saudi Arabia in I. Seragedin, E. Shluger, J. Brown (eds.) in *Historic Cities and Sacred Sites Cultural Roots for Urban Futures,* Washington DC: The World Bank pp.180-185

Shukla S. 2001. Locations for South Asian Diasporas, *Annual Review of Anthropology,* Vol 30, pp.551-572

Shurmer-Smith P. 2002. *Doing Cultural Geography,* London: Sage Publishing

Shurmer-Smith P. and Hannam K. 1994. *Worlds of Desire Realms of Power: A cultural geography,* London: Edward Arnold

Sirojudin, S. *Global Networks* 2009, "Economic Theories of Emigration" in *Journal of Human Behavior in the Social Environment,* Vol 19: pp.702-712

Snel E., Engberson G. and Leerkes A. 2006. Transnational Involvement and Social Integration, 6 (3) pp. 285-308

Soysal Y. 1994. *Limits of Citizenship: Migrants and Postnational Membership in Europe,* Chicago, IL: University of Chicago

Suarez-Orozco M. 2003. Right Moves? Immigration, Globalization, Utopia and Dystopia in P. Pessar (ed.) *American Arrivals: Anthropolog Engages the New Immigrant,* Santa Fe: School of American Research Press pp.45-74

Taylor C. 2004. *Moderm Social Imagineries,* Duke University Press

Taylor J 1976. *The Half-way Generation, London:* NFER Publishing Company

Telang S. 1967. *The Coloured Immigrant in Newcastle upon Tyne,* Newcastle upon Tyne: City Planning Officer

Tesfahuney M. 1998. Mobility, Racism and Geopolitics, *Political Geography*, 17 (5) pp.499-515

Thieme S. 2008. Sustaining Livelihoods in Multi-Local Settings: Possible TheoreticaLinkages Between Transnational Migration and Livelihood Studies, *Mobilities*, 3 (1) pp.51-71

Thrift N. 1990. Transport and Communications 1730-1914 in R. Butlin and R. Dodgshon (eds.) *An Historical Geography of England and Wales*, London: Academic Press Second Edition

Thrift N. 1996. *Spatial Formations*, London: Sage Publishing

Thrift N. 1997. The Still Point: Resistance, Expressive Embodiment and Dance in S.Pile and Keith M. (eds.) *Geographies of Resistance*, London: Routledge pp.124-51

Tibi B. 2009. *Islam's Predicament with Modernity: Religious Reform Cultural Change* London: Routledge

Timothy D. 2001. *Tourism and Political Boundaries* London: Routledge

Tolia-Kelly D. 2004. Materializing Post-Colonial Geographies: 'Examining the Textural Landscapes of Migration in the South Asian Home, *Geoform* Vol 35 pp.675-688

Tolia-Kelly D. P. 2006. A Journey Through the Material Geographies of Diaspora Cultures: Four Modes of Environmental Memory in K. Burrell, and P. Panayi, (eds.) *Histories and Memories: Migrants and Their Histories in Britain*, London: St Martins Press

Tuan Y. 1977. *Space and Place: the Perspective of Experience*, London: Edward Arnold

Tuan Y. 1978. Space, Time, Place: A Humanistic Perpective, in T. Carlstein, D. Parkes and N. Thrift (eds.) *Timing Space and Spacing Time 1*, London: Arnold

Tuan Y.F. 1989. *Morality and Imagination: Paradoxes of Progress*, Madison: University of Wisconsin Press

Turner B. 2007. The Enclave Society: Towards a Sociology of Immobility European, *Journal of Social Theory*, 10 (2) pp.287-303

Turner B. 2010. Enclosures, Enclaves and Entrapment, *Sociological Inquiry*, 80 (2) pp.241-260

Urry J. 1990. *The Tourist Gaze, London :* Sage Publications Ltd. Reprinted 2002

Urry J. 2000. *Sociology Beyond Societies: Mobilities for the 21st Century*, London: Routledge

Urry J. 2007. *Mobilities*, London: Polity Press.

Urry J. 2010. Mobile Sociology, *British Journal of Sociology* Vol 61 pp.347-366

Vertovec S. 2001. Transnationalism and Identity, *Journal of Ethnic and Migration Studies*, 27 (4) pp. 573-582

Waters M. and Jimenez T. 2005. Assessing Immigrant Assimilation: New Empirical and Theoretical Challenges, *Annual Review of Sociology*, Vol 31 pp.105-125

Watsons J. 1977. *Between Two Cultures: Migrants and Minorities in Britain*, Oxford: Basil Blackwell.

William B. and Hall M. 2002. *Special Interest Tourism* London: Belhaven Press

Werbner P. 1999. Global Pathways: Working Class Cosmopolitans and the Creation of Transnational Ethnic Worlds, *Social Anthropology*, Vol 7 pp. 17-36

Werbner P. 2001. The Limits of Cultural Hybridity: On Ritual Monsters, Peotic Licence and Contested Postcolonial Purifications, *The Journal of the Royal Anthropological Institute*, 7(1) pp133-152 http://www.jstor.org/stable/2660840. Last accessed: 23th March 2009

Werbner P. 2005. The Translocation of Culture: 'community cohesion' and the force of multiculturalism in history, *The Editorial Board of the Sociological Review* Oxford: Blackwell publishing

Wolf M. 2001. Will the Nation State Survive Globalisation, *Foreign Affairs* 80 (1), pp. 178-190

Wylie J. 2002. An essay on Ascending Glastonbury Tor, *Geoforum*, Vol 33 pp. 441-454

Zelinsky W. 1973. *A Cultural Geography of the United States*, Eaglewood Cliffs, NJ: Prentice Hall